THE DEVELOPMENT OF CORPORATE DESIGN

THE DEVELOPMENT OF CORPORATE DESIGN

Brand Identity, Graphic Design and Professionalism in Post-war Britain

DAVID PRESTON

BLOOMSBURY VISUAL ARTS
LONDON • NEW YORK • OXFORD • NEW DELHI • SYDNEY

BLOOMSBURY VISUAL ARTS
Bloomsbury Publishing Plc, 50 Bedford Square, London, WC1B 3DP, UK
Bloomsbury Publishing Inc, 1385 Broadway, New York, NY 10018, USA
Bloomsbury Publishing Ireland, 29 Earlsfort Terrace, Dublin 2, D02 AY28, Ireland

BLOOMSBURY, BLOOMSBURY VISUAL ARTS and the Diana logo are trademarks of
Bloomsbury Publishing Plc

First published in Great Britain 2026

Copyright © David Preston, 2026

David Preston has asserted his right under the Copyright,
Designs and Patents Act, 1988, to be identified as Author of this work.

For legal purposes the Acknowledgements on p. xvii constitute an
extension of this copyright page.

Cover design by Daniel Benneworth-Gray

All rights reserved. No part of this publication may be: i) reproduced or transmitted in
any form, electronic or mechanical, including photocopying, recording or by means of
any information storage or retrieval system without prior permission in writing from
the publishers; or ii) used or reproduced in any way for the training, development or
operation of artificial intelligence (AI) technologies, including generative AI technologies.
The rights holders expressly reserve this publication from the text and data mining
exception as per Article 4(3) of the Digital Single Market Directive (EU) 2019/790.

Bloomsbury Publishing Plc does not have any control over, or responsibility for,
any third-party websites referred to or in this book. All internet addresses given
in this book were correct at the time of going to press. The author and publisher
regret any inconvenience caused if addresses have changed or sites have
ceased to exist, but can accept no responsibility for any such changes.

A catalogue record for this book is available from the British Library.

A catalog record for this book is available from the Library of Congress.

ISBN:	HB:	978-1-3503-8468-2
	PB:	978-1-3503-8467-5
	ePDF:	978-1-3503-8470-5
	eBook:	978-1-3503-8469-9

Typeset by Integra Software Services Pvt. Ltd.
Printed and bound in India

For product safety related questions contact productsafety@bloomsbury.com.

To find out more about our authors and books visit www.bloomsbury.com
and sign up for our newsletters.

To Tamsin

CONTENTS

List of illustrations ix
List of tables xv
Acknowledgements xvii

PART ONE
IDENTITY PROGRAMMES IN CONTEXT 1

1   Introduction 3

2   A macro history of corporate branding 22

3   Brand identity in Britain 37

PART TWO
IDENTITY PROGRAMMES IN PRACTICE 67

4   Reconfiguring practice: the systematic methods of Henrion Design Associates 77

5   Coordinated but not standardized: the practical rationality of Hans Schleger & Associates 118

6   Setting standards: Design Research Unit and the design manual as an instrument of control 158

PART THREE
THEMES, THREADS AND LEGACIES 205

7   Recurrent themes and threads 207

8   The legacy of post-war corporate design methods 216

Notes 227
References 237
Index 251

ILLUSTRATIONS

1.1 Unpublished poster proposal for Gleem toothpaste, F. H. K. Henrion, 1959 4

1.2 Brand identity programme for Pest Control of Cambridge, by Henrion Design Associates, excerpt from *Design* magazine, issue 84 5

1.3 Example of a comprehensive brand identity programme produced by Design Research Unit for Ilford. As featured in Alec Davis's (1952: 37) article for the *Penrose Annual* 8

1.4 Double-page spread from Alec Davis's (1956: 20–1) feature for *Design* magazine on 'Factors in house style', with examples on the use of colour, pattern, borders, trademarks and symbols, and lettering 9

2.1 Exhibition catalogue for 'Das Firmengesicht' (The Face of the Firm), exhibition of international advertising graphics in Berlin, 1954 34

3.1 Double-page spread from 'An Account of the LNER Type Standardization', *The Monotype Recorder*, Vol 36, No 4, Winter 1932 47

3.2 Cover of the special London Transport issue of the trade journal *Art & Industry*, October 1946 50

3.3 Double-page spread from Norbert Dutton's (1946: 112–13) feature on London Transport, with numerous illustrations by Ronald Ingles 52

3.4 An example of the use of a standard corporate typeface, in this case, Cyclone for British Overseas Airways Corporation (BOAC). As featured in Alec Davis's (1952: 38) article for the *Penrose Annual*. The illustrations featured top-left and bottom-right also featured in Davis's (1950a) earlier article for *Design* magazine 56

- **3.5** Double-page spread from Ashley Havinden's article for the *Penrose Annual*, 'The Importance of "Company Handwriting"' 60
- **3.6** F. H. K. Henrion's cover design for the 'House Style' special issue of *Design* magazine, issue 95, edited by Alec Davis (1956) 62
- **3.7** Double-page spread from the 'House Style' special issue of *Design* magazine, issue 95, edited by Alec Davis (1956) 63
- **4.1** 'Four Hands' wartime poster by F. H. K. Henrion distributed in Europe after D-Day. Client: US Office of War Information, 1944 78
- **4.2** Portrait of Henrion in his early forties by Wolfgang Suschitzky, bromide print, 1955, 14 3/4 in. x 11 1/2 in. (375 mm x 292 mm), NPG P559 80
- **4.3** View into the design studio extended on top of the Henrion household, undated 82
- **4.4** Henrion pictured in his late forties with employees from Henrion Design Associates, as featured in *Design* magazine, issue 177, 1963 83
- **4.5** Front cover of Henrion and Parkin's (1967) text *Design Coordination and Corporate Image* 86
- **4.6** Sample spread from *Design Coordination and Corporate Image* (Henrion and Parkin, 1967: 34–5) 87
- **4.7** Opening spread from 'Systematic Methods in Design Co-ordination', from *DIA Yearbook 1967/68* (Henrion and Parkin, 1968: 30–1) 88
- **4.8** 'Rotary filing system for Blue Circle Cement', *DIA Yearbook 1967/68* (Henrion and Parkin, 1968: 34) 96
- **4.9** 'Cards from the Post Office design library', *DIA Yearbook 1967/68* (Henrion and Parkin, 1968: 38) 97
- **4.10** An example of the design work for Blue Circle Cement created as a result of their systematic methods, as featured in *IDEA* magazine No 114, 1972 98
- **4.11** Diagram of Post Office design survey, *DIA Yearbook 1967/68* (Henrion and Parkin, 1968: 36) 99

ILLUSTRATIONS   xi

4.12 'One of eight magnetic boards used for network planning for the Blue Circle design co-ordination programme', from *DIA Yearbook 1967/68* (Henrion and Parkin, 1968: 40) 102

4.13 'A specially constructed display stand with rotating felt screens carrying hundreds of colour photographs of design items belonging to the Blue Circle Group', from *DIA Yearbook 1967/68* (Henrion and Parkin, 1968: 34) 105

4.14 Evolutionary mapping of the KLM logo development process, from *DIA Yearbook 1967/68* (Henrion and Parkin, 1968: 41) 106

4.15 'Comparative analyses of old and new KLM symbols', from *DIA Yearbook 1967/68* (Henrion and Parkin, 1968: 40) 109

4.16 'Test of recognisability of KLM symbol when blurred by horizontal movement' and 'Comparative tests of old and new symbols when out of focus, such as in poor visibility conditions', both from *DIA Yearbook 1967/68* (Henrion and Parkin, 1968: 41) 110

4.17 Excerpt from *Design Coordination and Corporate Image* showcasing a small selection of design applications from the KLM brand identity programme 113

4.18 Henrion Design Associates' 'House Style Manual' for KLM, c.1967 114

5.1 Photographic portrait of Hans Schleger 119

5.2 Newspaper advertisement for Schleger's services in New York, publicized under his pseudonym Zéró 120

5.3 Uncredited press advertisement for Mac Fisheries used to announce new store openings between 1951 and 1954, from Mather and Crowther Guard Books 122

5.4 A selection of some of the logo variants deployed by Hans Schleger & Associates in their work for Mac Fisheries, with original logo design top centre 126

5.5 Press advertisement for Mac Fisheries by HSA, 1952, from Mather and Crowther Guard Books 127

5.6 Press advertisement for Mac Fisheries by HSA, c.1953, from Mather and Crowther Guard Books 128

5.7 1955 press advertisement for Mac Fisheries by HSA, from Mather and Crowther Guard Books. Note the combination of the detailed Kruger Gray logo at the bottom and the loose illustrative Schleger logo variant at the top 129

5.8 HSA's packaging scheme for Mac Fisheries, late 1950s 131

5.9 Schleger's 'Looming Up' advertisement for Weber and Heilbroner, c.1925 134

5.10 Schleger's 'Mills! Mills! Mills!' advertisement for Weber and Heilbroner, c.1925 135

5.11 HSA poster for Edinburgh International Festival, 1970, showing how the trademark was initially deployed in a restrained manner 136

5.12 HSA poster for Edinburgh International Festival, 1973, showing how the trademark was deployed with greater fluidity, with the birds now leaving the castle 137

5.13 HSA poster for Edinburgh International Festival, 1975, showing how the trademark was increasingly abstracted over subsequent iterations of the campaign 138

5.14 Mac Fisheries leaflet design illustrated by Hans Schleger 140

5.15 Mac Fisheries leaflet design illustrated by Pat Schleger 141

5.16 Typographic advertisement for Mac Fisheries from *Kilburn Times*, 23 October 1953, from Mather and Crowther Guard Books 143

5.17 A Mac Fisheries advertisement featuring a Mac Chicken character created by Leslie Watson in the style of the HSA scheme 144

5.18 An example of the photo-realistic product packaging style as featured in a Mac Fisheries advertisement created by lettering artist Leslie Watson 145

5.19 Double-page spread from *Graphik* magazine (Maiwald, 1953a: 22–3) 146

5.20 Double-page spread from *Graphik* magazine (Maiwald, 1953a: 24–5) 147

5.21 'Mac Fisheries present Mac Fish', advertisement from *Graphik* magazine article (Maiwald, 1953a: 24) 148

ILLUSTRATIONS   xiii

5.22 'Mac Fisheries present Mac Fish', advertisement, Bristol test area, 1952, from Mather and Crowther Guard Books 149

6.1 The employees of DRU photographed together in 1968 165

6.2 The DRU directorate in a meeting, with Misha Black far left, Milner Gray third from left, and Dorothy Goslett third from right 166

6.3 An early identity programme for the photographic company Ilford, created by DRU in 1946 173

6.4 The opening page of DRU's report for Courage (Gray, 1950: 1) 175

6.5 Beer labels for Courage, designed by DRU, c.1950 176

6.6 Opening page of DRU's report for Watneys (Gray, 1956: 1) 180

6.7 The exterior of a Watneys public house designed according to DRU's identity principles 182

6.8 Watneys corporate identity manual, produced by DRU in 1966 183

6.9 Front cover of 'Manual for Magdalen Street' (Black, 1958) 184

6.10 Opening page of Magdalen Street manual (Black, 1958: 1) 185

6.11 Page of colour swatches from the Magdalen Street manual, 'Colours: Group One' (Black, 1958: 5) 187

6.12 One of several fold-out spreads with sample lettering, Magdalen Street manual (Black, 1958: 1a–1b) 188

6.13 'Lettering and Fascia Treatments', Magdalen Street manual (Black, 1958: 11) 188

6.14 Photograph of 'The new face of British Railways' exhibition held at The Design Centre, London, 1964 191

6.15 'The new face of British Railways', wall sheet explaining aspects of the British Railways 'house style' 192

6.16 DRU's preliminary design manual for the British Railways Board, November 1964 (Gray, 1964) 193

6.17 Opening page of the preliminary Design Manual for the British Railways Board (Gray, 1964: 2.01) 194

6.18 Covers from two of the ring-bound editions of the later British Rail manuals, together with a sample spread with fold-out page feature, c. 1965 195

6.19 Sample page from the preliminary manual on 'Standard House Colours' (Gray, 1964: 2.04) 197

6.20 Sample page from the preliminary manual focused on the symbol (Gray, 1964: 2.1) 198

6.21 Set of three design manuals housed in a cardboard sleeve, c. 1965 198

TABLES

1 Central concepts and keywords from early formative British texts on programmatic branding 65

2 Analysis of consultant design groups active between 1945 and 1970. Fields marked in black indicate fulfilled criteria, dark grey fields represent partial fulfilment, pale grey fields represent unfulfilled selection criteria 72

ACKNOWLEDGEMENTS

This book originates from research conducted during my PhD undertaken at University of the Arts London, which benefitted greatly from the guidance and support of my supervisors Jamie Brassett and Sean Nixon, so special thanks goes to them.

Thanks also go to my colleagues in Graphic Communication Design at Central Saint Martins who have encouraged and supported the development of my research over the past two decades. Special mention to Phil Baines, Catherine Dixon, Paul Rennie, Rathna Ramanathan, Rebecca Wright, Peter Hall, Rebecca Ross and Kira Salter. Many other colleagues, staff and students have helped to shape my ideas during this time, but I cannot list them all here.

Thanks to Leah Armstrong, Chiara Barbieri and Kasia Jeżowska for offering feedback on early drafts of this book. I also want to thank Ruth Artmonsky, who has been a continual source of inspiration to me.

I would like to express my gratitude to those who have granted permission to reproduce images which enhance this book. I am also indebted to those who have helped me to navigate the various archives used during my research. The reproduction of imagery within the book would not be possible without the support of Central Saint Martins, UAL.

I want to thank my team at Bloomsbury, particularly Louise Baird-Smith for commissioning the book, along with Hattie Morrison, Joseph Skingsley and Suzie Nash, who have all worked to support its development.

I would also like to thank the anonymous peer reviewers for their insightful comments and suggestions which have helped to strengthen the arguments in this book.

PART ONE
IDENTITY PROGRAMMES IN CONTEXT

1
INTRODUCTION

The emergence of brand identity programmes

The end of the ideas poster

In London, 1959, the British graphic designer F. H. K. Henrion is said to have presented a poster design proposal for Gleem toothpaste to his client, the American advertising firm Erwin, Wasey, Ruthrauff & Ryan. This painterly design featuring a swirl of toothpaste squeezed directly from the tube to form a perfect white smile was not exceptional in and of itself (Figure 1.1), being strongly representative of the kind of jobbing work that had been typical of commercial artists in pre-war Britain, yet this rather unremarkable design would come to signify a remarkable moment in this German émigré's career. The story goes that Henrion's client responded to the proposal by claiming that the design was 'too good' for them. What they needed, apparently, was not a strong individualistic ideas poster, but rather an altogether simpler design, featuring the actors from the brand's television commercial and constituting one part of a total or holistic campaign.

The most curious aspect of this anecdote is the surprised reaction with which Henrion greeted the knock-back, later lamenting that holistic design programmes had come to supersede concept-led individual design artefacts, referring to this incident as 'the end of the ideas poster'. Having completed his first extensive brand identity programme for Pest Control of Cambridge in 1953 (Figure 1.2), the disdain with which he greeted the withering status of the individual design artefact is intriguing; the irony that he had, by this point, been championing the merits of a coordinated approach to corporate design for at least five years seemingly lost on him. Not that this incident held him back, far from it. Over the coming decade he went on to establish a reputation as a pioneer of corporate design, cementing his reputation with several high-profile international design jobs, not least the brand identity programme for the Dutch airline KLM and the publication of the seminal textbook, *Design Coordination and Corporate Image* with his employee Alan Parkin.

Figure 1.1 Unpublished poster proposal for Gleem toothpaste, F. H. K. Henrion, 1959. Courtesy of the Estate of F. H. K. Henrion.

Why begin this book with Henrion's pithy anecdote about the end of the ideas poster? Well, the rise of the all-encompassing corporate communications programme at the expense of the heroic individual design artefact emphasizes a shift that is central to the premise of this volume. The emergence of programmatic brand identity during the post-war period in Britain was interlinked with several other changes occurring during the same period, which, when combined, had a significant influence on how design would come to be practised in the future.

Alongside the emergence of programmatic branding came two other important developments. The first was a strong trend towards group practice within design; complex and ambitious holistic brand identity programmes would demand an upscaling of the design workforce, with collaboration and teamwork now becoming critical to success. The second important development came in the shifting professional status of design, and particularly graphic design, which was to become closely linked with the imperative of visual unification at the heart of brand identity programmes. Tracing connections between these threads of development, this book aims to establish how the materiality of graphic designers' work was transformed as brand identity design became a central tenet of their

Figure 1.2 Brand identity programme for Pest Control of Cambridge, by Henrion Design Associates, excerpt from *Design* magazine, issue 84. Courtesy of the Estate of F. H. K. Henrion.

practice. By considering the collaborative nature of corporate design labour, the book moves beyond what is a long-standing tradition of viewing creativity from a purely individualist perspective.

Focusing on branding practices in the post-war era, the book addresses the underestimated significance of post-war graphic designers who spearheaded the development of innovative new programmatic approaches to corporate design in Britain. While many scholars have recognized the importance of the 1980s in terms of the impact of brands on society, generally the period that preceded this has been neglected, with scholars downplaying the significance of early pioneers like Henrion, suggesting that they were simply 'ahead of their time' (Moor, 2007: 30).[1] Drawing on empirical research I contest this assertion, arguing that practitioners such as Henrion played a critical role in establishing the patterns of corporate design practice that were deepened in the following decades. As such I contend that the 1950s and 1960s have been erroneously overlooked. My supposition being that although branding had, by the 1980s, reached unprecedented levels of significance as a symbol of social, cultural and economic capital, it was the earlier era that had set in place the foundations from which the ultimate idea of the brand as a form of 'new religion' could proliferate.[2] In this sense, while those scholars who have focused on the 1980s have served to underscore the powerful effects of neoliberalism, this book can be seen as an attempt to address a pre-history of such neoliberal corporate design practices. The book develops from this premise, focusing on the first, formative stage of brand identity design activity in Britain. It explores in detail the operational methods, group structures and client–designer relations of those practitioners most heavily involved in the establishment of the new programmatic approach to designing brands. Through a series of case studies, the role of certain key groups will be investigated to establish the role they played in defining the practice of brand identity design in Britain during the post-war period.

Although the book focuses on ways of practice within Britain, relations with other nations and cultures are considered. The key protagonists featured all practised within Britain, but many originated from outside the country, hailing from nations such as Germany or Azerbaijan. As such, the influence of European design ideals and the importance of émigré designers cannot be overstated. Transatlantic connections between Britain and the United States (US) are also reflected upon, particularly in relation to the role of advertising as both a complementary and a competing profession to graphic design. Although the US was generally more advanced in treating design as a commercialized practice, this book shows that post-war British designers played a much more critical role in advancing the discourse and methods of programmatic brand identity design than has previously been thought. While developments in the US can be seen to loosely mirror those of Britain, much of the key literature and milestone publications emanated from practitioners clustered around the London design scene.

The transition from sculptural artefacts to technological systems

Chronicling the emergence of brand consultancy, the book explains how the development and proliferation of brand identity programmes transformed the working methods and principles of practising graphic designers working in post-war Britain. It is commonly understood that the practice of designing brands

INTRODUCTION 7

may be traced through many centuries to the ancient act of branding cattle; meanwhile the design of symbols to represent individual companies or products also pre-dates the period surveyed here, thus perhaps raising questions as to why the focal period of this book does not begin earlier. By concentrating on a 25-year period after the end of World War II, this volume aims to challenge the dominant logo-centric approach to understanding the history of brands. Rather than examining the design of corporate logos, it instead charts the development of a coordinated and programmatic approach to brand design whereby multiple artefacts are brought into alignment under a unified visual identity system.

While some organizations in Britain, such as London Transport or The London & North Eastern Railway (LNER), had made early attempts to coordinate their appearance before the Second World War, these efforts were an exception to the norm. Most organizations operating in the first part of the century had neither the capital, nor the infrastructure, nor the awareness to commission design programmes of this nature and it was not until the 1950s and 1960s that such ideas were realized on an unprecedented scale. As such, the development of corporate branding was a post-war phenomenon, as recognized by scholars from both Britain and the US.[3] This volume concentrates on a period from the mid-1940s onwards, when opportunities for designers to embark upon such programmes began to emerge as a response to the burgeoning culture of reconstruction that followed the end of the war. After the war individual 'commercial artists' of the inter-war period, such as Henrion, began to move away from one-off design commissions for posters, adverts and such like, taking on corporate design programmes of increasing scope and scale.[4] According to design methods theorist Bruce Archer (1965), design underwent a transition during this time away from a sculptural or artefactual paradigm, towards a more technological and systematic one.

Even before the Second World War had ended plans were in place to meet the increase in demand for design services that would follow, with the consultancy Design Research Unit (DRU) having been conceived precisely to address such opportunities. Initially conceived in 1942 and formed in 1943, by 1946 DRU were embarking upon their first comprehensive brand identity programme for the photographic company Ilford (Figure 1.3). This would constitute the first of many such schemes carried out by them over the coming decades.[5] Programmes such as these were distinct from the typical identities of pre-war in that they set out to consolidate a vast network of design artefacts through the application of a specific palette of visual elements. So, whereas most pre-war identity schemes had typically consisted of little more than a trademark repetitively badged across a range of artefacts, the post-war programmes gradually sought to apply more sophisticated, nuanced and controlled aesthetic codes that would include a broader palette of visual elements. This meant moving away from an over-reliance on the trademark or symbol in order to incorporate other visual

Figure 1.3 Example of a comprehensive brand identity programme produced by Design Research Unit for Ilford. As featured in Alec Davis's (1952: 37) article for the *Penrose Annual*. Courtesy of Scott Brownrigg.

elements, like colour, pattern, borders and lettering as important factors within a unified brand identity (Figure 1.4).

In the years that followed, British designers embraced the concept of comprehensive brand identity programmes, actively promoting the idea that they could coordinate a client's design and marketing collateral. Consequently, the scale of design commissions began to grow relatively rapidly. As Michael Middleton (1967: 82) explains:

> In a complex world the unit of design tends to grow ever larger, embracing not merely individual objects but whole ranges of objects. A 'corporate identity programme' will bring, buildings, products, printed matter and all of the aspects of an organisation into a common design framework.

In order to tackle the inherent complexity of such large design programmes, practitioners adapted their working methods to enable them to work more efficiently. Over time a distinctive discourse emerged around the discipline, as well

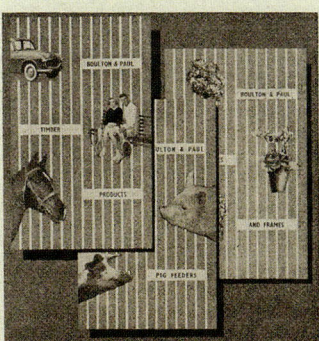

Figure 1.4 Double-page spread from Alec Davis's (1956: 20–1) feature for *Design* magazine on 'Factors in house style', with examples on the use of colour, pattern, borders, trademarks and symbols, and lettering. Item held by the University of Brighton Design Archives.

as techno-rational methods and processes that would enable more practitioners to embrace the new practice. During this period practitioners in Britain were at the forefront of efforts to transform programmatic brand identity design into a recognized practice with its own codified methods. The design of brand identity programmes became a staple activity for British group consultancies in the 1950s and 1960s and articles in the major journals and annuals of the day spread knowledge about what was now considered an important new field of design. The all-encompassing identity programme with its holistic approach to the corporation came to take on ever-greater significance for those design practitioners with any genuine sense of commercial ambition.

By the end of the 1960s the programmatic approach to brand identity design was firmly established, with Henrion and Parkin (1967) publishing the first major book dedicated to the subject incorporating examples of best practice from Britain, alongside those from the United States, Europe and Japan. They described the process of creating a brand identity programme as an act of 'design coordination', a process which they understood as an attempt to control and order a series of branded design artefacts. Although Henrion and Parkin primarily use the term 'design coordination' to emphasize the alignment of design artefacts, the concept can also be understood as one concerned with the alignment of the design workforce and the processual complexity of their work. In this respect, design coordination can be said to involve both the physical act of designing, and the administrative direction of such work, with this duality being a consistent theme throughout the latter chapters of this book.

The trend towards consultant group practice

As designers progressed from conceiving artefacts singly to conceiving them serially, the alignment of multiple designs became a key role for the designer, but the scope of such programmes grew quickly and soon overwhelmed individual freelance practitioners. In order to manage the challenges presented by the complex multiplicity of the corporations they worked for, many practitioners grouped together into teams in order to share their skill sets and enhance their capacity for work. According to Middleton (1967: 85) the concept of group practice in design took root as a direct response to the development of brand identity design, with ever-larger design programmes moving 'beyond the capacity of the individual designer' and collaboration becoming an inevitable by-product. This direct interlinkage between the growth of brand identity and group practice is one I look to examine throughout this book in order to test whether there is validity to Middleton's claim.[6]

As the breadth and depth of design commissions rapidly grew, collaborative group work became commonplace, with design consultants re-evaluating their ways and means of practice. The new, highly collaborative approach had a transformative impact on design practice, with rational methods and techniques being adopted to manage economic risk as the underlying motives and principles of the designers involved came under increasing question. As the number of practising design groups increased, so too did the relative size of these groups, with this surge towards group practice leading to changes in the fundamental dynamics of an occupation that had previously relied on practitioners working in relative isolation to one another and depended largely on personal intuition and the methods of fine art.[7]

There became a need to formalize working design processes and routines in order that practitioners could work more productively together as part of a collective innovation process. These developments occurred in parallel with the impetus of the Design Methods Movement, which had sought to understand and codify the design process.[8] The practice of brand identity design thus came to represent more than simply the coordination of a multitude of design objects, for in most cases the workforce had to be coordinated and managed in tandem with attempts to align systems of design artefacts.[9]

A note on terminology: house style, corporate identity and branding

Within Britain there have been three dominant historical phases in the terminological development of identity design. The first phase spans roughly from 1950 to 1970 and can be characterized as the 'house style' phase, during which this particular term became dominant. Following this was the 'corporate identity' phase, with this term coming to prominence between roughly 1970 and 1990.[10] From the 1990s onwards the term 'branding' gradually came to the fore. While these three practices are each demarcated by distinct terminological reference points and are discrete in terms of their broader ambitions, they do share similarities in the way that they each infer a certain control over the visual appearance of an organization.

During the period studied in this book the terminology deployed to describe the discipline remained unstable with no single term finding common acceptance. The term 'house style' would gradually become increasingly common, but it was many years before it was dominant. Between 1945 and 1955 the design press typically used phrases such as 'family likeness' or 'cumulative impression' to characterize the impact of projects of this nature. The term 'house style' was popularized in no small part due to the efforts of journalist and designer Alec Davis, whose many articles on the subject helped to establish the field. Particularly important was his special issue of *Design* magazine dedicated to the subject (Davis, 1956).

By the late 1960s new terms competed for traction, with Henrion and Parkin championing 'corporate image' and 'design coordination' as important new concepts in their influential book on the subject. Here they borrowed from developments in the US, where 'corporate image' was already an established term.[11] Towards the end of the decade lines began to be redrawn in terms of the focus and remit of the practice, with business and marketing concerns now sitting alongside the aesthetic drivers that had dominated earlier conceptions of the discipline. By the time the term 'corporate identity' came to favour in the 1970s the focus of the practice began to shift dramatically towards business and marketing concerns, with design increasingly becoming a secondary consideration for practitioners working in the field.[12] The term 'corporate identity' remained dominant through the 1980s and early 1990s, until 'branding' began to supplant it as the phrase we recognize today.

These discursive shifts are significant in that they suggest a changing of mindset, a purging of past baggage and an impetus towards the new. Moreover, they can be understood as reflective of the socio-economic context within which such work has been produced. The idea of 'house style' evokes a certain purity and innocence of the post-war era of reconstruction, wherein brand identity remained a relative cottage industry with a focus on craft and aesthetics.[13] 'Corporate identity', by contrast, is synonymous with the business mergers that became increasingly commonplace in the 1970s and 1980s, as well as the growing 'businessification' of design. The move to 'branding', meanwhile, can be understood as an attempt to downplay associations with the corporate world following an increase in anti-corporate sentiment towards the end of the century. This increased scepticism about corporate marketing is evident in publications of the time, including Klein's widely popular text *No Logo* and the magazine *Adbusters*, first published in 1989.

Throughout this book I refer to 'brand identity' to bridge the rhetorical shifts that occurred during the twentieth century. Although this term is not derived directly from the period of focus, it serves to align a plethora of competing terminology linked to specific phases in the subject's development.[14] The concept of 'brand identity' can be understood as analogous with both 'corporate identity' and 'visual identity' in the sense that each term is typically used to refer to the visual manifestation of a brand. Conversely 'brand image' may be interpreted as analogous with 'corporate image' as both phrases are typically used to refer to the public perception of the organization, as opposed to its visual appearance. We get into dangerous territory here as there is a lot of conflict in the way that these terms are used and defined by practitioners from different domains. For instance, some would argue that that corporate identity is about far more than visual appearance.

Brand identity and the professionalization of graphic design

As an extension of the graphic trademark, the design of brand identities programmes has usually been attributed to graphic designers more than those

INTRODUCTION

of a product, industrial design or architectural persuasion, for example. As Davis (1956: 19) explains:

> The basic [house] style will probably be created by an individual, though he may be guided by many others. It is likely that he will be primarily a typographer or graphic artist; theoretically it is also likely that he may be an interior decorator or a colour consultant, but in practice, this seldom seems to happen.

Davis's contention that typographers and graphic artists took a lead in the development of brand identity design is one that I will consider further within this book as I attempt to understand how and why the practice developed in the ways that it did.

Many histories of graphic design have focused on the development of visual communication as a generic activity, tracing their lineage far back to the ancient caves of Lascaux.[15] By comparison this book is framed from the perspective of graphic design's development as a recognized activity of professional labour. Although some practitioners in the US and Britain are known to have deployed the term 'graphic design' in the first half of the twentieth century, the term was not widely adopted in Britain until the mid- to late-1950s.[16] In Britain the Royal College of Art played an important role, introducing their 'School of Graphic Design' in 1948 under Richard Guyatt's stewardship.[17] Developments in the US closely mirrored those in London, with Yale said to have led the way with the development of their graphic design programme under the direction of department chair Josef Albers between 1950 and 1955.

British scholars Robin Kinross (1988) and Paul Stiff (2009) argue that graphic design only emerged as a distinct form of work in Britain during the post-war era. Here they distinguish between earlier commercial art practices, which Stiff characterizes as picture making for business, and the emergence of the new graphic design as a more technocratic and organizationally motivated form of design, wherein acts of planning, coordinating and specifying came to the fore. Here Stiff aligns the emergence of graphic design with the emergence of group work, describing a move away from design activity as a purely personal experience involving one man and his crayon or airbrush, towards a collaborative, shared practice in which team working was key.[18]

The surging interest in corporate communication design after the war was closely interlinked with the concerted efforts of practitioners to professionalize design. So as British 'commercial artists' of the pre-war period began to embrace a new identity as 'graphic designers', they sought to assert their independence from interrelated, but distinct occupations such as advertising and printing, thus gaining jurisdiction over their own field of work.[19] Embracing the opportunities of corporate branding was a means by which to allow more direct working relationships with their clients, enabling them to transform graphic design into a more tenable and stable occupation, cutting out the intermediaries who had commonly managed their work.

The methods and structure of this book

Design as a form of labour and the practice theoretical approach

In this book I examine and explain the working methods of three innovative design consultancies that each played a key role in establishing brand identity design as a central concern for designers in post-war Britain. I consider how the practices of the designers involved were transformed by the demands of complex brand communication programmes that crossed disciplines and media. Based on extensive archival research as well as interviews with relevant employees, my book shifts focus away from the oft-celebrated material artefacts produced by brand designers, concentrating instead on the ways that they went about their work. As such, it studies design as a form of labour and adopts a practice theoretical approach (Nicolini, 2012). In this sense it can be said to be concerned with design-as-practice (Kimbell, 2009). Designers' working documents and files are examined to reveal the rationale and logic behind their decision-making processes. This focus on 'ways of practice' allows us to see how the emergence of branding radically impacted the identities, routines and priorities of the designers involved.

Surprisingly few scholars have investigated design as a form of labour in the post-war era, with little attention given to the materiality of designer's work, or 'ways of practice' within their studio environments.[20] For those who have drawn attention to this period of history there has often been an emphasis on the virtuosity of design, with the practice understood as a liberated form of creative expression and subversiveness, as opposed to a more corporate or institutionalized form of labour. For instance, Rick Poynor's (2004) monograph *Communicate* focuses on graphic design from the 1960s, charting the work of those businesses small enough to retain some degree of personal or creative freedom. In celebrating independent, subversive practice at the expense of more commercially oriented practice, Poynor constructs a history of British graphics that is largely devoid of the corporate. Elsewhere, the V&A museum project 'British Design from 1948' champions the idea that British design has since the 1960s been defined by its subversive spirit (Breward, Fisher and Wood, 2012). These approaches have posited design as a practice closely associated with the creative expression of art, but in seeking to expunge the corporate, they have tended to overlook the occupational basis upon which design work has usually been founded.

INTRODUCTION 15

In this volume I do not seek to celebrate or valorize corporate design, but rather to bring it into the limelight in order to raise important questions about its past and its future. The subject of corporate design tends to evoke strong, polarized viewpoints, which may lead some to second-guess, or try to locate my position as author. To be clear, this volume is no celebration, but neither is it a critique or relentless anti-corporate treatise. Instead it seeks to tread a messier, knottier path, considering multiple perspectives and possibilities. As both a historian of design and an active design practitioner I attempt to bridge between the contextual awareness and deep knowledge of historians and the occupational and material knowledge of design practitioners that is often left tacit or unsaid. In so doing I endeavour to avoid what has been described as the 'redundancy of design history' (Julier and Narotzky, 1998), whereby the interests of historians become divorced from the principles and paradigms of the practice that they purport to study. My knowledge as a practitioner enables me to bring history and practice together in closer proximity. By examining the occupational basis of design and considering how it was transformed during this period my ultimate aim is to reveal relevant insights and raise pertinent questions for both historians of design as well as practising designers. In this sense I seek to develop a reciprocity between past, present and future concerns, while opening up a discursive space between design historians and practitioners.

One key barrier to understanding the occupational basis of design has been the long-standing pre-occupation with the formal aesthetic qualities of the work graphic designers produce. This fascination with over-arching aesthetic developments has undermined our understanding of how the routines and practices of design work have developed over the last century. As design historian Victor Margolin (1994) shows, many scholars have been overly attentive to the visual qualities of design, creating historical narratives that are propelled along by stylistic changes in the look and form of designs. So, while we know much about the ebbs and flows of various design movements across previous decades, as well as the significant contribution made by individual design heroes, far less is known about the ways in which designers' day-to-day practice routines have been conducted, or how they have changed over time and why. The focus of scholars on design artefacts and their impact on society has thus led to the patterns of working practice to be largely ignored.[21] As Margolin (1994: 233) puts it, 'Various publications have brought attention to the subject of graphic design history, but have not marked a course for the full explanation of how graphic design developed as a practice'.

This volume constitutes an attempt to address this lack of attention directed towards this history of practice. In it I focus on a key period of British design history, during which the working methods of graphic designers were radically transformed as they adopted systematic approaches to design in order to manage increasingly complex corporate communication design commissions.

The material artefacts and apparatuses that developed in result of the codification of design practice will constitute a central subject of study within this book, as I direct my attention towards the materiality of practice. Referencing historical artefacts used by design practitioners in the performance of their work, I will seek to develop a more materially aware understanding of design practice during the post-war period. Here I move focus away from the design artefacts produced as a result of the design process, turning my attention instead towards the tools and apparatus developed to carry out this work.

The material apparatus of design

Those studies that have considered the impact of tools and technology on the enactment of design work have often centred around the capacity of tools for mark-making of various kinds. This includes scholarship focused on apparatuses used to develop or extend human mark-making capabilities, from the pencil or airbrush (Laing and Saunders-Davies, 1986), to the computer (Labuz, 1993). Elsewhere there is a body of literature focused on the apparatuses that have enabled graphics to be reproduced on-mass via various print technologies (Twyman, 1970, 2013). Generally speaking, these studies into the tools of graphic design have developed from a concern with the formal aesthetics of designers' work, seeking to explain how tools have impacted the visual appearance of designed artefacts.

By comparison, this book focuses on the tools deployed by corporate design practitioners to manage the cognitive bases of their work and to substantiate it as a legitimate form of knowledge production and more than simply an aesthetic veneer. As such, the tools examined in this book have been used by practitioners to better define design problems, to rationalize or specify their responses to these problems and to organize their workflows, for instance. Although these tools are often unglamourous in their nature and typically of little immediate aesthetic interest, they are nevertheless valuable evidence of the patterns of practice.

In focusing on these kinds of entities I am championing the significance that material 'things' can have in establishing the patterns and routines of practice. Here I respond to Bruno Latour's (1992) contention that studies of organizational systems have historically been analysed almost exclusively without reference to the volumes of stuff involved. As Alex Preda elaborates, things and artefacts have historically tended to be treated as marginal, irrelevant or passive in terms of the production of social order. For Preda (1999: 351), such 'things' need to be reconsidered as active rather than passive social entities, as they have the capacity to 'bind human actors and participate in developing specific forms of social order because they allow for common practices to develop, stabilise and structure time'.

In order to interpret and understand these material artefacts I adopt strategies, concepts and methods from Management and Organization Studies (MOS) and Science and Technology Studies (STS). From MOS I take my broad-based strategy, which is a practice theoretical approach, while from STS I adopt 'inscription' as a core concept that enables me to consider how knowledge has been embedded in material artefacts deployed by the consultancies in question. More on these influences follows here.

Adopting a practice theoretical approach in accordance with the ideas of Theodore Schatzki (2002), Andreas Reckwitz (2002) and Davide Nicolini (2012) enables me to underscore the relevance of how ways of practice have changed over time. The basic unit of analysis will be practices, rather than practitioners, which makes this an atypical approach for graphic design history, which has tended to valorize practitioners. Practice theory is fundamentally an approach focused on the processual nature of practice, with practices being understood as bundled sets of activities hierarchically organized into nexuses of doings, sayings, tasks and projects. When I refer to practice, I refer to the everyday activities of designers at work, their actions, habits and rituals. Practice theory foregrounds activity and performance, affording a capacity to, 'describe important features of the world we inhabit as something that is routinely made and re-made in practice using tools, discourse, and our bodies' (Nicolini, 2012: 2). Alan Warde's (2014: 284) definition is also useful here, with practice being described by Warde as, 'practical and routine activity, embodied procedures, the material and instrumental aspects of life and mechanisms for the transmission of culture into action'.

To date, practice theory has been underused within design studies. Shove et al. (2007) provide an example of the potential, employing a practice theoretical approach in their study of the underplayed importance of designed artefacts in everyday life. While their work focuses on the everyday significance of designed products, this volume, by comparison, shines a light on the role that technological entities have played in supporting the development of brand identity design practices.

Debate abounds in terms of where agential power resides within practices, with proponents of Actor Network Theory viewing non-human objects as important actors with a level of agency that is equivalent to that of humans. By comparison self-proclaimed practice theorists tend to be more reticent about the agency of non-humans and typically view human agency as hierarchically dominant. As Postill (2010: 10) explains, most practice theorists define practices as, simply, 'arrays of activity in which the human body is the nexus'. The practice approach thus embraces mentalist and textualist ideas, seeing practice as neither internal, inside the head of actors as a mental or cognitive phenomenon, nor external in some form of structure or discourse. As Christian Bueger and Frank Gadinger (2015) elaborate:

> ... scholars [of practice theory] see practice as ontologically in between the inside and the outside. They identify the social in the mind (since individuals are carriers of practices), but also in symbolic structures (since practices form more or less extra-subjective structures and patterns of action).

This sense of practice theory as an approach that acknowledges the importance of the minds of the practitioners as well as the structures and discourses within which they operate sits well with my intentions, as a study of corporate design must consider both the internal and external operations of practitioners in order to provide an account of meaningful depth. Also significant is the fact that practice theorists recognize the potentially collective nature of knowledge. This is important given that I have identified group practice as a critical factor in the emergence of programmatic branding. Furthermore, practice theorists acknowledge action as a legitimate form of knowledge, giving credence to tacit knowledge and performativity, as well as more dominant forms of technically rational or explicated knowledge.

In this book we will see examples of practitioners who favoured both ends of the spectrum, with some embracing technical rationality, and others resisting demands to explicate their knowledge, favouring tacit and practical forms of rationality instead.[22] To account for the working routines of these practitioners I investigate the micro-practices of three representative design consultancies, thus 'zooming in' on practice to establish how designers responded to the challenges and opportunities of programmatic branding (I go on to discuss how the three design consultancies were identified in Part Two of the book). Through a process of 'zooming out' I seek to draw connections between the three group practices under study, before speculating about their impact on subsequent patterns of practice. In this process of zooming in and then out, I adopt what Nicolini (2009) terms the strong approach to practice. Here I seek to address criticisms levelled at so-called weak approaches to practice-based study that have been accused of producing rich descriptions of everyday work, but little value in terms of the meaning of that work, what makes it possible and why it is performed in the way that it is. By comparison the strong approach attempts to move beyond pure description in order to understand the broader significance of the practice.

De-scripting practice

To analyse the micro-practices of the three representative design consultancies I draw attention to apparatus mobilized in the performance of their work, borrowing theoretical ideas from STS in order to interpret these entities. This apparatus enables me to provide rich and detailed insights using technology as a means to observe the processual complexity of practice. My interest here is in how design consultancies utilized forms of technology to achieve their creative and commercial objectives. By technology, I refer not to technical machines per se, but rather to an expanded definition of technology as a system that involves 'organisation, procedures, symbols, new words, equations, and, most of all, a mindset' (Franklin, 1999: 3). Many of the tools observed in this book would not be understood as machines, and would likely be considered rudimentary in terms of their technological advancement; yet they represent important examples of how a new approach to brand identity was initiated with support from technical entities that helped to frame new ways of doing, saying and being.

To interpret these technical entities, I endeavour to decipher patterns of activity embedded or inscribed within them. The Latourian concept of 'inscription' is important here as it speaks to the way that objects, artefacts or things are prefigured, or scripted, with certain affordances, conditions or knowledge. In their study of the scientific laboratory as a site of knowledge production, Latour and Woolgar describe inscription as 'an operation more basic than writing'. They hold a particular interest in the 'inscription device', which they define as, 'any item of apparatus or particular configuration of such items which can transform a material substance into a figure or diagram which is directly usable by one of the members of the office space' (Latour and Woolgar, 1986: 51). Inscription devices are thus the technical entities that enable inscriptions to be made. Elsewhere, Latour (1983) has described inscriptions as written traces that make the perceptive judgment of others simpler.

Central to the power of inscription is its relative durability in comparison to thought or speech. So, while thought or speech can be viewed as transient, inscriptions are immutable and mobile, acting as mechanisms for the transmission of culture into action (Law, 1992). As Madeline Akrich (1992: 208) explains, 'like a film script, technical objects define a framework of action'. But just as these technical entities can define how action unfolds, they can also be used to describe and decipher action that has already occurred. Here I draw on Akrich's concept of 'de-scripting', which refers to the process by which knowledge that was previously 'black-boxed' or obscured from comprehension is revealed or understood. It is through this act of de-scripting that researchers gain entry to the black boxes of practice, thus reverse-engineering an understanding of practice pieced together from traces of the inscriptions left behind. My role is thus to de-script, decipher and decode the various inscriptions mobilized in practice by the design consultancies in question.

For Latour, inscription is an important concept for scholars who want to understand and unpick power relations between different social agents. One of the key facets of an inscription-based approach is the ability to address potentially disturbing material differences between the tools that are involved in a practice.

This makes it possible to investigate a wide range of different artefacts from a single consistent viewpoint. This is significant for my study as the tools mobilized by design coordination practitioners vary greatly in their medium, format and general material qualities.

The structure of the book

The book is comprised of three parts. Part One takes a zoomed-out stance in order to explain and contextualize the wider significance of brand identity programmes in terms of the historical development of design and branding practices in Britain and abroad. Part Two adopts a more zoomed-in, ground-up approach in order to closely examine how patterns of practice were developing and changing in the post-war period. Part Three then zooms back out to draw together themes and threads and look at the long-term legacy of these developments.

Chapter 2 reviews long-standing tropes and tendencies within the study of branding. The practice theoretical approach taken within this book is positioned in relation to more well-established approaches that are typical in the field. This chapter goes on to consider the history of programmatic branding, reviewing several important phases of development and explaining why the chosen period of emergence and codification is particularly important.

Chapter 3 focuses on programmatic approaches to brand identity design within Britain in the post-war period. It sets out an overview of changes occurring at the time with reference to recognized design personalities and groups. These changes are contextualized in relation to broader socio-economic developments within Britain. The emerging discourse of programmatic identity design is explored, with key texts examined to show how the subject was becoming established as a distinctive and recognizable practice of growing importance.

Part Two of the book begins with an explanation of how the three representative consultancies were selected for inclusion in this book. This leads into Chapter 4, which focuses on the work of Henrion Design Associates and the systematic methods they developed for their clients. This chapter explores the planning and design tools developed by an early design consultancy in their attempts to gain power over their clients and other competing professionals. We see how the consultancy reconfigured their practice around the business opportunities provided by brand identity design work, sharing and publicizing these methods through the design press and professional events.

Chapter 5 focuses on the work of Hans Schleger & Associates and their identity for the fishmonger Mac Fisheries created under the direction of the advertising agency Mather & Crowther. Collaborative documents are examined to reveal the power relations between advertising agencies, design consultancies and clients. This chapter provides a counterpoint to the other case studies, demonstrating a model of consultancy that resisted the rationalization and systematization of

INTRODUCTION

design. The group were strongly against standardization and homogeneity in design, and were able to create coordinated, but not standardized brand identity programmes that retained a sense of humour and humanity.

Chapter 6 focuses on the work of Design Research Unit and their evolving approach to brand identity manuals. Client reports show how they were initially against what they called the 'stereotyped' approach of homogenous chain store graphics, preferring to embrace and celebrate variety and multiplicity in their approach to brand identity design. Through examples we see how their founding principles were challenged, leading them to adopt more tightly controlled design programmes founded on the unified homogeneity they had earlier loathed. This chapter shows different approaches to controlling design through specification documents and guidelines – from the loose cooperative approach of 'recommendations', to the controlling approach of 'standards'.

Part Three begins with Chapter 7, which draws connections between the individual case studies, identifying recurrent themes and threads of interest. The process of synthesis that occurs here is important as it enables me to move beyond 'thick description' (Geertz, 1973) of isolated work scenarios to build a fuller picture of working patterns as a whole. The fight for professional jurisdiction is discussed in terms of the relationship between advertising, graphic design and design management. The role of the designer as a leader is considered in relation to the three presented examples. Models and methods of group working are analysed in relation to the examples and scenarios previously discussed. Finally, the changing motives and ideals of designers is considered in relation to their attitudes to socio-cultural and economic capital.

Chapter 8 brings this volume to a close, providing an overview of the enquiry, along with an exploration of the long-term legacy of post-war design methods and their impact on contemporary branding design practice. The contribution of each case study is briefly summarized before I move on to consider the transition from the post-war period of emergence studied here to the phase of proliferation that occurred later in the 1970s and 1980s.

2
A MACRO HISTORY OF CORPORATE BRANDING

Overarching tropes in the treatment of brand identity

The subject of brand identity design has generated a vast amount of scholarly and professional literature, but this work tends to fall within certain recognizable categories. In this section I identify dominant tropes in the treatment of brand identity, recognizing three core tendencies within the field. The first looks at the overwhelming dominance of logos within literature about the design of brands. Secondly, I explore the celebratory showcase, an approach that valorizes designers' creative work as well as their unique expertise and know-how. Finally, I look to the development of business-based literature emerging from the domain of corporate communications and marketing. This section is not intended as an exhaustive review of literature, but rather a mapping of common approaches that have defined the ways the subject has been understood to date. By identifying strong tendencies within the field, I highlight areas of focus, as well as blind spots ripe for further exploration.

Taxonomies of trademarks and the obsession with corporate symbols

Logos and trademarks have long dominated discourse around the subject of design for brands. Although the act of branding is said to have originated many centuries ago, the term 'branding' only came to prominence towards the very end of the twentieth century around the time that Naomi Klein's (1999) book *No Logo* came to public consciousness. As a practice it has come to be inextricably linked in the public consciousness with the omnipresent corporate logos that adorn our environments. Such is the strength of the connection between branding and logos, that the two concepts have become largely synonymous with one another. This is evident in the mainstream press, where it is now common to compare the size of a branding fee with the seemingly insubstantial corporate logo that results from this.

While it true that logo design *can* be instrumental in building the public impression of an organization, it is more accurate to think of the logo as the tip of the proverbial iceberg. Corporate branding practice is usually based upon complex strategic planning, incorporating sophisticated visual unification systems in order to align hundreds or thousands of communication assets across diverse international markets and multiple communication channels. Logo design *can* prove to be a useful gateway to a fuller understanding of brand design, but the omnipresence of the logo as a powerful concept in society has more often proved to be a barrier to awareness of what brand communication design practice actually entails.

The tendency to treat brands in a logo-centric manner is not new and can be traced back long before 'branding' was the preferred term of choice. Many of the first books published on the subject of brand identity were dedicated to the design of logos, or trademarks as they were then more often known. Egbert Jacobsen (1952) edited one such volume called *Seven Designers Look at Trademark Design*, within which several prominent North American practitioners set out their take on the process of creating a trademark. What has since followed appears to have been an inexhaustible stream of inventories from across the globe, each extensively cataloguing the corporate symbols of their time. Key examples here include works by Kamekura (1965), Ricci and Ferrari (1973), Kuwayama (1973), Wildbur (1979), Klanten (2002), Evamy (2007) and Hyland and Bateman (2011). Whether originating from Asia, North America or Europe, each of the publications in this long canon of inventories share a common will to collate and classify a range of corporate symbols with the fervour of an enthusiastic collector. However, in their efforts to capture great breadth and variety, texts such as these extract corporate symbols from their socio-cultural context, removing much of their meaning and reducing them to studies in form. These catalogues of trademarks are representative of the strong logo-centric tendency when it comes to thinking about the design of brands.

While some texts about logos have adopted formats distinct from the taxonomic catalogue – the logo design textbook being a pertinent one – the inventory approach is arguably most dominant.[1] I highlight this logo-centric trend in order to draw attention to the overbearing tendencies affecting the discipline that have limited the manner with which it has been studied and understood to date. Such has been the obsession with logos, that it is only in recent decades that dynamic brand programmes have gained more widespread attention from authors in the field, with examples like Ulrike Felsing's (2010) *Dynamic Identities in Cultural and Public Contexts*, Irene van Nes's (2012) *Dynamic Identities,* and Martin Lorenz's (2021) *Flexible Visual Systems*. Contemporary examples such as these show a trend towards design programmes that not only offer visual unification, but also dynamism and variability.

Case studies, gurus and celebrations of success

Aside from the literature focused on corporate logos, also prevalent are those texts emanating from specific corporations or organizations. Where taxonomies of trademarks have located corporate branding firmly within the realm of graphic design, the case study format has tended to place the subject as a more divergent discipline, taking in architecture, product design and event design, for example. These texts tend to be hagiographic in nature, presenting a one-sided story of events that unquestioningly valorizes their chosen subjects. Most literature in the corporate design field is of a journalistic, pro-corporate outlook, with case studies for large multinational clients being showcased in a slick fashion with glossy photos and small amounts of explanatory text. Key examples here are Lubliner's (1994) *Global Corporate Identity*, along with Nakanishi's (1979, 1985) earlier volumes on *Corporate Design Systems*.

Also prevalent in the field are those books adopting the trope of the self-promotional showcase. These texts are produced by either single design agencies, such as Pentagram, or specific corporations, such as Olivetti, IBM, Philips or Braun.[2] Texts such as these celebrate the success of design companies and their clients, often acting as a marketing device to garner interest in the brand or the agencies who developed them. Showcase texts such as these have usually been sponsored or self-published by the subjects of the studies themselves and this goes a long way to explaining their typically one-sided nature. Such is the nature of publishing, that if you want extensive access and image permission rights to a design archive you will almost certainly be expected to celebrate the creative genius of the designers involved. This tradition continues today with publishers like Unit Editions who celebrate the work of heroic design individuals like Henrion (Shaughnessy, 2013), as well as renowned design groups like Pentagram (Shaughnessy, 2023) and North (Perkins, 2024).

Equally problematic in terms of their partiality are the 'how-to-do-it', or 'guru' texts that have emanated from figureheads in the industry who tend to have a vested interested in promoting the services of their own companies, whether explicitly or not. Early British exemplars of this ilk include Michael Farr's (1966) *Design Management*, F. H. K. Henrion and Alan Parkin's (1967) *Design Coordination and Corporate Image,* Ole Eksell's (1967) *Corporate Design Programs*, James Pilditch's (1970) *Communication by Design*, and Wally Olins's (1978) *The Corporate Personality*.

Wally Olins has proved to be a particularly influential figure in the development and proliferation of corporate branding, writing about the importance of design as an element of business strategy. Olins, who in 1965 co-founded the corporate design agency Wolff Olins with Michael Wolff, wrote prolifically on the subject over several decades and is widely considered to have taken a leading role in the development of the discipline. *The Corporate Personality* is considered seminal in the field, with corporate communications scholar John M. T. Balmer (2014: 6) proclaiming that, 'an understanding of this book is critical to an understanding of the roots of corporate identity scholarship and, moreover, to a discernment of corporate identity that goes beyond graphic design and a concern with visual identity schemes and company logos'.

Decades earlier, design academic Steve Baker (1989: 275, original emphasis) claimed, 'what corporate identity currently *is*, I would contend, is largely the result of the ways in which Wally Olins defined the field in 1978 in his first book, *The Corporate Personality*'. Though this reads like praise when taken out of context, it was far from it. Baker was actually attempting to hold Olins to account for what he saw as the issues that had dogged the discipline's development and restricted the ways in which it had been understood, using his article to dismantle Olins's arguments and highlight the contradictions, inconsistencies and generalizations found in the book. Baker took issue with Olins's pro-corporate outlook and argued that the text lacked nuance and credibility, being hindered by Olins's self-aggrandizing 'chummy' prose style and over-riding commercial motives. His main concern with the text was the lack of internal logic and alignment to Olins's ideas, which for Baker, resulted in leaks, gaps and areas of silence not addressed.

Given the perceived deficiencies Baker underlines, one might wonder why the text proved so influential. Baker suggests it was Olins's position as the chairman of Britain's best known, market-leading corporate identity consultants that propelled the book on to such great renown; a suggestion that has credibility, as the ever-increasing financial rewards involved for those at the leading edge of the discipline would have lent Olins's words great sway. Olins was also considered an aggressive self-publicist, which could only have helped in the successful promotion of his book.

Olins developed his own personal canon of publications over many decades, but it was his practitioner books on branding pre-2000 that were especially influential in explaining the criticality of corporate identity to organizations and their management. As such, Balmer argues that Olins's work inspired and greatly influenced the first generation of corporate communications and corporate marketing academics. Olins certainly played a role in broadening the conceptualization of corporate identity from a discipline narrowly rooted in graphic design, to one that plays an important role in the wider marketing mix. Thus, we see Olins (1979: 209) emphasizing the notion that corporate identity is concerned equally with behaviour *and* appearance:

> Corporate identity – real corporate identity that is – is about behaviour as much as appearance, and certainly about reality, as much as symbolism. Whenever behaviour and appearance are linked real corporate identity emerges.

This move to shift focus away from what Olins saw as the thin veneer of the graphic image and towards a deeper conceptualization of business identity, led the discipline to radically develop in scope and ambition in the decades that followed. As corporate design consultants began to consider their clients' corporate policies on a much broader level, this led to a rise in the status of the corporate design consultant, with design and branding increasingly viewed as a legitimate concern for the board room.

Corporate identity and branding as facets of corporate communications and marketing

From the 'guru' texts of practitioners like James Pilditch and Wally Olins emerged a new domain of literature more scholarly in its approach. This canon of work is best represented by the work of the aforementioned John M. T. Balmer (2001, 2010, 2014), who epitomizes the new breed of academically minded business scholars working from the 1990s onwards. The long list of journals to which Balmer has contributed gives a sense of the contexts within which such scholarship resides, with publications focused on brand management, corporate communications, marketing and business ethics, for example.

Examining the disciplinary literature from the late twentieth century reveals a developing schism between those texts produced by practising brand identity designers and those texts emanating from the first generation of corporate communication scholars. From this new breed of marketing academics a strand of literature emerged around the turn of the millennium that came to serve a different kind of professional for whom design was only a facet of the broader marketing mix.[3] When Balmer suggests that his work is directed at scholars and practitioners alike, the practitioners he has in mind would appear to be broad-based branding professionals as opposed to those tasked with the fabrication of brand identity programmes. It is not that Balmer's work is without worth for designers, but rather that the cultures and priorities of corporate communication scholars and practising brand identity designers diverged significantly over time. This fractured state of affairs is evident in the kinds of journals and conferences that branding design practitioners have contributed to. In contrast to the long list of peer-reviewed journals in which Balmer has been published, those branding design practitioners engaging in a broader disciplinary dialogue tend to contribute to design-industry-focused magazines and journals such as *Design Week*, *Creative Review* and *Eye*, as well as industry-led conferences, such as TYPO and Brand New. In doing so they have often tended to publicize the work and the approach of their own businesses first and foremost, establishing themselves as aspirational design personalities.

As corporate communications scholars sought to develop a body of literature aligned with the interests of broad-based branding and marketing professionals, by contrast, the more specific discourse around brand identity design has become increasingly insular and self-serving. There are some exceptions to this tendency wherein scholarship and practice have sought to find a greater sense of coherence. For example, design firm Moving Brands (2009) adopted a more formal tone when releasing what they described as their first 'paper'. This was not a paper in the scholarly sense, but rather a self-promotional publication with imagery showcasing their portfolio of work and textual snippets of their broad creative philosophy. Three years later they released a 'white paper' (Moving Brands, 2012) summarizing a presentation given at an insurance industry forum for global businesses. Though including references for further reading and being entirely text based, the modular format of this second paper reads like a set of expanded, bullet-pointed principles. The subtle shift in language from 'paper' to 'white paper' can be seen to imply a desire to align more closely with governmental or industry-driven expertise rather than academic research per se.

Isolated examples such as this show a willingness or curiosity on behalf of design practitioners to engage in disciplinary dialogue, but they also emphasize the significant cultural differences between practising brand identity design professionals and practising marketing experts and scholars. While agencies like Moving Brands should be applauded for trying to find a middle ground between the conventions and expectations of academic practice and those of commercial practice, their efforts only serve to underline the dearth of scholarly material serving the interests of brand identity design practitioners. This deficit leaves significant gaps that I seek to address in this book.

Wally Olins is one of the few early design professionals to have worked in such gaps with any conviction, contributing to refereed journals and books later in his career. This is less surprising when one considers that he read History at Oxford and was once noted as, 'the only design consultant that I know who's never had a design training' (Alan Eden-Green, cited in Olins, 1979: 208). In this respect, Olins is reflective of the increasingly strategic and business-led orientation of branding. Equally he can be seen as representative of a broadening in the scope and remit of brand identity design as the century progressed. As design activity increasingly became a board-level concern, opportunities emerged for strategic, business-savvy individuals like Olins to enter the fray. Indeed, he was by no means the first, or only one to do so, with British consultants like Michael Farr and James Pilditch also gaining similar influence earlier in the 1960s.

Practitioners working in academia and design research have made their own unique contribution to literature in the field, often seeking to question and interrogate the status quo. Examples like Metahaven's *Uncorporate Identity* (van der Velden and Kruk, 2009) point to a tradition wherein communication design researchers have sought to explore alternate conceptions of brand oriented more around social purpose. Metahaven's critique of corporate identity has been highly influential in European design schools, but regrettably their publication became known as much for its visual style as its verbal arguments.

More recently, Jason Grant and Oliver Vodeb's (2023) book on post-branding set out to propose a new set of ideals for a more conscientious approach to brand that would counter fundamentalist marketplace semiotics. Their premise built upon three key strategies they describe as, transparency and open-source principles, participatory design approaches, and diversity and commoning. These strategies are conceived to counter issues associated with corporate design and demonstrate ways to challenge the hegemony of neoliberal ideology within branding practices.

These contemporary examples demonstrate how designers within academia have used their position to posit alternate models that reject the entrenched principles of corporate design culture. It is notable that these particular examples operate at the margins, looking in at corporate design practice from outside. In this sense they tend to speak to those who welcome their anti-corporate sentiment, but arguably texts such as these have little impact on practitioners actually working within these domains.

The history of brand identity design as a programmatic endeavour

While it is widely accepted that the brand-mark as a symbol of identification has existed for many centuries, the activity of creating a comprehensive brand identity programme is understood as a more recent notion. Given that debate surrounds the question of how far back such a tendency can be traced, here I map out four distinct schools of thought, locating the different key moments of development for each. These schools of thought can be summarized as follows: Broad antecedents – pre-twentieth century, Founding Fathers – early twentieth century, Codification – the post-war years, Proliferation – the 1980s. The following sections draw out the key reference points and axioms upon which these schools of thought depend.

Broad antecedents – pre-twentieth century

Firstly, there are those who have attempted to trace back the tendency for comprehensive programmatic identity schemes through the centuries. For example, Olins (1978: 18) loosely argues that a historical precedent was set by various religious groups that had used art to project and control their appearance. He goes on to claim that the second phase of the Industrial Revolution was more significant, with large and complex enterprises being formed that couldn't be controlled by existing techniques. He suggests that the English railways of the 1850s were especially important, as they were in large part responsible for pioneering the activity of brand identity design – as well as many of the broader facets of modern management – and that their work marked the beginning of the age of corporate identity. Such companies expressed a unity of style made apparent by the consistent colouring of vehicle liveries, broad architectural and typographic similarities, as well as distinctive crockery and cutlery within the dining cars of the trains.

Though the efforts of such railway companies provide an interesting foregrounding to events that would follow, I side with those commentators such as Avril Blake (1986) and Wibo Bakker (2005) who have argued that these activities were more tentative or gestural in their ambitions and should not be considered comprehensive or programmatic attempts at visual unification, but rather early exploratory steps.

Founding Fathers – early twentieth century

Next in line are those scholars who have suggested that the early twentieth century marked the key period in which comprehensive brand identity programmes emerged. In this bracket fall Philip B. Meggs (1983), Richard Hollis (1994) and Jonathan Woodham (1997). Many histories of corporate design have been dominated by Peter Behrens's work for the electrical firm Allgemeine Elektricitäts-Gesellschaft (AEG), with graphic design historians lauding this as the first ever brand identity programme.

Working as AEG's artistic adviser from 1907 onwards, Behrens was responsible for a broad range of designs, from monumental architectural structures to more modest printed catalogues and posters. Aside from the scope and multidisciplinary nature of this work, what marked it out from that of its predecessors – such as the English railway companies – was the coherence of its overall approach. This uniformity was achieved in part through the standardization of two key design components: the corporate logo and bespoke typeface.

AEG's use of a corporate logo was not in itself an innovation, yet this particular design, shaped like a honeycomb, distinguished itself through the visual alignment it maintained with other designs produced within the programme. As design historian Frederic Schwarz (1996) explains, Behrens applied the logo not only to products and catalogues, but also to buildings, such as the AEG's turbine hall. Further to this, Behrens allowed the structure of his designs to be informed by the honeycomb shape of the logo. This can be seen in the corporate architecture of the AEG turbine hall, where the angles of the roof structure mirror the angles of the trademark. It is also evident in some of the company's products, such as the coffee pots Behrens designed for the firm. Alongside the logo, Behrens developed his own unique alphabet for AEG that would be released as a mechanized typeface. Behrens Antiqua, as it was called, was unconventional in design and helped to differentiate the company from its competitors.

The most critical aspect of Behrens's work for AEG was the consistent and controlled way that the two core design components – the logo and the typeface – were applied. Using grid structures derived from architectural theory, Behrens was able to construct a wide range of design artefacts united by a common structural backbone. Whilst grids such as these had been used extensively in architecture before, Behrens's dogmatic application of these structures was unprecedented in the domain of brand identity and played a significant role in the creation of his highly rational and ordered identity for AEG.[4]

Another powerful and oft-cited example from the early twentieth century is the identity of the Nazi party. Several authors have argued that this design work constitutes one of the most 'successful' visual identities of the twentieth century. The party's handbook, *Organizationsbuch der NSDAP*, has been considered amongst the first identity manuals, but as design historian Steven Heller claims, the identity was not as strictly unitary as we are often led to believe. He explains: 'The Nazis brand may indeed be uniformly distinctive, but for all the significance they placed on graphic design, there was more variety and greater leeway than one might think' (Heller, 2011). Aside from these questions around its design qualities and relative homogeneity and control, this undoubtedly remains a forceful example, as well as a warning, of the powerful potential of communication design programmes such as this.

Aside from Behrens's design programme emanating from Germany, there are several other canonical international examples persistently put forward by design historians. These have included Frank Pick's stewardship of London Transport from 1908 onwards, North American Walter Dorwin Teague's designs for Texaco in the 1930s, Adriano Olivetti's direction of Italian firm Olivetti in the 1930s, and Walter Paepcke's patronage of Container Corporation of America from the late 1930s. But for each of these canonical examples, there are other, oft-neglected cases that are due further consideration. For instance, in Britain, little-known examples include the standardized lettering of W. H. Smith, c. 1903; Tootal's bespoke alphabet design, c.1911; the early lettering and colour scheme of Mac Fisheries, c.1920; and the typographic standardization of the London & North Eastern Railway (LNER) and its coordinated poster campaigns, c.1930.

In continental Europe some work has already been done to establish the roots of brand identity design in particular countries. Design historian Carlo Vinti (2007) has provided a detailed account of pioneering brand identity work in Italy, while Wibo Bakker (2011a) has produced equivalent work on such developments in

A MACRO HISTORY OF CORPORATE BRANDING

the Netherlands. Bakker argues against the international canon referenced above (AEG, London Transport, Texaco, Olivetti and Container Corporation), claiming that such firms have been wrongly identified as pioneers of the discipline. He suggests that the central concern of these firms was to present themselves through 'good design' and that because they were not concerned with 'visual unification', their work should not be considered corporate identity. According to Bakker, designers and historians have placed undue significance on these works due to the quality of individual design pieces and the renown of the individual designers involved.

Whilst there may be a case to argue that this book could be reframed, beginning earlier to incorporate preliminary examples, I have chosen to concentrate attention on the post-war years during which brand identity design practices became more fully established. As Kinross (1988) and Stiff (2009) explain, this latter post-war period was critical in terms of the development and commercialization of graphic design consultancy in Britain. Moreover, Balmer (1998) supports the idea that this era was critical, stating that the period from 1950 to 1970 was the first important phase in the evolutionary development of corporate identity. Others have also shared this view, as we will see in the next short section.

Codification – the post-war years

Next, there are those who claim that the early examples of AEG and Olivetti, for instance, are isolated and exceptional cases and that brand identity on a broader level only found true relevance in the years following the Second World War. For example, Avril Blake (1986: 42) claims the following:

> The idea that design could be used as a business tool, to express a firm's unique identity through all aspects of its operation, had existed before the war, but its realisation was very much a post-war phenomenon and developed on a large scale only during these ten or fifteen years.

Blake's observations here reflect the significant socio-economic changes that occurred in Britain during the post-war era, with the ongoing climate of reconstruction leading to increased investment in industry as the country sought to develop its economic performance. Consequently, new opportunities arose for ambitious designers to harness the potential of design as a force for renewal, with the drive towards 'modernization' enabling practitioners to explore programmatic approaches to brand identity design.

Blake's comments are significant as they set out a key foundational premise upon which this book develops from, this being that brand identity only developed as a significant and recognizable practice in the post-war era. Elsewhere the

North American designer Saul Bass (cited in Meggs, 1990: 4) recognizes a similar pattern in America to the one that Blake identifies in Britain, suggesting that:

> Corporate identity as a clear discipline is a post-World War II phenomenon. It's only thirty or forty years old. During this period, its grown from a cottage industry to an institutionalized form, has become an acknowledged component of business activity.

Given that the US is often understood to have been ahead of the curve in terms of the commercialization of design, Bass's comments are notable, suggesting that the development of brand identity in North America was more in line with Britain than might first be assumed. The range of brand identity design literature emanating from both countries in the post-war period reveals that, if anything, Britain was slightly ahead of the US, at least in terms of the codification and dissemination of knowledge surrounding the discipline.

In Britain, design practitioner and writer Alec Davis took on a leading role in establishing the terrain, contributing a series of important articles on the subject, which are discussed in more detail later in this book. The pinnacle of these efforts was his special issue of *Design* magazine, published in September 1956. This text was relatively insular in its choice of content, with little reference to developments occurring outside Britain. In the US, meanwhile, the design and marketing agency Lippincott & Margulies (1958a, 1958b) took a leading role with their efforts to codify 'corporate identity' in their self-promotional publication, *Sense*. Over two special issues in 1958 they sought to clarify the rhetoric surrounding the discipline, providing examples of effective brand identity programmes, and even offering guidance around the appropriate use of corporate identity manuals. This was a significant milestone in the development of brand identity in the US, coming some two years after *Design* magazine's 'House Style' special.

Arguably the most influential post-war practitioner in the US was designer Paul Rand, known for his brand identity programmes for clients like IBM, UPS and ABC. Unlike the new consultant design groups in Britain, Rand preferred to work alone, seeing limitations to collaborative large-scale teamwork. He wrote in the British trade journal *Art & Industry* (Rand, 1947) of the need for a single designer to oversee each design composition. As he saw it, a design would lose its unity of style and purpose when different practitioners were in charge of separate design components that were only later brought together as one.

Although he preferred to work alone with (albeit with the aid of an assistant or two), Rand's career success depended on his working relationship with the industrial designer Eliot Noyes, who played an integral role in many of his most celebrated brand identities. Together Noyes and Rand developed a comprehensive approach that incorporated graphics on an equal footing alongside the more well-established domain of industrial design. Their work continued in the tradition of Peter Behrens at AEG, with Behrens' ideologies being passed on to Noyes through his professor at Harvard, Walter Gropius, founder of the Bauhaus school.

Although Rand was a major influence both within and beyond US borders, his knowledge of brand identity remained largely implicit in his work, with his writing about design touching on a wide range of subjects, but never really codifying a unique or specific approach to brand design that others could adhere to. His article 'The Trademark as an Illustrative Device' (Rand, 1952) shows his early awareness of brand systems and his inclination towards playfulness and flexibility, with play being a common theme he often circled back to in his writing.

By the late 1950s and early 1960s the concept of 'corporate image' came to dominate discourse in the US and was closely linked with in-house public relations, planning and marketing departments. In its May–June 1959 edition, the US magazine *Print* came out with a special edition dedicated to the subject ('Corporate Image Issue', 1959), featuring contributions from Europeans, including the British-based graphic designer, Willy de Majo. The trend towards 'corporate image' as an exercise in management and public relations is also exemplified by American Lee Hastings Britol's (1960) book, *Developing the Corporate Image: A Management Guide to Public Relations*.

Prior to the publication of the literature described above, Germany had led the way in the summer of 1954 with 'Das Firmengesicht', an international exhibition dedicated to 'The Face of the Firm' (Wills, 1954) (Figure 2.1).[5] The exhibition was structured around the corporations involved, as opposed to the featured designers, and included British work by designers Lewitt-Him for Schweppes and Hans Schleger for Mac Fisheries (focused on later in this book), as well as representation from Simpson of Piccadilly and Wolsey of Leicester. This work sat alongside designs from North America (Columbia Broadcasting System, Container Corporation of America, Hermann Miller, Knoll), Switzerland (Geigy), France (Cinzano), Italy (Olivetti) and Germany (Volkswagen). Swiss chemical company Ciba-Geigy is still recognized as an examplar of programmatic branding, with work by designers including Max Schmid, Markus Kutter and Karl Gerstner celebrated in a contemporary volume dedicated to the company's branding and marketing (Janser and Junod, 2009).

During the 1960s several practitioners sought to further consolidate the body of subject-specific knowledge surrounding the discipline, publishing comprehensive texts dedicated to the subject. This included *Design Coordination and Corporate Image* by Henrion and Parkin (1967), as well as Swedish designer Ole Eksell's (1967) more modest 'how-to' text of the same year, *Corporate Design Programs*. These efforts to codify brand identity design as a programmatic practice clearly indicate the growing significance of the field. Henrion and Parkin's book liberally demonstrates this growing stature with reference to numerous international case

Figure 2.1 Exhibition catalogue for 'Das Firmengesicht' (The Face of the Firm), exhibition of international advertising graphics in Berlin, 1954. Author's collection.

studies. From this we can see that US exemplars include George Nelson's work for Herman Miller (c. 1947), Eliot Noyes and Paul Rand's programmes for IBM (c. 1955) and Westinghouse (c. 1959), Lester Beall and Clifford Stead Jr. for Rohm and Haas (c. 1965) and Saul Bass & Associates for Celenase (c. 1966). In Italy exemplars include Giovanni Pintori for Olivetti (c. 1946), Erberto Carboni for Barilla (c. 1952), Eugenio Carmi for Italsider (c. 1958) and various international designers for Pirelli (1960s). In Germany exemplars include Otl Aicher for Braun (1950s) and Anton Stankowski for Lunch Bier (c. 1965), while in the Netherlands we have Total Design for Pam (c. 1964) and Pieter Brattinga for Steendrukkerij de Jong (undated). In Switzerland we have Hans Hilfiker for Therma (c. 1958) and Donald Brun for Anker Bier (undated), in Japan, Katzumie Masaru for the Tokyo Olympic Games (1964) and in Sweden, Olle Eksell for Mazetti (c. 1956). One interesting note on these international examples is that they are almost exclusively credited to individual design practitioners as opposed to design groups, which appears to have been a trend specific to Britain.

James Pilditch was another British author whose texts would help to concretize the status of the discipline, with *Communication by Design* (1970) developing on the ideas of Henrion and Parkin, albeit within a more business minded paradigm. Pilditch's firm, Allied International Designers, founded in 1959 became a major player in the field, ushering in the next major shift when they became the first design company to be listed on the stock exchange in 1980.

Proliferation – the 1980s

Finally, there are those who have argued that the 1980s were the critical juncture at which corporate design reached unprecedented levels of success and influence. Of special note here is the work of design scholar Liz Moor (2007) and her text *The Rise of Brands*, which provides an overview of the development of branding as a phenomenon, drawing particular attention to the late twentieth century. Moor's text provides a credible and comparatively extensive overview of the practice; tracing its development from an ancient act that signified ownership, to its proliferation in contemporary society, where, she says, it has come to represent an abstract form of communication that transcends the purely visual. Whilst her text is comprehensive and convincing in many respects, it lacks detail with regard to the formative development of contemporary practice in Britain or elsewhere. She references the work of British practitioners Henrion and Parkin, giving credence to their ideas in a chapter of her book titled: 'Brands and Media: the Idea of "Design Coordination"' (Moor, 2007: 30). However, Moor's efforts to explain Henrion and Parkin's concepts are only cursory, with their significance downplayed due to their tendency to overlook the social, political or economic concerns of corporate branding.

Moor claims that the writing of Henrion and Parkin, together with that of other early British scholars in the field, such as Pilditch, was simply ahead of its time, arguing that the corporate identity industry grew significantly only in the 1980s following a sharp rise in corporate mergers. This statement may well hold a certain truth, but it seems anomalous that Moor's research, which purports to examine the emergence of the branding industry, fails to address in any substantial detail the efforts of practitioners who played a significant role in defining the territory prior to its later dramatic growth.

Elsewhere, Woodham (1997: 141) gives credence to Henrion's role as a pioneer in the field, while suggesting that the business of corporate identity creation developed dramatically in accordance with the growth of multinational corporations, adding that this was, 'an aspect of the design profession that became increasingly significant in the post-Second World War period'. This point of emphasis seems in contrast with Moor's approach where the 1980s are singled out as the critical point of developmental significance. Guy Julier (2000, 2017) also decides to overlook the role of the British post-war 'pioneers', preferring to focus instead on the booming 1980s as a period in which neoliberal practices began to develop in Britain. Julier provides detailed empirical evidence to support his assertion that the 1980s were the point at which design consultancy, and subsequently brand identity practice, reached critical mass.

Although the 1980s represents an unprecedented period during which corporate branding became more proliferous and fully entrenched in mainstream culture, it is my contention that the earlier formative phase of development after the Second World War is more significant in terms of the formation and development of patterns of practice in this area. So while Julier's work examines neoliberal design in the latter phase of the twentieth century, this book is concerned with how the foundations of these neoliberal practices were established.

Summary

In summary, though gestural attempts to coordinate brand image were made in earlier centuries, the first sustained attempts towards programmatic brand identity came in the twentieth century. In the first half of the century these efforts were few and far between and tended to be relatively one-dimensional, with Behrens's scheme for AEG being exceptional for its strict methods and unitary characteristics across multiple media and formats. The formative period after the Second World War, from 1945–1970, proved to be decisive in the setting the practical and ideological development course for the discipline. By comparison, the latter phase, from 1970 onwards, was significant as an era of proliferation in which these ideals were further concretized. The brief overview of schools of thought set out here makes clear that this formative period of development after the Second World War has to date tended to be overlooked, presenting a gap that this book addresses. So, although the work of Moor and Julier are important reference points – particularly given their socio-economic perspective on design and branding – I seek to question their pre-occupation with the 1980s in order to consider more fully the influence of earlier decades.

3
BRAND IDENTITY IN BRITAIN

Locating brand identity programmes in the post-war socio-economic context

From austerity to liberation

Many historical studies of the twentieth century can be distinguished by certain strong thematic concerns, with particular arguments recurring so regularly that they have developed to become recognizable tropes. Commenting on this phenomenon, design historians Conekin, Mort and Walters (1999: 4) opine that the historiography of post-war Britain has projected 'a series of comfortable and familiar images of the period which are intrinsically recognisable'. They identify the following themes that they claim have set the terms of enquiry: economic growth and modernization, the decline of the British Empire, the development of political consensus, affluence, the rise of the welfare state, and concomitant patterns of social stability. Here I will seek to situate the development of corporate branding practices in relation to such themes.

While Britain had once been considered an economic superpower, factors such as the decline of the Empire and the end of the industrial revolution gradually saw Britain recede into the background, with the US taking centre stage as the new global superpower. The study of Britain's economic decline is well developed, if highly contested. Notable works here include Wiener's (1981) cultural critique, *English Culture and the Decline of the Industrial Spirit, 1850–1980*, written from the perspective of Margaret Thatcher's Britain, as well as Rubinstein's (1993) counter-thesis, *Capitalism, Culture and Decline in Britain, 1750–1990*. These studies represent macroscopic attempts by scholars to understand Britain's transition from an industrial superpower to a relative also-ran, underlining economic historians' preoccupations with what Rubinstein has described as 'the central question of post-1870 British history' (2001: 348). There is little consensus in this domain, with scholars debating the severity of Britain's economic decline and the reasons behind it.

Historians Lawrence Black and Hugh Pemberton (2004) have claimed that the preoccupation with various notions of national decline have hindered understanding of post-war Britain. They argue that affluence is in fact a more productive lens through which to examine the period, claiming that a focus on the domestic, rather than the international, would help to further our grasp of the cultural implications of ever-increasing post-war consumerism. Crafts and Mills (1996) support this view, using statistical evidence to argue that the trend rate of economic growth was more rapid after 1950 than it had been prior to 1940.[1]

Design historical accounts have tended towards more microscopic approaches to socio-economic history, with Maguire and Woodham (1997) concentrating on the 'Britain Can Make It' exhibition of 1946 in order to account for the cultural politics of design in the post-war era. They describe the inter-war period in Britain as one beset with structural weaknesses, citing the following factors as impediments to growth:

> The chronic lack of investment, the plethora of small-scale producers, the almost total absence of marketing skills and strategies, the outdated technology and distrust of formal education, the myriad market structures and stress on marginal product differentiation.
>
> (Maguire and Woodham, 1997: 30)

Furthermore, they argue that British manufacturing practices lagged well behind those of the US during the 1940s and that with nine million Britons either in the armed forces or directly producing for them, Britain became ill-equipped to meet the demands of peacetime production. The key to industrial regeneration after the war was seen to lie in the recapturing and development of export markets, but this would depend on a rapid increase in productivity. Whereas American manufacturing exhibited high levels of standardization, in Britain the virtual absence of standardization was allied to higher costs and lower productivity. Britain's economic troubles only worsened after the war, with the nation becoming increasingly dependent on America. Having taken a substantial loan in the immediate aftermath of the war, the initiation of the Marshall Plan in 1948 further concretized Britain's deep reliance on their transatlantic neighbours. These economic difficulties carried through into the domestic realm, where the extension of rationing above and beyond war-time levels indicated the severity of the problems.

The theme of austerity has been one that has strongly coloured much historical study of the post-war era. In his trilogy of books covering the arts in Britain from 1939 to 1975, cultural historian Robert Hewison (1977, 1981, 1986) divides the post-war epoch into two fundamental periods split between the immediate austerity of recovery and the liberating creative expression of the 1960s – as I will go on to show, this divide has developed to become a deeply entrenched one that is mirrored across much of the literature in the field. Building on the notion of popular myths, Hewison (1986) concludes his series by explaining that each of the decades he has studied has its own 'moment of myth'. These myths, he argues, retain a certain validity in the sense that they reflect an imaginative, rather than a literal truth. So, in the 1940s the myth centres around the pride and communality of suffering during the Blitz, whilst in the 1950s it surrounds the aggressive ambition of the Angry Young Man, and finally, in the 1960s, he argues that it was the idea of Swinging London that came to typify the period.

Though he sees the popular myth of the 'Swinging Sixties' as being attributable to a shorter period of the decade running from 1963 to 1967, Hewison also acknowledges that the influence of this so-called 'Swinging' period continued well into the following decade. He draws attention to the fact that the hedonistic stereotype of the 1960s as a time of pleasure, of colour after the drab austerity of the 1950s, of growing affluence, of cultural confidence and expansion, developed alongside another strand of personal liberation that he refers to as the oppositional culture of the underground.

Similarities can be seen here in the work of historian Arthur Marwick (1982), who frames the austerity of the post-war period around notions of social consensus. Like Hewison, he characterizes the 1960s as a time of freedom that precedes the later troubles of the 1970s.[2] Further parallels are found in the work of social historian David Kynaston (2007, 2009, 2013), who, in his more contemporary series of texts has suggested that British society continued to live in the shadow of the war until around 1957. Whilst the first four volumes in his series are characterized by the notions of 'austerity' (1945–51) and 'family' (1951–57), his more recent work centres around 'modernity' (1957–62), projecting an image of British society dominated by a new-found materialism. The rise of consumerism that Kynaston (2013) articulates is closely linked with the burgeoning pop- and counter-culture that Hewison has elaborated on, for these emergent cultural scenes that emphasized personal liberation were dependent on new-found patterns of material consumption, despite often proclaiming to be directly opposed to such ideas. Hewison (1986) argues that the affirmative and celebratory tempo of change during the 1960s was not sustainable in the long term, having been founded on a fantasy based on the illusion of unending economic expansion. Here he emphasizes the ambiguity and tension present during the decade, particularly between hedonistic ideals and the realities of what he describes as a society in decline.

Within the more specific field of design history the theme of modernization has been particularly well presented, with Breward, Fisher and Wood's (2012) work being fairly typical. In their catalogue for 'British Design from 1948', they argue that the Second World War had an immensely powerful impact on the social, economic and physical fabric of Britain, explaining that a new culture of design emerged after the war which was characterized by a drive towards modernization. Though they claim that the 1951 Festival of Britain epitomized this progressive and utopian vision of a modernized Britain, they go on to suggest that the Coronation of 1953 provided a reminder of the power and taste of traditional British values, hence drawing attention to the tensions that were present during the period between progressive ideals of modernization and nostalgic values of the past.[3] Their account portrays the 1940s and 1950s as a period in which designers were determined to create a new and better world, underlining the social imperatives of design practitioners active during the period. However, the optimistic, democratic and highly principled attitudes of these practitioners are said to have waned over time, with the authors emphasizing the tendency towards individualism and creative anarchy that transpired in the 1960s, 1970s and 1980s.

In dividing this period of history into two distinct eras (the 1940s–1950s and the 1960s–1980s) the authors emphasize the major themes of their exhibition, that is, 'reconstruction' and 'revolution' – two of the most readily recognized tropes of British design historiography, which can be seen to mirror Hewison's divide between austerity and liberation. Breward, Fisher and Wood suggest that the subversive spirit prevalent in the latter period was particularly significant in the ongoing development of design practice, coming to define the field. This so-called subversive strand of practice has received considerable attention from design historians, not only in broad survey exhibitions of design, such as the V&A's, but equally in more focused studies of graphic design, such as the 'Communicate' exhibition at the Barbican. I will attempt to debunk the idea that subversiveness has defined British design since the 1960s, demonstrating how in actuality patterns of practice within design tended to become more routinized and formulaic from the 1960s onwards. So, although Britain may have come to be regarded as a country of subversive design and designers, my research suggests that, for the most part, graphic design as a practical activity became increasingly conformist in the decades following the war.

I am mindful not to further reinforce a polarity between commercialism and independence/subversiveness, for in practice there is an inevitable overlap between these realms. For example, while Ken Garland – a key figure in Poynor's independent design project – has been much-heralded as an ethical, independent graphic designer, he has himself downplayed this dimension of his work, highlighting that his practice has been multi-faceted, embracing both social and commercial concerns (Shaughnessy, 2012). An example of Garland's commercial prowess can be found in the extensive work he completed for Michael Farr's design management business during the 1960s.

Americanization

As a result of the ongoing economic challenges of the post-war period the sophistication of the American industrial system with its better-developed management theory, production methods, marketing skills and productivity, became increasingly alluring to policy makers in Britain, with Maguire and Woodham (1997) suggesting that national survival depended on the fastest possible adoption of much of the American system. Although the notion of 'Americanization' has often been posited as a direct process of imposition through which American marketing methods were imposed, or at least adopted wholesale, in practice the lineage of influence is less straightforward. Throughout its history, design consultancy has, we are told, largely mirrored the business approaches and organizational strategies found in the advertising and marketing industries, albeit with some years' time lapse. Thus Julier (2000) explains how an American model of practice had been established in advertising in the first half of the twentieth century that was later 'transplanted' from the US to Britain, primarily through the expansion of American offices into Europe. Others have explored the extent to which American models of practice influenced Britain, with Nixon (2013) arguing that the channels of influence were not unidirectional as is often thought to be the case. Nixon shows that American advertising practices had actually taken distinctive directions in Britain, with less of a wholesale transfer taking place, and more a reworking and hybridization occurring.[4] Still, patterns of practice established in the US clearly had an important influence on the development of advertising and design consultancy in Britain, which is unsurprising given the complex political and economic entanglement between the two nations during the period.

In her historical review of consultant design practice, design historian Penny Sparke (1983) suggests that America led the way in relation to the establishment of independent design consultancies conceived to serve the needs of corporate clients. So while design practitioners in the US had developed multi-disciplinary design consultancies in the 1920s and 1930s, practitioners in Britain were much slower to adopt these ideas in any serious way, with the trend for group practice only really becoming noticeable in Britain by the mid-to-late 1950s.[5] Julier (2000) suggests this discrepancy was likely due to the smaller, less affluent economic market of Britain by comparison to the wide and stable distribution base of America. During this period the myth of American design was beginning to encroach on traditional British values, with design from the US being perceived by many Britons to act against the interests of consumers and society as a whole, employing as it did principles such as built-in obsolescence and superficial styling. Many design practitioners were concerned by the commercially-oriented nature of American industrial design, with Maguire and Woodham (1997) explaining how few, if any, members of Britain's Council of Industrial Design had agreed with the influential American Raymond Loewy's assertion that aesthetics consists of a beautiful sales curve shooting upwards. Designers in Britain had become aware of the concerns around Americanization through the design press, with commentators like the American Edgar Kaufmann Jr. (1948) warning Britons of the perils of superfluous commercially driven styling. Practitioners in Britain were equally anxious about the infiltration of North American competitors into the marketplace, with the industrial designer Loewy having set a precedent for success during the inter-war years. As a result, they were generally slow to follow the commercial lines of the US consultant designer model, with the design group Bassett Gray a rare pre-war exception to this rule. This group, founded in 1922, would later evolve to become the Design Research Unit whose methods are studied in detail later in this book.[6]

Much of the early antipathy to American commercialism was directed towards product and industrial design, but, by the 1950s, critics from within North America had begun to turn their attention towards the commercialism of advertising and graphic design. For example, Canadian cultural theorist Marshall McLuhan (1951) sought to reveal the symbolism behind various communication design artefacts, whilst underlining the wider implications of such works on society. Vance Packard (1957), meanwhile, sought to expose the secrets of the advertising and public relations industry in his seminal text, *The Hidden Persuaders*, documenting how psychological techniques were used in post-war North America to manipulate consumers and induce desire for products. The techniques Packard described can be traced back to the work of public relations pioneer Edward Bernays, who had pioneered these strategies, publishing his first book on the subject early in the 1920s (Bernays, 1923). It was Packard's text that brought these morally questionable sales tactics firmly into the public eye in the post-war era, gaining notoriety as an early anti-consumerist doctrine, not just in the US, but also in Britain, where the book gained popularity following its publication in 1960.

While British advertising practitioners had been willing to adopt advertising practices from the US, albeit in their own ways, the design community had greater difficulty reconciling the 'hard sell' tactics of American consumer culture with what they saw as the serious social purpose of design. This explains the relatively slow development of consultant design activity in Britain, with it taking until the late-1950s to the mid-1960s until any momentum developed around consultant group practice. Julier (2000) points to a raft of British design consultancies founded during this time, singling out James Pilditch's Allied International Designers as pacesetters, but he overlooks those groups founded in the 1940s and 1950s, focusing the lion's share of his energy on the 1980s, a period he has scrutinized again in his more recent text on the neoliberalization of design (Julier, 2017). Sparke (1983) meanwhile, has acknowledged the isolated instances of consultant design in Britain during the 1940s, but skirts over developments in the 1950s as a whole. She contends that consultant design in Britain emerged out of the graphic design scene, just as it had done earlier in America.

In practice, key US designers had come from a range of backgrounds in theatre, advertising, graphics, fashion and furniture design (Gantz, 2014). For instance, Walter Dorwin Teague had specialized in decorative design and typography for advertising before developing his consultant design group around industrial design. Raymond Loewy began his career in window display design before developing a multi-national consultancy focused on industrial design. Norman Bel Geddes began in theatre design before shifting to industrial products, with Henry Dreyfuss following a similar path, first acting as an apprentice to Bel Geddes, before becoming a major competitor. Donald Deskey (born 1894) began in window design and interiors before moving to industrial design and graphics. Harold Van Doren (born 1895) was unusual in specializing in industrial design from the early stages of his career.[7] Each of these key players adapted their career to capitalize on demand from the market, developing a commercialized form of design that centred around the aesthetic 'streamlining' of products. The development of consultant group practice in America during the inter-war years thus stemmed from a group of applied artists who aligned themselves with the creation of industrial design products. Together they took on areas of practice not covered by architects, including appliances and consumer goods, furniture and interiors, transport and heavy equipment, exhibitions and visual communications.

In Britain, by comparison, the trend towards consultant group practice was more allied to the professional development of graphic design and the proliferation of brand identity programmes, with the target of visual unification playing to the strengths of communication designers. In Part Two of this book we see how this played out in practice through design consultants' responses to developments in the Americanization of British culture, with particular attention directed to how the imperatives of practitioners changed over time and how these shifting attitudes impacted the patterns of their day-to-day practice.

Professionalism and commercialism

During the 1960s and 1970s attitudes of British designers (both graphic designers and designers in a broader sense) can be seen to have diverged significantly, as the discipline became more established as a central tenet of the marketing industry. Many of the shifting perspectives of the period are reflected in practitioners' differing attitudes towards professionalism. Although the professional body of designers, the Society of Industrial Artists (SIA), had been founded as early as 1930, membership reached unprecedented levels after the war as the status of the designer began to improve and business opportunities expanded. The surge of interest in design professionalism had, by the 1960s, led to questions emerging around the ethics of professionalism and precisely whose interests the Society ought to serve. Many of the older generation who had been members prior to the war continued to be cautious of the influence of US commercialism on the development of the British scene, but while some supported the need for designers to meet the demands of society in order to be considered legitimate and responsible professionals, others were more motivated by commercial opportunities emerging within the industry.

The SIA put in place a strict code of conduct forbidding its members from certain ungentlemanly or aggressively business-like behaviour, including a ruling that prohibited self-promotional activities.[8] Such policies were not popular with all members, with some of the younger generation questioning what they saw as the Society's staid and reserved attitudes to competition. Furthermore, there was a sense in which the principles of the Society protected those more established members, reinforcing the status quo and thus limiting opportunities for entrepreneurial young designers trying to find a rung on the ladder. While some of the younger generation felt constrained by the strict code of the Society – Terence Conran is noted to have been forced to withdraw his membership in 1963 for an infringement to the ruling on advertising and self-promotion, having been caught touting his services through printed advertisements – other newcomers failed to see the relevance of professional status and questioned the increasingly commercial imperatives of the profession.[9]

Ken Garland's (1964) oft-cited 'First Things First' manifesto has been canonized for its open and direct critique of the increasing commercialism within design and advertising of the 1960s, yet Garland's call-to-action was also, in part, a response to the apathy in which he viewed the SIA's professional project. 'First Things First' had initially been aired at an event at the Institute of Contemporary Arts, entitled 'Why you should join the SIA'. Growing tired of what he saw as the 'prophetizing' of the older generation, Garland recalls how he been ready to leave the event, but instead decided to write down what he really thought about design. At the conclusion of the meeting when he shared his ideas aloud, they proved to be divisive among the audience – though several people had encouraged him to publish his provocation, which he later did. Critiquing the commercial motives of the profession, Garland called for a reversal of priorities, whereby high-pressure consumer selling would be shunned in favour of more useful and lasting forms of communication. In airing his views Garland's motivation was, he argues, not to position design in opposition to advertising or commerce, or to seek the abolishment of high-pressure advertising entirely, but rather to remind designers of their political and ethical responsibilities. In this sense he sought to steer a course towards a more socially conscious form of design. Given that the SIA's professional project claimed to be motivated by the betterment of society (Gray,

1970; Middleton, Lord and Pilditch, 1971), it is ironic that Garland sought to reject the SIA as an institution, while simultaneously championing many of the very same ideas it promoted. This course of events can be seen to reflect the shifting identity of the SIA as an organization that battled with conflicting perspectives as it drew in a steadily increasing body of membership.

As graphic design began to gain traction as a recognized professional activity the practice went through a gradual process of increasing commercialization from which the highly prized cultural capital of 'commercial art' came to be challenged by more explicit drives towards the imperatives of economic capital. This process of commercialization can be seen to develop in tandem with the growing professionalism of practitioners in post-war Britain. Robin Kinross (1988) sets out this transition in a compelling way, explaining how the practice had finally lost what was seen as its undesirable tag of commercialism, but seemingly become more commercial in the process as 'graphic design' was gradually established.

The developing discourse of brand identity in Britain

To determine how brand identity design emerged as a meaningful practice in the post-war era I will now analyse a series of texts published within British design trade journals and annuals of the day. These texts played a critical role in the codification of brand identity design, demonstrating how an occupational community began to converge around the practice. Furthermore, they provide critical evidence of the significant rhetorical changes that occurred within the British brand identity design scene during this early phase of emergence.

Six texts are analysed from four separate authors and four distinct publications. These texts cover a period from 1932 to 1956 and are as follows:

> Beatrice Warde (1932) 'An Account of the LNER Type Standardization', *The Monotype Recorder*.
>
> Norbert Dutton (1946) 'Living Design—London Transport', *Art & Industry*.
>
> Alec Davis (1950a) 'Printing Design and the Print User', *Design*.
>
> Alec Davis (1952) 'Typography and House Style in Industry', *The Penrose Annual*.
>
> Ashley Havinden (1955) 'The Importance of "Company Handwriting"', *The Penrose Annual*.
>
> Alec Davis (1956) 'House Style', *Design*.

In studying these texts, I follow design historian Alice Twemlow (2013: 2), who argues that vernacular texts ought to be included within design history's purview, 'not just as raw primary source material, but also as the central point of study'. The texts included here map the initial emergence of the house style phase of brand identity design that can be attributed to the 1950s and 1960s in Britain, a period during which 'house style' would become the dominant terminological reference point. I have included one text that predates the Second World War in order to lay the groundwork for the developments that followed during the focal period presented in the book. This text became an important reference point for champions of the discipline, with those writing in the 1950s referring back to it. In this sense this article about the type standardization of the LNER took on new meaning and significance for later commentators who sought to promote brand identity design as an important new discipline. This work can thus be understood in reference to the idea of a pre-adaptation, in as much that the text was reframed to serve a purpose for which it had not initially been intended. It is with this text that we begin.

1932: Beatrice Warde, 'An Account of the LNER Type Standardization'

Published in *The Monotype Recorder* in 1932, 'An Account of the LNER Type Standardization' is a six-page article documenting the implementation of a scheme to coordinate the typographic appearance of the London & North Eastern Railway (LNER), one of the 'big four' railway companies operating in Britain between 1923 and 1948. While this was arguably not the first comprehensive visual identity programme attempted in Britain, the article in question was an important early attempt to codify the methods of such an approach. While the author of the article is not credited in the publication, the work has been widely attributed as the work of Beatrice Warde who oversaw Monotype's publicity at the time.[10] Warde was notably a close associate of Eric Gill, whose typeface was chosen as the vehicle for the rail company's visual unification programme.

Warde began her article with an explanation of the basic premise of the programme, explaining how the standardization of a single typeface enabled the firm to achieve a recognizable 'group personality':

> In standardising its typography, the London and North Eastern Railway has not only made possible a number of economies but also has given the public at large a visual image of one 'group personality' which is even more valuable than the emerald green livery borne Northward by the iron dragons of King's Cross.

She refers to 'group personality' on three occasions in her article, emphasizing the potential for a standardized design programme to create a 'cumulative recognition' among consumers. For Warde, this recognition delivers significant social benefits, with the standardized personality acting as a means of greater clarity and efficiency benefitting end-users. In explaining the decision to standardize a sans-serif typeface, as opposed to a serif type, Warde says:

> What did arise was the mental picture of a passenger being jostled on a crowded platform on a winter evening, and trying with one eye on the station clock to verify the connections of a given train; a picture of another passenger running his eye over fifteen excursion leaflets that are printed perhaps by fifteen different printers; glancing from them to the station announcement, to the destination board of the train, to a 16-sheet poster issued by the company and being given in every case a sense of continuity and consistency, a sense that something had been said to him with as little fuss and distraction as possible.

Central to the success of the programme was the ambition to create a consistent appearance based around common usage of Gill Sans. For Warde, Gill Sans, was 'the most efficient conveyor of thought', and would communicate most clearly and effectively with passengers. (Figure 3.1)

Figure 3.1 Double-page spread from 'An Account of the LNER Type Standardization', *The Monotype Recorder*, Vol 36, No 4, Winter 1932. Item held by Science Museum Group Collection.

Such was Warde's zeal for the operation, that at times, her account reads as if the programme were of her own making, the manner in which certain design decisions are recounted implying that she had some personal involvement in the programme – in her role as Publicity Manager for Monotype (the distributors of Eric Gill's typeface design and publishers of The *Monotype Recorder*) it is likely that she had inside knowledge of the operation. As a spokesperson for Monotype, it would also clearly have been in her interests to celebrate Gill's typeface and the programme more broadly, especially as she was a known ally of Gill.

The programme is put forth by Warde as a reform of great modernity and extraordinary significance:

> This article deals with an example of genuine typographic modernity: a reform which is radical (i.e. root-deep in economic fact) and far reaching in its effect. [...] When a vast railway system contrives that 10,000 different booklets, leaflets, and other pieces should be almost automatically designed (or say constructed) well and in a recognisable unity [...] the result is extraordinarily significant.

It is hard to contest the view that the transition from designing 10,000 items individually, to designing them systematically and *en masse*, was one of significance. For Warde, designing a single piece of print carefully and tastefully was no longer a modern or noteworthy achievement and what was truly modern was the large organization that was so powerful that it was able to impose standard rules upon its print suppliers. This, she proposes, was the only occurrence of genuine economic or practical significance taking place within the business of twentieth century printing.

In the given account, the standardization of design exhibited by the LNER suggests a shift away from artistic approaches to design and towards more strategic, systematic and pre-planned methods. In Warde's mind this technocratic turn would involve the demotion of the creative typographer, as forewarned in the first sentences of the article, 'It is not an article for typographic artists, because it describes a new phenomenon in typography which to a great extent leaves the artist out of the picture'. The rhetoric of the piece is notable for the way it reflects (and anticipates) the systems turn that took place later within design circles, particularly under the guise of the Design Methods movement (Cross, 1993). The themes dealt with reflect closely on the work of Bruce Archer (1965, 1968), for example, particularly his influential text *Systematic Methods for Designers*.

As Warde outlines, standardization offered the LNER several tangible benefits, including: (1) the visual unification of disparate design outputs, making the company's offer more widely recognized and distinctive; (2) the raising of design standards – as print items were often relatively unconsidered in their construction, standardizing these could result in a higher quality of design; (3) time savings – as construction becomes a relatively automated process, the total design time involved is cut; (4) cost savings – time savings in the design stage carry through into financial gain for clients.

These organizational benefits did not necessarily impact positively on designers, with concern raised for more artistically minded practitioners who the author understood to be resistant to their work being constrained or channelled into standardized forms. Particular tensions between artistic individuality and standardization were insinuated by Warde in reference to the plight of the organization's poster artists: 'even those temperamental brethren, the poster artists, are learning that the neutral Gill Sans is safe to use as lettering with almost any pictorial effect'. In practice, the LNER's poster artists interpreted Gill's typeface with a greater freedom than Warde implies, with examples evident in which the artists appear to have entirely overlooked or ignored Gill's design, creating hand-rendered lettering of no resemblance to Gill's typeface. Even those artists that followed the Gill template often rendered their attempts with seeming indifference, manipulating the letterforms to fit around the pictorial content of their designs.

The article focused almost exclusively upon the role of typography as a coordinating force, fleetingly mentioning the role of colour when touching upon the standardized green liveries of the LNER's locomotives that were already in existence. Posters brought out under the previous director William Teasdale are also mentioned in terms of how they had helped to bring the 'group personality of the line into the public conscience'. In 1927 Teasdale had put five of the company's most prolific designers on an exclusive contract, with his intention being to limit the variety of pictorial representation evident in the organization's publicity – he was hoping to attain what he referred to, in correspondence with his top five artists, as the 'LNER Look'.[11]

For Warde, standardization was seen as a way to control creative typographers, commercial artists and what she considered uncultured and ill-disciplined printers, inclined to wander from the cause. Advancements in technology, and in particular the tendency for printers to hold an increasing number of alternate typefaces, led Warde to believe that practitioners were presented with, 'a thousand temptations to typographic vulgarity'. Standardizing a typeface, rather than a style, she believed, would afford greater specificity and accuracy of results, allowing a sense of discipline and order to come to the fore. There is an interesting collision here between the liberating effects of new technology and the oppressive tendencies of standardization. This balancing act between what should be specified, and what should be left free-to-choose, would become a dominant theme surrounding the development of brand identity design throughout the twentieth century.

1946: Norbert Dutton, 'Living Design – London Transport'

Norbert Dutton's article of 1946, 'Living Design', was an early attempt to valorize the coherent brand identity of London Transport (Figure 3.2).[12] This argument would later become a mainstay within histories of brand identity, with the organization becoming a canonical example of international standing, discussed regularly alongside other seminal identities of the early twentieth century, such as AEG in Germany, Olivetti in Italy and the Container Corporation of America in the US.

Dutton's (1946) work was not the first piece of journalism to recognize the company's design policy, with G. W. Stonier (1935) having run a broadly similar – though much shorter – feature in the same journal a decade earlier. Still, Dutton appears to have been the first to systematically analyse the breadth and value of the company's full brand image in such a manner. The way he describes the identity is complex and multi-faceted. Unlike Warde, he does not describe a unitary programme of standardization, as the London Transport approach

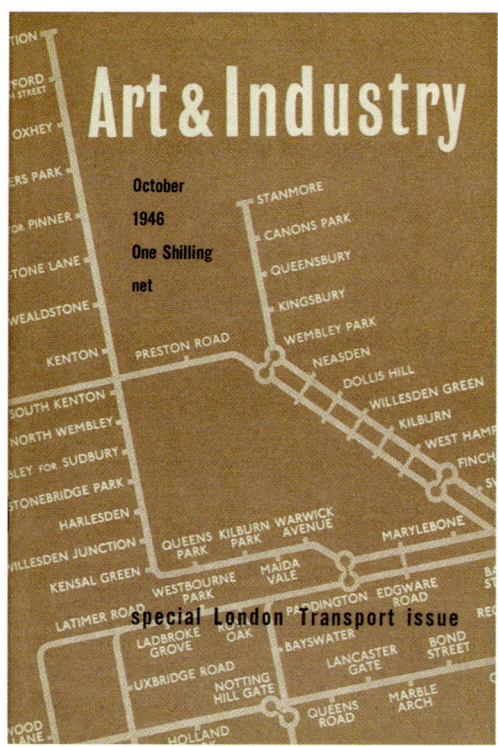

Figure 3.2 Cover of the special London Transport issue of the trade journal *Art & Industry*, October 1946. Author's collection.

was, for him, 'never merely the application of a formula'; instead, he sees it as more nuanced, accommodating a multiplicity of approaches within a wider holistic harmony. For others, brand identity would come to represent continuity, standardization and formulaic patterning systems, but for Dutton, it represented something looser and more susceptible to change. The brand identity that he described was not simply a style, but rather, a 'living idiom', for, as he argued, a single style would be 'doomed to sterility'.[13] This notion of the living organizational idiom is in contrast with the dominant paradigm of brand identity endorsed by most other authors during the twentieth century. A paradigm that has, to this day, revolved around aesthetic unification founded primarily on consistency (just as the LNER text had earlier explained and as many subsequent authors have restated).

Dutton's concept of brand identity was not straightforward, as he sought to hold conflicting ideals together in unison, showing his appetite for an idiom that was 'infinitely flexible', while also recognizing the importance of the 'unmistakable', 'recognizable unity' that could be achieved through the application of consistent or recurring design elements. These contrasting concepts of flexibility and repetition appear paradoxical, but he attempted to show that they were not mutually exclusive and could co-exist within one brand. He presents the London Transport's design idiom as a multi-disciplinary one that encompasses the design of vehicles, buildings, street furniture, interiors, fabrics and graphics. Whereas others have often focused on brand identities that are predominantly graphic or typographic, he embraces multiple media with equal conviction. In his eyes, the London Transport's policy is all-embracing, and this helps to explain why he believed so adamantly that flexibility was required to implement a successful brand. It is worth noting that as an organization, London Transport had made purposeful efforts ever since their formation to coordinate a range of disparate services that had previously run as separate entities. As such it was a major organizational imperative to present themselves as one unified and seamless service.[14]

Dutton understood rigorous design detail to be of great importance to the coordinated impression of an organization. Citing the humble platform bench as an example, he claims that by incorporating the station nameplate into the bench's design (in an identical size and appearance to that used upon the walls of the station) that the bench 'falls into place within the larger pattern'. Here he describes a modular method, in which recurrent modules build up to create a recognizable pattern. This technique emerges again when he describes ticket machine designs as units: 'the unit becomes, as it were, a module from which composite patterns are constructed'.[15] He clearly believed that these modular acts of repetition helped to create visual unity, and for Dutton, this was exemplified most clearly in the consistent application of graphic forms: 'The adoption of a single style of lettering, and the recurring use of the London Transport symbol

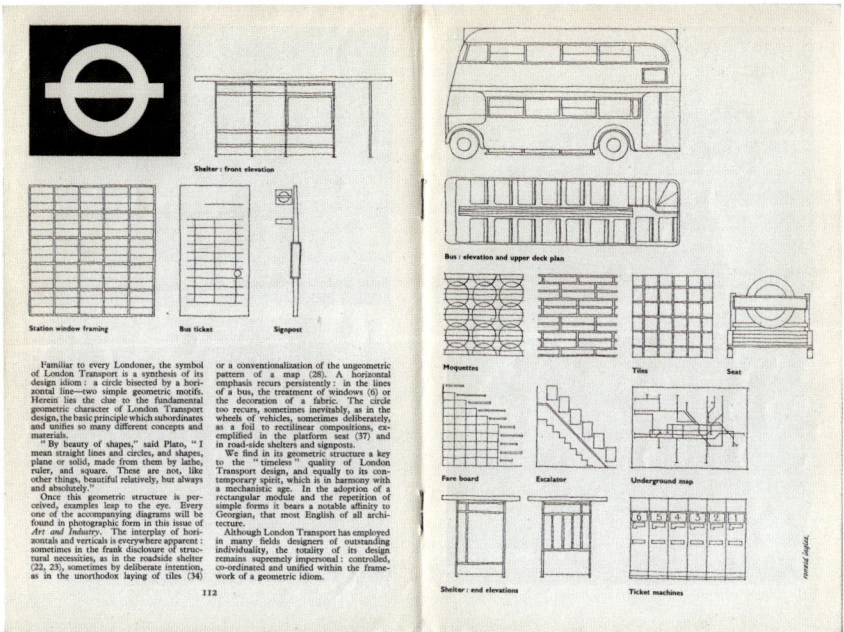

Figure 3.3 Double-page spread from Norbert Dutton's (1946: 112–13) feature on London Transport, with numerous illustrations by Ronald Ingles. Courtesy of Scott Brownrigg.

as a decorative motif, contribute powerfully to a visual unity.' As such, he made a strong case for the importance of graphic design as a force for effective visual unification. His claims imply that repetitively applied graphic forms may allow greater freedom for other design domains, such as architectural, environmental or vehicular design.

In many respects the idiom that he recounts is fundamentally a graphic phenomenon. This is reinforced by the illustrated graphic he uses to substantiate his central thesis that the idiom of London Transport is essentially geometric (Figure 3.3). This illustration is used to persuade the reader that the many manifestations of the organization are united by an ever-present geometry derived from the organizations symbol. As he explains:

> Familiar to every Londoner, the symbol of London Transport is the synthesis of its design idiom: a circle bisected by a horizontal line – two simple geometric motifs. Herein lies the clue to the fundamental geometric character of London Transport design, the basic principles which subordinates and unifies so many different concepts and materials. [...] Once this geometric structure is perceived, examples leap to the eye. Every one of the accompanying diagrams will be found in photographic form in this issue of *Art & Industry*. The interplay

of horizontals and verticals is everywhere apparent [...] Although London Transport has employed in many fields designers of outstanding individuality, the totality of its design remains supremely impersonal: controlled, co-ordinated and unified within the framework of a geometric idiom.

The most vexing aspect of Dutton's text is the lack of clarity with which he describes the construction of the London Transport idiom. He claims that it was achieved by 'effort not accident', adding that the design of the whole transport system had been 'carefully planned'; yet he suggests that the principles that underlay the idiom were unknown to the designers responsible for implementing it. As he explains:

> Analysis must surely yield some unifying principle behind an achievement so rare in the whole history of design. And indeed it does: but a principle so subtle as to have escaped the conscious perception of even those designers who have been most closely concerned in its application.

This leads to questions as to how such carefully conceived intentions could be implemented by designers who themselves were unaware of the idiom. Perhaps what he was trying to express was that the individual designers were unaware of how their work tied into the bigger picture carefully orchestrated by Chief Executive, Frank Pick.

Canonical historical narratives (Barman, 1979; Salcr, 1999) have portrayed Pick as an influential champion of design who led a team of practitioners towards the production of this sophisticated and pioneering brand identity; yet some have questioned the integrity of this narrative, pointing to discrepancies in its accuracy. For instance, typographic scholars Colin Banks (1994) and Justin Howes (2000) have shared empirical evidence showing that the London Transport typeface – long considered an early cornerstone of the identity – was simply not intended as a unifying design device. In fact, far from being conceived as a flexible alphabet that could to be applied across multiple media and contexts, Pick had commissioned Edward Johnston to design a one-inch tall alphabet tailored for use on the organization's printed publicity posters. As it turned out, such was the unorthodox nature of the design, printers – who were generally unaccustomed to working with sans-serif movable type – were unsuccessful in their attempts to compose the type on the company's posters. Fortuitously, the design suited signage and wayfinding applications better, and over several years, its use spread to an ever-greater range of applications. The evidence provided by Banks undermines Dutton's claim that Pick had commissioned a standard alphabet for use on its stations. It is concerns such as these, around the precision with which brand identity design as a discipline has been understood, that have led the Dutch design historian Wibo Bakker (2005) to question the long-established canon of early corporate pioneers.

1950: Alec Davis, 'Printing Design and the Print User'

Journalist and designer Alec Davis demonstrated a keen interest in brand identity throughout his career, contributing many articles on the subject through which he began to codify the principles of a programmatic approach to brand identity design. Davis became the chief proponent of coordinated design principles in 1950s Britain. Through his articles in the pages of *Design* magazine (Davis, 1950a, 1950b, 1956, 1959) and the *Penrose Annual* (Davis, 1952), he began to codify the principles of house style. Davis articulated the growing significance of this emergent concept, with his articles widely disseminated across the design community in Britain through the vehicle of the Council of Industrial Design's popular magazine. Davis could be considered the first writer, certainly in Britain, to systematically formalize and define design coordination as a distinct approach to industrial design.

Born in Lincolnshire in 1912, Davis was a designer and journalist who spent his working life in London. He studied Journalism in London before freelancing for various publications in a range of editorial roles.[16] In 1949, he became the founding editor of *Design* magazine, but this role was short lived, with him relinquishing the position after three years.[17] Still, he continued to be involved with the magazine after this time, contributing numerous features over the coming decade, many of which were written on the subject of house style, with nine features appearing in *Design*, including a full special issue dedicated to the subject.

In February 1950 Davis's first article referencing the term 'house style' was published under the title 'Printing Design and the Print User' (Davis, 1950a). Although he used the term 'house style' just once in his text – indicating that he was tentative about his selection of terminology – his intention to champion the pursuit of a more holistic approach to identity design was clear, as intimated by his introductory blurb:

> Good design in business printing means something more than the occasional commissioning of booklet covers or poster designs by Famous Artists: it implies a consistent design policy – reflected in all forms of printed matter from price lists to packing slips.

Davis claimed that every single piece of printed design produced by an organization was of great importance, no matter how seemingly small and insignificant it may appear. For Davis, even delivery notes and packing slips needed to be carefully considered, as these neglected forms of printed matter all helped to give an impression of the firm that uses them. This argument for a holistic approach impacting upon all manifestations of the organization, no matter how small, is an interesting and important one, adding weight to his concept of a 'consistent design policy'. According to Davis, another argument for house style is that it could afford economies of production, leading him to suggest that 'good design need cost no more than bad [...] it will often reduce costs because it involves a measure of simplification'. By standardizing colours, formats or materials, cost savings could be made, with Davis referring to a particular case that resulted in a saving of sixty per cent on the client's original expenditure. Next, he goes on to suggest that a holistic approach to design need not be limited to the realm of printed matter:

> In those firms whose printed matter is consistently of a high standard of design, there is almost always an overall-design policy which is equally evident in non-printed matter: ideally the two are planned side by side. The possibility of developing a likeness between letterheads and, say, machine tools or biscuits or razor-blades may not be immediately obvious, but these diverse manufactured goods (and most others) carry some form of wording.

Here, Davis formulates his most convincing argument. Fusing the need for house style to be cross-disciplinary with his specialist discipline of typography, he implies that typography can provide the means of achieving consistency across the range of products on which it is used. He provides three examples of companies that successfully standardized the wording appearing across all of their design channels through the use of one specific corporate typeface: Johnston Sans for London Transport, Cyclone for British Overseas Airways Corporation (BOAC) (Figure 3.4) and Albertus for Sainsbury's.

Davis employs a range of phrases to denote the results of a house style programme, such as 'family resemblance', 'overall-design policy' or 'reminder advertising', but he also draws upon a broader range of rhetoric to describe the act of coordination itself, e.g. 'rationalisation', 'simplification' and 'standardising'. The word 'uniform' appears once, but the word 'coordination' notably does not feature. Davis circles around the topic of house style, with his writing lacking the command, structure and focus that would follow in his later work. Though he asserts multiple agendas in his text, no over-riding argument comes through. The main body of the article is introduced with Davis declaring the importance of an audience within printed design work, what he refers to as 'the print user'. Given the prominence of this term within the title of the text, it is odd that he fails to explore the notion in any significant detail.[18] Instead he is drawn down seemingly diffuse avenues of thought, initially championing the value of consistent design policy, before

Figure 3.4 An example of the use of a standard corporate typeface, in this case, Cyclone for British Overseas Airways Corporation (BOAC). As featured in Alec Davis's (1952: 38) article for the *Penrose Annual*. The illustrations featured top-left and bottom-right also featured in Davis's (1950a) earlier article for *Design* magazine. Author's collection.

concluding with a seemingly unrelated call for the printing trade to embrace the professional typographic designer. Though he attempts to connect the two concepts, the convoluted manner in which he does so leaves the article confused and lacking impact.

The three illustrated examples of work included in the article all refer to typography and/or lettering, with work for Marconi being the sole example in which another means of brand unity beyond typography is referenced, that being colour. As Davis promotes typography as the primary means through which design can be coordinated, he dedicates, roughly, three of his seven text columns to the subject. This bias was most likely related to his professional expertise. As a 'typographical adviser' it would have been in his interests to champion his own subject area, hence why he chose to use the final two columns of his article as a forum to voice his belief that the professional typographer ought to be more warmly embraced by the printing trade.

1952: Alec Davis, 'Typography and House Style in Industry'

Some five months after his first text for *Design*, Davis (1950b) had his article 'Van lettering as part of a consistent Design Policy' published. Featuring six examples (J. Sainsbury, North Eastern Gas Board, HP Sauce, Ilford, Maconochie's and Dunn's of Bromley), this was a minor feature of two pages, focused on just one element of a holistic programme, that being van livery. Davis decided to include one small image of another design artefact from each organization alongside larger images of the six vans. The writing focused primarily on the quality of the lettering as opposed to the quality of the identity as a whole, with just one of the six paragraphs addressing the issue of consistent design policy.

Davis's (1952) second substantial article on house style for the *Penrose Annual*, 'Typography and House Style in Industry', is similar to his first article for *Design*, with many of the same case studies and illustrations appearing in both texts. This text is more heavily illustrated, with four rather than three case studies and a greater number of pictures used to illustrate each case. Perhaps the most significant development is the inclusion of the term 'house style' in the title of this work, with Davis becoming more reliant on the phrase and employing it four times in his text. From this point forward, the term becomes his descriptor of choice, recurring in the title of nine subsequent texts, all written by him over the following eight-year period:

'Typography and House Style in Industry' (Davis, 1952)
'House Style – A Special Issue' (Davis, 1956)
'House Style for Household Appliances' (Davis, 1957a)
'House Style for Confectionary' (Davis, 1957b)
'House Styles Evolving' (Davis, 1957c)
'House Style for a Printer' (Davis, 1957d)
'House Style Programmes and Progress' (Davis, 1958a)
'House Style by Remote Control' (Davis, 1958b)
'House Style: The Face of the Firm' (Davis, 1959)
'Public House Style' (Davis, 1960)

Much of the rhetoric used in 'Printing Design and the Print User', was repeated in 'Typography and House Style in Industry', with the word 'style' becoming more dominant and appearing nine times. More important still is the way Davis links notions of consistency with increased consumer recognition. These two concepts are linked in symbiosis within each text, as evidenced by the following two excerpts:

> The initials of British Overseas Airways Corporation are made easily *recognisable* by the Corporation's *consistent* use of one type-face.
>
> (Davis, 1950a: 3; emphasis added)

> In recent years much stress has been laid on the desirability of a firm's having a *consistent* design policy in all its activities, so that a house style is *recognisable* in its products, its premises, and its printed matter.
>
> (Davis, 1952: 36; emphasis added)

Thus, Davis explains that consistent design treatment leads to audience recognition. As such, house style is achieved by applying the same style consistently, in order that it is built up through repetition, to become recognizable and thus associated with the organization in question.

1955: Ashley Havinden, 'The Importance of "Company Handwriting"'

Ashley Havinden, born in Kent in 1903, worked for advertising agency W. S. Crawford in London for practically the entirety of his working life. Starting as a trainee, he quickly rose to become Art Director of what some consider the most creative British advertising agency of the first half of the twentieth century.[19] As a member of numerous professional organizations and a frequent speaker at industry events, Havinden commanded respect amongst the design and advertising communities, being a protagonist in the development of brand identity programmes in Britain. While the programmes he developed as Art Director of Crawfords helped to push aesthetic boundaries, his writing provided an opportunity for him to share his expertise with a wider community of designers and art directors. In the 1952–3 annual, *Designers in Britain 4*, Havinden (1952–3) claims:

> Repetition is the basis of modern commerce – a totally different conception to the ephemeral success of a popular dance tune which is 'here today and gone tomorrow'. If the sale of a product is to be consistently repeated then the appearance of the product itself, even the factory in which it is made, as well as all the ancillary activities to do with reminding the public about it (such as the packaging, posters, press advertising, printed matter, exhibitions, window displays) must also be co-ordinated and present a consistently attractive appearance.

From the perspective of today's saturated brand environment, Havinden's earnest call for coordinated and consistent visual identity programmes appears unremarkable, but this is precisely what is interesting about his statement – it emphasizes that brand unification was not the norm within post-war British society. Here we have a highly regarded, avant-garde practitioner calling out for a new approach to design practice centred around repetition.

Havinden develops these ideas further in a later piece published in the *Penrose Annual* in 1955. This article, 'The Importance of "Company Handwriting"', serves two important functions for Havinden. Firstly, it set out in detail his conception of the coherent, recognizable brand identities he referred to as 'company handwriting'. Second, in exclusively showcasing the work of his own agency within the featured case studies, he explicitly promotes himself and his employers. See, for instance, the featured brand identity work for the client KLM (Figure 3.5).

When Havinden refers to a company's 'handwriting', he is not insinuating that lettering or typography should be used to achieve a unifying design style. Rather, he seeks to draw a comparison between the readily recognized appearance of an acquaintance's handwriting and the kind of consistent visual identity that would benefit business organizations. As he explains: 'Just as a man's script is recognisable at once by his friends, whatever he is writing, so a company's variegated approaches to the public should assume a familiar and readily identifiable form'. Havinden is perhaps unaware that his term, 'company handwriting', harked back to what are commonly considered the very first commercially branded products. As Davis (1956) explains, traders centuries earlier had inscribed their own signatures upon their goods in order that these goods would be recognized as originating from them. These signatures were literally the companies' handwriting, and in many cases, they would act as a certification of the product's quality.

Havinden began his article with a robust argument for the financial waste inherent in advertising work that was not coordinated, stating that individual advertisements must be clearly recognized as belonging to the service or product that they advertised in order that they may be effective:

> Some £230,000,000 were spent in 1953 on advertising in Britain. I wonder how much of this was good value? One just has to look at the poorly designed posters in the streets and the unco-ordinated advertisements in the newspapers and magazines to see how little of that advertising money fulfils its function in arresting the attention and capturing the goodwill of the public. A large proportion of all advertising is not as effective as it could be, in the first place because it lacks a focus that will be recognisable at once and associate itself, in the mind of the casual reader or passer-by, with the product or service to be advertised. All advertising for branded-goods, however varied, should be consistent in theme and should have an unmistakable appearance. We might call this appearance the 'company handwriting'.

As with Davis, he clearly believes 'recognition' to be a key concept, employing the term eight times and repeatedly explaining how consistency could be used

Figure 3.5 Double-page spread from Ashley Havinden's article for the *Penrose Annual*, 'The Importance of "Company Handwriting"'. Author's collection.

to breed familiarity and so increase public recognition. Other key terms in his article are: 'unmistakable', 'cumulative effect', 'cohesion' and 'pattern'. 'House style' is a term notable only for its absence here, reflecting that the term had yet to become commonplace.

Like Davis, Havinden highlights the role of the audience when he refers to 'the casual reader or passer-by'. Both authors identify the perception of the audience as a key criterion for defining whether a brand identity programme may be considered as coordinated or not. Havinden claims that only if a programme is perceived to be coordinated by its audience can it be considered effective, and thus likely to capture the 'goodwill of the public'. His reference to goodwill can be interpreted in relation to our current notion of 'brand loyalty' – a term that implies a consumer's continued allegiance to the products and services of a single organization.[20]

Whereas Warde (1932) and Davis's (1950a, 1952) texts both focused solely on typography as a coordinating device, Havinden touched on a range of means by which coordination could be achieved, including: symbols, logotypes, patterns and the style of illustrative or photographic content. He even considered the cropping of imagery as a means to achieve unity, explaining: 'As a further unifying device it was decided to show "Daks" trousers always in photographs cut just above the waist'.

For Havinden, brand identity involved more than simply the imposition of a consistent style; thus he highlights that there must also be an association between the 'handwriting' and each individual product that it appears upon. As such he draws attention to the flattening out that can occur when a single style is imposed insensitively across multiple artefacts and media (i.e. what suits one artefact may not suit all). Here, the balance between rigidity and adaptability that Dutton advocated for emerges again, with Havinden's reference to an 'infinity of variations', reflecting Dutton's 'infinite flexibility':

> [...] a unifying style, consistently applied, helps to co-ordinate, consciously or unconsciously, all the 'messages' a firm sends out to the public in every phase of its activities and gives them a cumulative effect that immeasurably enhances their value. No effort should be spared, therefore, to make this style as striking and, at the same time, as simple as possible, to allow for the infinity of variations it may have to assume.

This is noteworthy as a number of active design practitioners continue to question the ongoing preoccupation with consistency, reiterating that brand identity design is about coherence, rather than strict, totalizing consistency (Steel, 2016).

1956: Alec Davis, 'House Style'

Alec Davis's most potent contribution to the codification of corporate image-making came in September 1956 when he released a special issue of *Design* magazine dedicated solely to the subject of house style. The contents page of the text read more like an introductory textbook than a monthly magazine, with sections titled under the following questions: 'Why is it important?', 'Who should have it?' and 'Where should it be evident'. Other features focus on contemporary and historical examples, the 'pitfalls and possibilities' of house style, and finally, a summary of the contemporary context, titled, 'Where do we stand?'. Where Davis's early writing had been obfuscated by a lack of clarity and a tendency to stray off course, here his prose is concise. With the words 'House Style' emblazoned across the cover of the magazine (Figure 3.6) and repeated nine times upon the contents page alone, there is an indication that what had in 1950 been a relatively unorthodox new concept, was in 1956 a blossoming, readily recognized field of practice.[21]

Figure 3.6 F. H. K. Henrion's cover design for the 'House Style' special issue of *Design* magazine, issue 95, edited by Alec Davis (1956). Item held by the University of Brighton Design Archives.

BRAND IDENTITY IN BRITAIN

Davis's introduction to the issue demonstrates his new-found dexterity with the language of house style; yet in spite of the unfamiliar eloquence of his prose, his message remains similar to his earlier work, with a familiar reliance on terms such as: 'recognisable', 'consistency', 'style' and 'unity' (Figure 3.7). The opening paragraph of the introduction closely mirrors the sentiment of his first text written in 1950, with the words 'consistent' again being allied with consumer 'recognition': 'If the style is good, consistent and at the same time flexible, it can do much to promote sales through a wider public recognition and increased good will'.

One word that Davis had not deployed before was 'flexible' and this would introduce a new critical dimension to his existing patter. To this point his prose had centred exclusively on the notion of consistency, with words like 'uniformity' and 'standardisation' beckoning for a design that privileged rigour and order above all. Now, like Dutton before him, he recognized that a lack of flexibility could lead to sterility: 'A house style can therefore be a sound investment and a useful tool; but its edge must not be blunted by rigid standardisation'.

On the following spread, whilst discussing the role of design symbols, Davis supports his call for flexibility with reference to F. H. K. Henrion's work for the organization Bowater, stating that when 'properly designed they [house style programmes] can be adaptable'. Unfortunately, the illustrated examples provided failed to support the notion that the corporate symbol could provide

Figure 3.7 Double-page spread from the 'House Style' special issue of *Design* magazine, issue 95, edited by Alec Davis (1956). Item held by the University of Brighton Design Archives.

flexibility. Instead, the three photographs featured showed simply the same logo repetitively badged across different design artefacts. Aside from the necessary variations in scale and material, no significant adaptation or flexibility is evident. Nevertheless, Davis's recognition that house style, properly conceived, must balance consistent and variable elements was an important development that mirrored Dutton (1946) and Havinden's (1955) arguments.

Some twenty-four references appear in the 'further reading' section of the magazine, the earliest of these being Warde's LNER article of 1932. Two are from the 1940s, whilst the remaining twenty-one indicate work published between 1950 and 1956, with many of these only vaguely connected to the subject of house style.[22] Within this seventy-two-page special issue, Davis set out a comprehensive and rigorous documentation of house style, establishing in the process a basic taxonomy of the different means through which a house style could be delineated. Here he included five discrete 'factors': Colour, Pattern, Borders, Trademarks and Symbols, and lastly, Lettering, to which he would dedicate significantly more space than any of the other factors, believing it to be 'the most important single factor'.

Summary

Analysing the featured articles presented here has helped to establish how the practice of brand identity design began to develop around the middle of the century through the dissemination of texts available within popular trade journals and publications. The rhetorical developments traced here have shown the attempts made by practitioners to articulate and codify the phenomenon under question. Evident here is a process through which knowledge of a new, emergent practice is moving from an implicit, or relatively tacit form, to a more explicit, codified basis. Inherent in this transition is the emergence of a 'community of practice' (Lave and Wenger, 1991) developing gradually around brand identity design and supported by an expanding repertoire of inscriptions that record the growth of the practice and its associated ideals.

As can be seen in Table 1, the writers presented here sought to develop clear terminology to assert their position and while they refer to identity design in a wide range of ways, it is clear from my analysis that 'recognition' was a core driver for all the authors featured here. The first three examples highlight the important role of the consumer, referred to variously as: 'the traveller', 'the print-user' and the 'casual reader or passer-by'. As such, the perception of the audience is recognized to be a key criterion in discerning whether a corporate image programme may be considered as coordinated or not. Achieving the desired recognition is reliant, we are told, on the deployment of consistent, recurrent design elements that are carefully controlled or standardized.

Table 1 Central concepts and keywords from early formative British texts on programmatic branding.

Author	Central concepts	Keywords
Beatrice Warde (1932)	automatically designed cumulative recognition group personality recognisable unity	modernity reform standardising
Norbert Dutton (1946)	infinite flexibility living design living idiom recognisable unity	controlled coordinated formula module motifs pattern totality unified
Alec Davis (1950, 1952, 1956)	consistent design policy family resemblance house style overall-design policy reminder advertising	consistent flexible rationalisation recognition simplification standardising style uniform
Ashley Havinden (1955)	company handwriting cumulative effect infinity of variations unifying style	cohesion consistent co-ordinated identifiable repetition

We have seen through the examples presented here that corporate communication design was typically associated with notions of aesthetic uniformity. However, it is surprising how often the texts investigated here recognized flexibility, variety and dynamism as equally important features of successful brand identity programmes. In the case of Warde and the LNER, the focus was placed solely on how a consistent image based on typographic standardization could create a strong group personality. But for Dutton, consistency alone was not adequate as a means by which to unify a complex organization. It was the balance between repetition and flexibility in the London Transport identity that was paramount for Dutton. For him, variety must be matched with recurrent visual elements to create a living design idiom applied across multiple communication channels and design forms. In the case of Havinden, brand identity is understood as an expression of a company's handwriting. This handwriting, we are told, should be tailored to the needs of specific communication design artefacts and not simply imposed insensitively or inappropriately without question or thought. Alec Davis, meanwhile, was slower to recognize the need for variation or dynamism within complex identity programmes, but he played a critical role in promoting and disseminating 'house style' as an important new practice within Britain.

The texts presented here are useful as a precursor to the more detailed narratives that follow next, as they help to establish the context upon which these more detailed narratives play out. These various texts have shown that while identity design was beginning to be discussed by authors in the 1930s, it was genuinely flourishing as a recognized discipline by the mid-to-late 1950s. The codification of the practices evident within these texts substantiates this, not only through the writer's words, but also through the expanding range of case studies upon which these texts tease out their arguments.

PART TWO

IDENTITY PROGRAMMES IN PRACTICE

Identifying exemplars

The second part of this book 'zooms-in' to take a focused look at how brand identity was performed in practice during the post-war period. This part of the book can be said to concentrate on a history of design labour, which is distinct from the typical history-of-design approach derived from the traditions of art history. Depth of enquiry is prioritized over breadth, with three consultancies being outlined in considerable granular detail. This highly concentrated approach affords the opportunity to survey how the materiality of practice was transformed within studio practices during the post-war period. Rather than analysing design outputs produced by practitioners, or the wider socio-economic impact of their work, this strategy adopts a practice theoretical approach to the study of consultant design groups. This means the focus resides on practice itself and the unit of analysis is the consultancy's 'way of practice' as born out through the material artefacts mobilized by consultancies in the production of their work.

According to Nicolini (2012), a key benefit of the practice theoretical approach is the ability to develop rich descriptions of everyday work. This method privileges 'thick description' (Geertz, 1973), building a ground-up narrative of events, as opposed to a top-down meta-narrative. As such I resisted the tendency to impose over-arching thematics upon each case study. Given that this book maps a period of marked transition, the accounts of the consultancies are necessarily complex and at times contradictory, with few neat or easy conclusions drawn. Such an approach requires commitment from the reader to engage with the nuance of the material and to interpret arguments that are teased out gradually from the given evidence, rather than imposed at the outset. A byproduct of this approach is that the broader significance of the design consultancies comes through later, as I draw together recurrent themes and threads that connect the three consultancies in the chapter that follows the case studies. This strategy enables me to 'zoom in' and identify specific insights about the individual consultancies, while also making 'zoomed-out' generalizations about developments across the discipline as a whole, considering the wider influence of these consultancies and the methods that they employed.

Shifting focus away from designed outcomes and artefacts may feel awkward for some readers. While some will appreciate the focus on design labour, recognizing the value of the methods used and the potential for their adoption in other contexts, for others, the methodological shifts may feel undesirable, such is the tendency for histories of design to circle around artworks produced by creative practitioners. Instead of treating design as an artistic or cultural endeavour, my focus lies in the bureaucratic and managerial aspects of designers' work, where verbal, rather than visual documents have taken precedence and design is primarily a form of labour. Many of the images in this part of the book are not glamorous, nor heroic, but rather incidental files that constitute the unacknowledged workhorses of design consultancy life.

Designer's business files and operational documents are not generally considered significant or worth celebrating and as a result they are rarely preserved within archives of creative work. The accounts that follow here depend upon a selection of artefacts that happen to have been saved from disposal. In some cases this means working with published records of designer's working files, rather than the actual original documents; nevertheless, a certain pragmatism is required when developing a book of this nature and one can only work with what is available. The archival documents presented here often support the heroic individual narrative that I had hoped to move beyond; nevertheless I have sought to challenge this wherever possible.

In order to examine design consultancies with the requisite detail and nuance it was necessary to select a limited range of businesses and exclude several others. Ultimately three influential design consultancies were selected following an initial pilot study of twenty-one companies. An initial long-list of consultancies was drawn up from research in two major British trade journals of the time, *Design* (the Council of Industrial Design's magazine) and *Art & Industry*, as well as the print-focused yearbook, *The Penrose Annual*. Three consultancies were selected from this long-list on the basis that they exemplified certain pragmatic criteria. Of foremost concern were the following factors.

Case study selection

The consultancy was active for at least ten years during the post-war period

Although the concept of the corporate design programme had existed in Britain prior to the Second World War, the development and actualization of the concept did not attain any real significance until the early 1950s, as I showed in Part One. The decision to focus on the period after the war meant it was possible to consider the formative phase during which practitioners began to group together as active businesses. Groups formed after 1960 were excluded to ensure that enough data could be obtained in relation to the focal period. The intention was to explore the inauguration and development of programmatic brand identity as a group practice, rather than the later proliferation within contemporary society from the 1970s onwards. Several influential firms have been excluded on this basis, including Wolff Olins and Minale Tattersfield, both of whom were formed in 1965.[1] Also notable are Pentagram, who had existed in an earlier guise from 1962, but only recognized under this name from 1972. Given that these consultancies came to the fore towards the end of the post-war era, they are best understood as examples of the later proliferation of brand consultancy. Whilst design consultancies can be seen to grow in size, significance and number from 1970, the earlier period of corporate design activity has more potential in allowing us to understand how patterns of consultant practice emerged and evolved from the outset.

The group was founded in and operated from a base in Britain

The decision to focus on design practice within a single nation was taken partly in acknowledgement of the cultural distinctions between practices performed across different countries and continents, and the sense that a global survey would be too thinly spread. Focusing on branding practices within a specific nation allows enough scope to develop the necessary analysis of everyday practice routines. As I have already shown, practitioners in Britain were at the forefront of innovation in terms of the codification of brand identity programmes; so whilst the influence of the US has been widely recognized, the role of British practitioners within this domain is largely unrecognized and underexplored. This decision rules out the inclusion of the companies of

American practitioners like Raymond Loewy (who was known for industrial design) and Walter Landor, who developed premises in Britain after earlier success with consultant design in the United States. Other notable exclusions are US consultants Lippincott & Margulies, formed in 1945; and Brownjohn, Chermayeff & Geismar, formed in 1957; as well as Swiss consultants Gerstner+Kutter, formed in 1958 (later GGK).

The group was comprised of at least five employees

As it is my intention to explore the dualistic relationship between consultant design groups and the groups of design artefacts they produced (their brand identity programmes), individual practitioners and companies of less than five staff members have been excluded. This has ruled out one-man teams who operated with the odd assistant as and when necessary, for instance, H. A. Rothholz is a notable example. Several individual freelance practitioners made a name for themselves as brand identity designers, but the output of these designers is relatively insubstantial by comparison to the groups formed during the same period. Given the limited resources at their disposal, these individuals struggled to influence patterns of practice to the same degree as larger consultant groups who had bigger resource pools to draw upon and more public exposure to influence others.

The group was commercially significant, well regarded within the design industry and contributed to the development and codification of the discipline

As I am interested in the tenability of graphic design as an independent and commercially viable profession, I focus on those groups who achieved commercial renown. Given the difficulties of acquiring company records indicating economic performance, this metric is gauged largely on the profile of the groups' clientele. In terms of the regard in which the group were held, I have considered to what extent they received coverage within the design press of the day and whether their employees held positions of authority in the industry (as, for example, presidents of relevant organizations or societies). In terms of their role in developing and codifying the discipline I have considered the extent to which they were regarded as 'pioneers' in their field and whether they published texts or spoke publicly about the discipline. I have excluded Banks and Miles on the basis that whilst they were well regarded and commercially significant, they contributed less to the codification and conceptual development of the discipline.

IDENTITY PROGRAMMES IN PRACTICE

A major proportion of work created by the group during the period could be considered brand identity design, with a particular emphasis on visual unification

As it is my intention to explicate the relationship between brand identity programmes and graphic design professionalism, I chose to focus on companies operating within these domains. This criterion excludes Crawfords advertising agency, who despite carrying a reputation for the pedigree of their graphic work, operated within the professional realm of advertising. Other companies ruled out here include multi-disciplinary organizations that provided graphic expertise as a minor component of their offering, for example: Gaby Schreiber, Lucienne & Robin Day, Conran Design Group and the companies of Richard Lonsdale-Hands. One group given careful consideration was Michael Farr (Design Integration), but as brand identity design was not a central component of their company offering they did not strongly fulfil this criterion.

Sufficient research material is available on the group in the form of archival documents and published works

Given that opportunity to learn represents a key aspect of case study selection (Stake, 2005), it is important to consider the availability of access to empirical data about the group in question. Thus, ideally archival documents, and to a lesser extent, published works, would be accessible in relation to the group's activities. Allied International Designers have been excluded on the basis that no archive of works is accessible – while company director James Pilditch published widely, his design consultancy operations have not been documented or recorded. Likewise, while an archive exists on the work of Willy de Majo (2009), this collection at the University of Brighton Design Archives was not accessible at the time of enquiry.

Finalizing the selection

Having analysed the initial sample of twenty-one groups from the pilot study (Table 2), the three consultancies identified as representative examples are: the Design Research Unit (DRU), Henrion Design Associates (HDA) and Hans Schleger & Associates (HSA). These groups fulfil the selection criteria outlined above most strongly and offer a broad cross-section of different ways of practising brand identity design in Britain. As such they are appropriate instrumental examples, that together represent the general phenomenon under

	Active 10 years plus 1945–1970	Founded in Britain	Comprised of at least 5 employees	Significant to discipline	Brand identity focus	Archival access
Lonsdale-Hands Organisation (c. 1937)	■	■	■	■	▦	▢
Design Research Unit (1943)	●	●	●	●	●	●
Gaby Schreiber Associates (1943)	■	■	■	■	▦	■
London Typographical Designers (1945)	■	■	▦	■	■	■
W. M. de Majo Associates (1946)	■	■	■	■	▦	■
Henrion Design Associates (1948)	●	●	●	●	●	●
Hans Schleger & Associates (1954)	●	●	●	●	●	●
Woudhuysen Ltd. (1954)	▦	■	▦	▦	▦	▢
Conran Design Group (1956)	■	■	■	■	▦	▢
Banks & Miles (1958)	■	■	■	■	▦	■
Allied International Designers (1959)	■	■	■	■	▦	■
BDMW (1959)	▦	■	■	■	▦	■
H.A. Rothholz & Associates (1960)	■	■	▢	▦	▦	■
Michael Farr Design Integration (1961)	▦	■	■	■	▦	■
Fletcher/Forbes/Gill (Pentagram) (1962)	▦	■	▢	■	▦	■
Ken Garland & Associates (1962)	▦	■	▢	■	▦	■
Kinner Calvert Associates (1964)	▦	■	▦	■	▦	■
HSAG Design Ltd. (1964)	▦	■	■	■	▦	▢
Minale Tattersfield (1964)	▦	■	■	■	▦	▦
Wolff Olins (1965)	▦	■	■	■	■	▦
Cato Peters O'Brien (Michael Peters) (1965)	▦	■	▦	▦	▦	▦

Table 2 Analysis of consultant design groups active between 1945 and 1970. Fields marked in black indicate fulfilled criteria, dark grey fields represent partial fulfilment, pale grey fields represent unfulfilled selection criteria

study. Excluding those groups formed after 1960 enables a more carefully interrogation of the transmutation of graphic design practitioners in the post-war era.

Analysing 'ways of practice'

Although the key protagonists behind the formation of the three selected case groups have each passed away, removing the opportunity for direct-from-source data collection, two key sources of data remain available: archival documents (including published texts authored by the protagonists) and first-hand oral accounts from those who worked within these consultant groups. Here I describe how I collected and employed these two forms of data in my enquiry.

Archival documents were employed as material evidence of practice, with an emphasis placed on the processual complexity of practice. As such, a key technological tool or set of tools was selected for each group as a means by which to examine that particular practice in action. Hence, I sought to identify technological entities that embodied the procedural routines and organizational mindsets of the groups in question, while considering whether these 'things' provided the requisite opportunity to learn. The technological entities I employ are as follows. For Henrion Design Associates, a range of methods and tools are analysed – including visualization aids, indexing systems and workflow plans – to show how design groups were adapting to new project requirements. Particular attention is paid to the coordination of design artefacts (non-humans) and the organization of the design workforce (humans). For Hans Schleger & Associates, a pair of advertising agency Guard Books – catalogues complied to record the development of a specific advertising campaign – are analysed to reveal power relations in the triadic working relationship between the advertising agency (Mather and Crowther), the design consultancy (HSA) and their commercial client (the fishmonger Mac Fisheries). Particular attention is paid here to the coordination of design artefacts within HSA's brand identity programme for Mac Fisheries. For the Design Research Unit, a selection of project reports and manuals are analysed to show how specification documents and files influenced the development of brand identity design practices. Particular attention is paid to the nature of communications between DRU, their clients and collaborators, as well as to the way specification documents evolved and developed during the period.

As explained in Part One, this work builds on strategies, concepts and methods from Management and Organization Studies (MOS), as well as Science and Technology Studies (STS). The broad-based approach is a practice theoretical one in accordance with the ideas of Davide Nicolini (2012) and other scholars working in MOS. From STS, meanwhile, I adopt core concepts around the power of inscription (Latour, 1983) and how the act of de-scripting (Akrich, 1992) enables knowledge to be revealed that has been black-boxed or obscured from full comprehension. As I seek to understand different ways of practising brand identity through the lens of technical apparatus, I attempt to question and challenge these representations of action. As I am reliant on historical representations of practice (as manifested in material stuff), it is imperative to consider how much slippage there is likely to have been between the representation and the reality of that activity. It is equally important to consider the active role that designers have played in shaping the ways in which their practices have been understood. Many companies have used their approach to practice as a marketing tool in publicizing their business, and as such, each representation is interpreted with care and criticality here.

While material technology (in an expanded sense) forms the base of evidence on which each chapter depends, I also draw upon other material artefacts to support my arguments; these include the physical outputs of design coordination programmes, i.e. graphic design work sometimes referred to as branding 'collateral'. As this book positions itself as a history of practice, as opposed to a history of objects, I am mindful to avoid over-emphasizing the importance of these outputs of the design process. It is equally important to note that while these technological entities may be critical actors in my study – constituting the means by which I view practice – I am not telling a history of these objects either, but rather the history of design practice that they enabled.

While de-scripted technological entities are central to my interpretation of the consultancies presented here, I am not dependent on them, for this is where first-hand oral accounts come into frame. Although the leaders of the three consultancies have passed away, relevant practitioners who worked with the organizations in question were identified for interview. To gain insight from these individuals, qualitative semi-structured interviews were conducted to glean key insights about ways of practice within these groups. Although the interviews provide qualitative data that would otherwise be unattainable (as well as some limited quantitative data), the accounts provided are liable to be biased or distorted by the passing of time, providing fragmentary evidence. It is important to acknowledge that interviewees will not provide 'a passive depository of facts', but rather, as oral historian, Alessandro Portelli (1998: 69) explains, in drawing on their memories, interviewees will be engaged in 'an active process of creation of meanings'. This does not negate the value of the data they provide, but rather it serves to underscore the importance of the researcher's particular means of interpretation. Thus, it is important to factor in the possibility of bias, and consider the motives of the interviewee, as well

IDENTITY PROGRAMMES IN PRACTICE

as their relationship to the subject of the interview, with particular care required when interviewing those who may have a particularly strong reason to promote, critique or defend the subject.

Given the partiality of any material gleaned from semi-structured interviews, it was decided that recorded oral accounts would be used as a supplementary source; Blaikie (2009) classifies this as an embedded method, in as much that it is supplementary to the core method. As such, this data was used in conjunction with the empirical data captured from my archival research. Here I conduct what Denzin (1989) refers to as 'between-method' methodological triangulation – in other words the data produced from multiple methods is compared through triangulation. Although I use the interviews as a supportive and complementary method, this is not to say that the archival material does not have its own deficits. As Durepos and Mills (2012: 255) explain, 'archives are socially constructed sites, which are manicured according to the conventions of archivists and house limited documents, archives can be understood as concealing as much as they reveal'. In view of this, the rigour and rationale with which this qualitative archival data is interpreted is key to testing the validity of my findings. My goal was to triangulate between the archival research and data gleaned from semi-structured interviews to test the validity of both sets of findings.

What follows here is a critical interrogation of the three selected design consultant groups. What will become apparent when the cases are later compared is that the technical entities deployed in each practice govern working relationships between the designer, client and other intermediaries. First, we look at the example of F. H. K. Henrion's consultancy Henrion Design Associates (HDA). Next comes an examination of Hans Schleger & Associates (HSA) led by the commercial artist Hans Schleger. Finally, we conclude with the group of Misha Black and Milner Gray, the Design Research Unit (DRU). Each of these case studies reveals a distinct approach to the practice of brand identity design.

In the case of HDA we will see how graphic design consultants learnt from the advertising industry to gain jurisdiction for their own profession, to win their own clients and to communicate with these clients in a more persuasive manner. Here we see the designer seek to claim a more powerful role in the relationship with their clients, whereby opportunities to rule or govern the brand identity design process are afforded. The case of HSA demonstrates how during the 1950s it was common for graphic designers to be governed by advertising agents acting as intermediaries between the client and the designer. HSA present us with an individualistic approach to brand identity that privileges dynamism and variety as much as consistency, order and control. This provides an example that runs counter to the dominant discourse of the era, which celebrated control and consistency above all else. The case of the DRU, meanwhile, shows us how designers transitioned from soft, tentative and organic forms of governance to more mechanistic and technocratic forms. We see how the DRU as a consultant design group moved away from a distrust of homogenization, or what they call the 'stereotyped' approach, slowly embracing concepts of standardization, consistency and control.

4
RECONFIGURING PRACTICE: THE SYSTEMATIC METHODS OF HENRION DESIGN ASSOCIATES

In this case we will see how Henrion Design Associates embraced brand identity design head-on, transforming their way of practice to make the most of emerging opportunities in the corporate design sector. By adopting methods from Operations Research and the Design Methods Movement, they were able to develop productive working routines, claim jurisdiction over the field of work and gain power over their clients in terms of the governance of the design programmes that they created. In order to rule relations over these clients they developed a wide range of systematic tools that would present their practice as technically and scientifically rational.

The development of Henrion Design Associates

Biographical background

Henrion Design Associates were a consultant design group founded in 1951 by the established commercial artist Frederic Henri Kay Henrion, commonly shortened to F. H. K. Henrion. Henrion was born of a French mother and a German father in Nuremberg, Germany, 1914. After training as a textile designer in Paris during 1933, he went on to study under the renowned poster artist Paul Colin. During his time in Paris, he also worked under artists Jean Carlu and A. M. Cassandre. Together this triad of poster artists were considered giants of pre-war

French graphics. Henrion was set to follow in their footsteps and become a commercial artist in the mould of Colin or Cassandre, but by 1936 he had left Paris for Tel Aviv, citing the situation of civil war created by the sit-down strikes of Parisian metalworkers. In Tel Aviv he would design posters and exhibition materials for the French pavilion of the Levant Fair. Here his designs were seen by the Crown Agents for the British colonies, and shortly after, Henrion was on his way to London, hired by the Crown Agents to promote the merits of citrus fruit.

In London he shared a flat with a German friend of a similar age, Walter Landauer, (later known later by his anglicized surname, Landor) who had arrived in London as a teenager and been directed towards Goldsmiths College to study packaging design under Milner Gray's tuition.[1] He would go on to become a key innovator in the inauguration of brand identity practices in the United States setting up his agency under his anglicized surname. While Landor flourished in North America, Henrion remained in London for the remainder of his career, establishing himself first as a poster artist of the highest repute (Figure 4.1), and then later, as one of the most prominent and prolific pioneers of corporate identity in Britain.

Shortly after arriving in London in 1936 Henrion had worked under the direction of Misha Black, preparing designs for a 1938 exhibition for MARS,

Figure 4.1 'Four Hands' wartime poster by F. H. K. Henrion distributed in Europe after D-Day. Client: US Office of War Information, 1944. Author's collection. Courtesy of the Estate of F. H. K. Henrion.

the Modern Architectural Research Society. Along with Walter Landor and Milner Gray, Black was a partner in the design group the Industrial Design Partnership (IDP). These close-knit interpersonal relations would ease Henrion into his next significant appointment as a graphic and exhibition designer working under Milner Gray at the Ministry of Information during the Second World War. During the war Henrion divided his time between the Ministry of Information and the US Office of War Information, where he was involved in putting together magazines for the American armed forces.

Henrion's close association with Black and Gray would not last beyond the cessation of war, as by the 1950s his new consultant group, Henrion Design Associates (HDA) had begun to compete directly with the Design Research Unit (DRU), the group of Black and Gray which had been in operation since 1945.[2] Together with Hans Schleger & Associates, the groups of HDA and DRU were especially influential in developing brand identity design as a programmatic concern focused on coordination and visual unification. Furthermore, through his writing with colleague Alan Parkin, Henrion made a lasting contribution to the codification and proliferation of brand identity design practice. He would also play an important role in the professional organization of design, taking on positions of stature in various influential organizations, including President of the Society of Industrial Artists and Designers (1960–2), President of Alliance Graphique Internationale (1963–6), President of Icograda (1968–70) and Vice President of the RSA (1971–3). He was also heavily involved with design education over a forty-year period, most significantly at the Central School of Arts and Crafts, the Royal College of Art and the London College of Printing.

From the 'intuitive' individual to the 'rational' group

During his early career as a design practitioner, Henrion would become accustomed to working independently in a state of relative isolation, embellishing each design work with his own personal signature as a mark of authorship. He had worked on occasion under the command of other designers, such as Misha Black or Milner Gray, but for the most part his clients were the design patrons of large organizations, such as Stephen Tallents at the General Post Office, for example (Artmonsky, 2011). His first comprehensive experience of collaboration came during preparations for the Festival of Britain of 1951, where he oversaw the design of two pavilions, those representing 'The Natural Scene' and 'Country'. Here he worked alongside other designers, artists and illustrators. In his capacity as the lead designer for the two pavilions he was responsible for directing, as well as collaborating with, other practitioners. He had experienced some collaboration before, particularly through his work for exhibitions like

MARS in 1938 and 'Britain Can Make It' in 1946, but the Festival required an unprecedented level of coordination and teamwork. In this respect it provided fertile ground for designers to share their first experience of designing in large cross-disciplinary teams.

During the period leading up to the Festival, Henrion moved to establish himself as more than simply a lone freelance artist for hire, operating from 1948 onwards under the moniker of 'Studio H'. This change appears to have been primarily a symbolic gesture, for despite the new name, his business operation does not seem to have changed in any significant way. As such, he continued to work in much the same manner as before, essentially as a lone commercial artist, albeit now with the assistance of a small number of associates. Here he followed the master and apprentice model that he had been accustomed to when working for the heroic Parisian poster artists of the 1930s.

In 1951 he changed the company name to Henrion Design Associates (HDA). This was a period of transition, as it took several years to build up the steady base of client work to meet his ambitions. In 1955 he was photographed by renowned documentarian Wolfgang Suschitzky (Figure 4.2).[3] Posed at work in

Figure 4.2 Portrait of Henrion in his early forties by Wolfgang Suschitzky, bromide print, 1955, 14 3/4 in. x 11 1/2 in. (375 mm x 292 mm), NPG P559. Copyright the estate of W. Suschitzky, courtesy of Fotohof.

his studio, he is presented as an artisan in practical clothing with the flourish of a bow tie around his neck and a drawing pencil in hand. By this time he was working with associates under his command, but the image frames him as a heroic individual surrounded by paints and paintbrushes and with his virtuoso artworks behind. This public image of the corporate communication designer at work would change dramatically over coming decades.

Henrion gradually built up the consultancy work and in 1954 he took up the post of Director of Visual Planning for the advertising agency Erwin Wasey, a large American firm with a London office on Park Lane.[4] He held this post part-time for four years, with his colleagues including the typographer and teacher Edward Wright and the renowned children's illustrator Eric Hill. As Director of Visual Planning, Henrion was given his own private office and would liaise directly with the agency's high-powered clientele, of which KLM were a significant example. He would learn a great deal about the practices and methods of the commercial world during this appointment, not least the importance of making a persuasive case to clients. Later he recalled how Erwin Wasey had helped him to gain 'a unique insight into the US advertising and marketing approach', going on to explain, 'I learned to understand and, at times, use with circumspection, the advertising, marketing research jargon in discussing design' (Henrion, 1979: 7).

As he developed his own group consultancy during the 1950s and 1960s, Henrion would go on to develop elaborate techniques to support and substantiate his creative design work and to convince clients of the technical rationality of his work. These techniques can be seen to relate directly back to the practices of American advertising, and in particular, the knowledge he had gained during his time at Erwin Wasey; with Henrion noting the importance of Erwin Wasey for his career, referring to his 'four years' intensive learning of the advertising scene'.

Vance Packard (1957) famously described advertising practitioners in post-war North America as the 'Hidden Persuaders', and Henrion's exposure to these very same ideas – such as motivational research, depth psychology and subliminal tactics – evidently influenced the long-term approach of his own company. This is significant for two key reasons. Firstly, it is indicative of the transmission of transatlantic influence spreading from the US to London. Secondly, it signifies the wider role that advertising played in supporting the long-term development and growth of graphic design as an independent and tenable practice in Britain.

In 1951 when Henrion changed the name of the business to Henrion Design Associates he began to consider the merits of offering clients a more comprehensive service focused on the unification of their brand image. Another important revelation came at this time for Henrion when he acknowledged that for his company to secure lucrative long-term contracts with clients, they would need to present themselves in a manner akin to the clients for whom they wished to work. In other words, rather than presenting themselves as a loose grouping of commercial artists, as Bassett Gray or IDP had done previously, for example, they should appear more like a commercial organization themselves. When later asked why the Dutch national airline KLM had hired a British design firm (HDA) rather than a Dutch alternative, Henrion told the Dutch designer Wim Crouwel (cited in Roberts, 2005: 61), 'institutions like to talk to institutions'.[5]

In order to appear more institutional, Henrion's group consultancy began to present themselves as a rational and robust business operation. By the 1960s their working routines had developed to reflect the collaborative and systematic demands of the corporate work they now undertook, thus modelling their working methods on those found in larger institutions. Where Henrion had previously worked independently and intuitively in the mould of a traditional commercial artist, his new group adopted a range of technocratic techniques to fulfil project demands and control the studio workflow. By 1962 Henrion had commissioned architects Team 4 (Richard Rogers, Su Rogers, Norman Foster, Wendy Foster) to design a studio extension on top of his home to accommodate his growing workforce (Figure 4.3).

Previously we saw Henrion depicted in his studio in 1955 with paint brushes at his side and the commercial art posters for which he was known on the studio walls behind him. This image captured by a celebrated documentary photographer tapped in to recognized stereotypes of the designer as a creative artisan. Fast-forward to 1963 (Figure 4.4) and we are presented with a different picture. Published in *Design* magazine in a feature on professional practice and

Figure 4.3 View into the design studio extended on top of the Henrion household, undated. Courtesy of the Estate of F. H. K. Henrion.

Figure 4.4 Henrion pictured in his late forties with employees from Henrion Design Associates, as featured in *Design* magazine, issue 177, 1963. Item held by the University of Brighton Design Archives.

the versatile designer, this new photograph can be understood as a promotional artefact seeking to reposition and reframe the designer as a collaborative and business-like professional. Now Henrion is flanked by five employees who are all smartly dressed. Although a similar bow tie remains in place around Henrion's neck, his dress sense is altogether sharper in the latter image, with a suit-jacket smartening up his appearance. In his hands he holds a mock-up of the livery design for a KLM aircraft (KLM being HDA's most important corporate client of the time) and behind him we see further examples of corporate design work for other clients. In the eight-year period between these two photographs we see a significant transition in the self-image of the graphic designer, as well as major changes to the organizational set-up of the design studio. No longer acting alone with his art materials at the drawing board, Henrion Design Associates is now to be understood as a fully fledged business operation ready to tackle major brand identity commissions from powerful corporate clients.

Several factors led to the significant operational changes represented in these two photographs, but amongst the most important was Henrion's decision to pursue holistic all-embracing design programmes for large national and multi-national organizations. Reflecting on his earlier career, Henrion (1990) recalls:

> Probably early Fifties, or mid-Fifties, I sat down with my five or six associates of the time and said, 'we seem to be working for many different clients doing

many different things', you know, doing exhibitions for one, letter paper for another, print for a third, packaging for a fourth etc. 'Wouldn't it make sense to have fewer clients and be in charge of all their physical manifestations?' I think the word corporate identity hadn't crossed the Atlantic yet, we called it House Style. Well we were very lucky to get KLM first, and then came BEA [British European Airways], Blue Circle Cement, London Electricity Board, one after the other. I mean we never made efforts to get work, one brought job usually brought the next one, very much unlike today.

Henrion's succinct account of events irons over any details or contradictions, condensing several decades into a few sentences and making the transition under scrutiny appear seamless. What is particularly evident is that, despite his apparent humility, he positions himself as an active agent in control of his own career development. This suggests that these events came to pass precisely because he willed them to; not that he was responding to external demands and opportunities presented by his prospective clientele. As such, he presents himself as, at least partly, responsible for the birthing of a new culture of design commissioning in which the systematic identity programme replaced the ad-hoc commissioning of individual design artefacts. This is significant as it indicates that graphic design practitioners were not only aware of opportunities around coordinated brand identity design, but also that they actively sought out such commissions, having identified that they could be beneficial to the prospects of their burgeoning businesses. This was also true in the case of the designer H. A. Rothholz, with papers from his personal archive showing that he actively cultivated and promoted the function of corporate visual unification that design coordination could offer.

To what extent Henrion, and other designers, were in fact responsible for leading the transition towards the commissioning of holistic identity programmes remains questionable. Although Henrion and many of his peers worked persistently to sell their clients the benefits of a coordinated design approach, it is also important to acknowledge the critical role of the commissioning client as an enabling agent. Without either the initiative or buy-in of the commissioning client the realization of more holistic, comprehensive design programmes would simply not have been possible. The relationship to advertising, and especially the advertising campaign as an ongoing concern, is pertinent here too, given that the wealthiest commercial clients were already well accustomed to commissioning long-term serialized advertising campaigns that would run over several months or years and across multiple platforms.[6] As such, the idea of a coordinated central concept, strategy or design policy, was not unprecedented, though graphic designers, such as Henrion, brought a very particular spin to the serial quality of mass marketing. While the advertising campaign as a vehicle of communication tends to have a temporal or even cyclical quality, being commonly linked to sales of a specific product or service, the brand identity programme is envisaged as a more permanent, holistic and concrete entity, with an emphasis on visual unity and the promise to control perceptions of an organization over time. This move from the serial advertising campaign to the serial brand image scheme can be understood as a shift from product identity to organizational identity.

It was this new totalizing impetus of 'design coordination', as Henrion and Parkin referred to it, which demanded the creation of a reconfigured approach to practice facilitated by new tools and technologies. Henrion and Parkin (1968: 33) emphasize this point in the introduction to their text for the *DIA Yearbook*, 'Systematic Methods in Design Co-ordination', stating: 'Every designer knows the creative and administrative problems of designing a single item. But when a task involves hundreds or even thousands of items then difficulties multiply enormously and a new approach must be defined and achieved'. I shall now go on to examine this 'new approach' to practice outlined by Henrion and Parkin in their paper for the *DIA Yearbook*.

'Systematic methods in design co-ordination'

'Systematic methods' in context

The late 1960s were a key phase of Henrion's working life, with his transmutation from lone commercial artist to leader of a successful graphic design group nearing completion. This period of his career can be viewed as the pinnacle of his brand identity work, with many projects for major clients either in progress or already complete. The publication of *Design Coordination and Corporate Image* (Henrion and Parkin, 1967) only further cemented Henrion's reputation as a pioneer in the field, being recognized as the first major publication of international scope dedicated to the subject (Bos and Bos, 2007; Bos, 2011). Although others had previously contributed to discourse on the subject, nationally and internationally – none more so than Alec Davis in Britain – the scale and ambition of this edition was unprecedented.[7]

Though *Design Coordination and Corporate Image* has proved its durability as an artefact, attaining a cult-like status in as much that it remains highly desirable for enthusiasts and collectors to this day, the significance of the DIA paper authored by Henrion and Parkin (1968) has to date been largely overlooked. As Bakker (2006: 5) explains, the DIA text 'is likely to have attracted less attention than the [Reinhold/Studio Vista] book'. This has meant that its significance has been under-valued and under-examined, and as such, the text is overdue scrutiny. Before going further, it is worth considering the intended audience of

Figure 4.5 Front cover of Henrion and Parkin's (1967) text *Design Coordination and Corporate Image*. Courtesy of the Estate of F. H. K. Henrion.

each of these two texts and the motives of the pair in authoring them. This will help to establish the intentions behind their publication, as well as the contexts within which they would likely have been received.

The book *Design Coordination and Corporate Image* (Figures 4.5 and 4.6) showcases the aesthetic qualities of design coordination as a phenomenon, surveying the field and setting out the key terminology as Henrion and Parkin understood it. The text charts the international scope of the discipline relatively well, albeit in a Western-centric manner. Overall, it is fundamentally a visual affair, with words treated as a necessary, but perfunctory accompaniment to the showcase of work on display. The visual force of the publication makes a strong case for the power of a unified company appearance, in as much that it provides many visual examples that demonstrate the graphic impact of coordinated brand identity programmes. In this sense the book reinforces Alec Davis's argument that a consistently applied design language can enhance the audience recognition of a particular brand or organization. Co-published by Reinhold Publishing Corporation in New York and Studio Vista in London, readers of the text likely constituted practising designers as well as students of

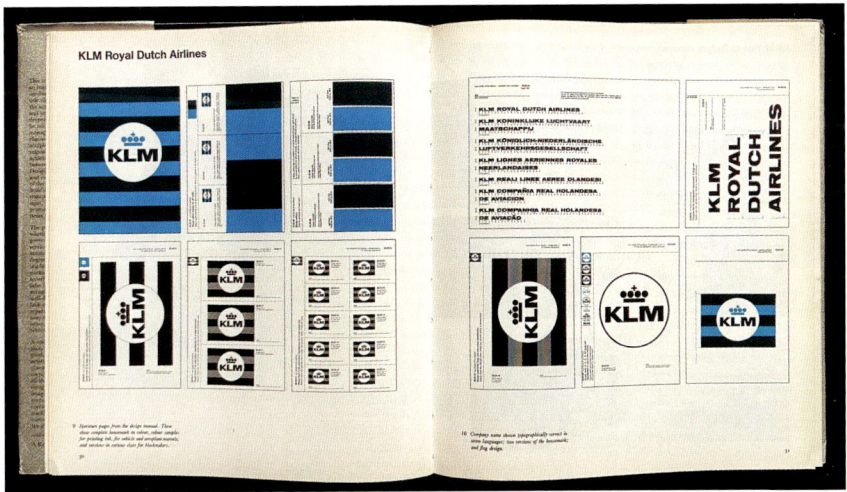

Figure 4.6 Sample spread from *Design Coordination and Corporate Image* (Henrion and Parkin, 1967: 34–5). Courtesy of the Estate of F. H. K. Henrion.

art and design.[8] Although the book presents itself as accessible to interested laypersons, as well as business and marketing professionals, it does not 'speak' to the reader in the same lucid tone that was later popularized by James Pilditch and Wally Olins, who captured a broader business-minded readership by writing about design from and for business perspectives.

If the Reinhold/Studio Vista text focused on visual end-product, then by comparison, the text for the *DIA Yearbook 1967/68* directed its focus to the processual complexity involved in achieving such an end-product (Figure 4.7). Founded in 1915, the Design & Industries Association (DIA) was an organization established with the intent of raising standards of industrial production in Britain, bringing together in closer unison manufacturers, designers, distributors, economists and critics. Directly inspired by the success of the Deutscher Werkbund, in Germany, the intention of the DIA was to harness the mutual advantages attainable from a close-knit association between design and industry.[9] As such members of the organization ranged from influential industry figures, such as London Transport's Frank Pick, Ambrose Heal of Heal's and Noel Carrington of Puffin Books, to design luminaries such as Misha Black, Gordon Russell and Charles Holden.

Given that the organization had been founded to unite the interests of design and industry, readership of the yearbook is likely to have comprised a mix of business professionals and designers. It is probable that the highly detailed, serious-minded nature of Henrion and Parkin's article made it more attractive to the yearbook's business-minded readership who were more inclined to the concerns of design management as opposed to visual or formalist concerns around graphic

Figure 4.7 Opening spread from 'Systematic Methods in Design Co-ordination', from *DIA Yearbook 1967/68* (Henrion and Parkin, 1968: 30–1). Photograph by the author. Item held by the University of Brighton Design Archives.

design. In this sense, while the Reinhold/Studio Vista book can be understood primarily as a graphic design text attractive to graphic design practitioners, the paper for the *DIA Yearbook* situates itself more in line with the kind of 'design thinking' literature prevalent in recent times, focusing as it does on the methods and operational aspects of design practice and their value to business.

How the DIA article came about is unclear. One can only speculate that Henrion's standing as a well-connected and sociable figurehead within the industry led to the commissioning of the piece. In agreeing to write for the yearbook his intention was presumably to further the status of his growing group practice, consolidating their reputation as not just industry-leading graphic design practitioners, but experts in a new field of their own making, that is: design coordination.

From 'carte blanche' to the 'chart before the course'

In beginning their text, 'Every designer knows the creative and administrative problems of designing a single item', Henrion and Parkin (1968: 33) can be seen

RECONFIGURING PRACTICE

to reach out an empathetic hand to fellow designers, sharing together in the unexpected complications of the design process; but taken in the context of their business readership, this turn of phrase can be seen as an analytical move to set up the competitive advantage HDA held over their competitors. As they go on to imply, any designer can design a single artefact, but only HDA are equipped to handle complex coordination schemes such as this.

After a short attempt to define some key terms and a roll call of recent client projects underscoring their credentials (Fisons, KLM, the Post Office, Blue Circle Cement and British European Airways), Henrion and Parkin continued their piece by outlining the premise of design coordination:

> The scale and complexity of these [design coordination] jobs pose a number of problems which cannot be solved by traditional intuitive methods. Often thousands of items are involved, and often the client himself does not know how far a new design policy can be applied and to how many items. This forced us to develop and apply techniques not normally used in design. These techniques apply less to the actual design stages, than to pre-design assembling of information and formulation of design requirements, than to design planning, progressing, and implementation.

Their comments around the limitations of 'traditional intuitive methods' are intriguing as they allude to what they view as the insufficiency of pre-existing methods, suggesting that designers' work to this point had lacked a sense of rationale and structure. Later they refer to the 'rationally structured' understanding that emerges from their own systematic methods.

The word 'rational' appears six times in this small-format 10-page text and is repeatedly valorized. The centrality of the term is emphasized further in a note about the office's employees, which states that of the ten staff members, three are 'mathematically trained "rationalisers"'. The reverence with which technical rationality is treated in the text is important, as it supports one of the core axioms of my research, that this period of British design history is significant as a moment in which, not only the language of design shifted markedly, but with it, the dominant paradigms underlying the profession. The growing interest in systems thinking that Henrion and Parkin develop upon had especially pronounced implications for graphic design practitioners given that their approach had been perceived to lack the scientific rigour or professionalism of their architectural or industrial design counterparts.

Comparing 'Systematic Methods in Design Co-ordination' with Henrion's paper for the International Design Conference at Aspen reveals just how far the dominant mindset of the discipline had shifted in little more than a decade. In 'Graphic Design in England', Henrion (1956) set out the differing approaches to the development of creative work taken by practitioners of different nationalities. According to Henrion, in North America creative work was developing from a 'chart before course' mentality, meaning that market research and statistics were governing the direction of creative design work. On the Continent, meanwhile, research and statistics were apparently of little concern, as they followed a 'carte blanche before course' model, with designers given free rein over creative work. Britain in 1956 was, according to Henrion, caught between these two states, with clients and advertising agents preferring to put the 'chart' first, and designers preferring the blank canvas. Henrion gives away his own position when referring to the forceful way the statistics-based, advertising mindset had 'invaded most fields of graphic design'.

More astonishingly, Henrion (1956: 2) confides that while British designers were using market research, they were not constrained by it should a superior idea or concept emerge independent of, or contrary to, this data:

> We pay a certain amount of attention to the background and the market requirements, market analyses and surveys, but we are prepared to throw these overboard if an intuitive idea of such quality turns up, which in spite of safe precedents (tried therefore trite), promises to capture attention in an original way, and draw it pertinently and wittily to the point of sale or information. This approach very often gives the best results equally in terms of sales and aesthetics. However, the more we get involved in mass media, be they magazines or television, the more we get involved in the network of charts dictating the course to take.

Henrion's depiction of market research thrown overboard is indicative of the thinly veiled disdain with which British-based creatives of the 1940s and early-1950s had treated more 'scientific' or rational approaches to design. Compare this with the following two excerpts from the DIA piece, where Henrion and Parkin (1968: 39 and 42) state:

> It is important for client and designer to agree on the requirements, and on how proposals are to be rationally evaluated, before design development begins. A large design programme is not simply a matter of having a bright idea and trying it on the client.

> We believe that the most challenging problem in any design job is to find the most appropriate systematic method of coping with it. [...] Important decisions which are only too often made subjectively on personal prejudice (called taste) should be made on the basis of more objective quantifiable evidence.

From the 'original', 'intuitive idea' of 'such quality' (Henrion, 1956), to the assertion that undertaking a large design programme is 'not simply a matter of having a bright idea and trying it on the client' (Henrion and Parkin, 1968), the evolving design philosophy of HDA could hardly have been more pronounced. Having previously slighted the invasion of the statistics-based US approach, Henrion now championed the merits of technical rationality and the systematic method. Given the turnaround in his ideology, one is reminded of Peter York's characterization of the pre-war sign-painter's transmutation into fully fledged 1960s management consultant. As York (1984: 34) remarks:

> These sixties designers were completely different. They'd ask you what your company really did, what its philosophy was and how people related to it, and ask to see the company archives and talk to the senior management. And they sent memos about it all. You'd think they were management consultants from the way they carried on, not sign-painters.

Parkin's role

The role of Henrion's employee Alan Parkin in the development of the consultancy's new ways of practice is worthy of further consideration given that he came from a background outside the typical art and design educational system, bringing with him different subject interests and expertise. Parkin apparently took a leading role in the development of both the *DIA Yearbook* text and the Reinhold/Studio Vista book, taking responsibility for writing the first drafts of both texts (Parkin, 2012).[10] Given that he is recognized as a co-author of both texts, it is clear to see that Henrion was keen to acknowledge his importance in the conception of these works (it would have been understandable had Henrion been given the sole credit given his reputation within the design scene).

Parkin's influence was not limited only to the authorship of the texts themselves but was also evident in the systematic methods and practices of the studio as described within the DIA Yearbook text. As Parkin explains, his role had differed to Henrion's other employees in that he was a more public facing member of the group. So, whilst the other designers at HDA were based strictly at the Pond Street studio, he was given his own business card (a luxury the others were not afforded) and accompanied Henrion to client meetings, working the slide carousel and supporting Henrion's design proposal presentations. Next, I will go on to examine Parkin's role more closely to consider the significance of his contribution.

It is notable that Parkin had come to work within the graphic design industry from an unorthodox background, graduating with a degree in Moral Sciences from Cambridge University. He had a long-standing interest in art and architecture and had won a Sanderson wallpaper competition soon after his graduation from Cambridge. This resulted in a brief spell of work with the designer and photographer, Humphrey Spender, before he later went on to work with commercial artist David Kaplan, the stepfather of a Cambridge friend. Next followed a spell working with commercial artist H. A. Rothholz, before his final position pre-Henrion as Production Editor of the *Architects' Journal*. Speaking about how he had come to be employed by Henrion, Parkin (2012) recalls a party held by a mutual contact at the Courtald Institute:

> There were all sorts of people there, including Henrion, who I had admired from a distance. I grew up in the Midlands and the only thing I knew about smart London stuff was what I read in magazines or heard on the radio. Henrion had done a series of advertisements for Windsor and Newton, or Reeves, I forget which, where there was a smart picture of him in his bow tie smiling, working with Reeves poster colours or something, saying 'I find them excellent'. It was in *Art and Industry*, a wonderful magazine. From being a schoolboy, I had this standing admiration for Henrion particularly, but also many of the other designers too. I knew who he was. This strange name F. H. K. Henrion, what kind of name is that?
>
> I did meet him at this party and started talking to him about what I had been doing. I'd had a year in Italy, a scholarship post-Cambridge, where I was trying to do something between graphics and logic really. An elaborate thing, it didn't come to anything. He was very interested, because he was interested in all sorts of things. It so happened he had just landed this job for KLM and was really quite alarmed about how it was all going to be done and he saw the opportunity of getting somebody in to help on that side of things – the organisation and the writing stuff. He said what are you doing? At that time I was production editor at the *Architects' Journal*. I'd been there about a year. He said would you like to come and work with me and I said, 'sure I would', it was as simple as that. We got going straight away on the KLM things. I was fairly good on the graphics side. I was a bit too careless, I wasn't a professional standard for lettering or typography or anything like that. I'd always had an interest in that, I knew what was what. It was really this organisation … presentation … that stuff.

Parkin joined HDA in 1961 when the group was already two years into the KLM consultancy. This could explain why there is relatively little coverage given over to the methods behind the KLM work in the *DIA Yearbook* text; in terms of complex systematic thinking, it is the work for Blue Circle Cement and the Post Office that receive greatest coverage. Parkin was interested in developments in computing and cybernetics, having exhibited as an artist at the Institute of Contemporary Arts show, *Cybernetic Serendipity: the computer and the arts*, curated by Jasia Reichardt (1968). Furthermore, his writing was likely influenced by Bruce Archer's articles for *Design* magazine that were later published in one volume under the title: 'Systematic method for designers'.[11] The resemblance between the title of Archer's seminal text and the Henrion and Parkin *DIA Yearbook* text is simply too striking to be ignored:

> Systematic Method for Designers (Archer, 1965)
> Systematic Methods in Design Co-ordination (Henrion and Parkin, 1968)

The close similarity between the two titles suggests that Henrion and Parkin were jumping on a bandwagon that had developed from Archer's earlier work. Such was the fervour for Archer's work that it had led to 'unprecedented' demand for his writing, with new printings of the publication being publicized in *Design* magazine (*Systematic method for designers*, 1965: 73).

Given that Parkin's interest in mathematics and cybernetic theory had inspired Henrion to employ him, it is apparent that he acted as a kind of scientific foil for Henrion. Yet Parkin (2012) downplays his influence on the group, and when asked directly about his role, simply claims that:

> My input would have been that I was an admirer of the British Standards Institution, who for many years had been producing these very bleak, very stark, very cut-down little grey covered standards [...] where in extremely precise and careful terminology they defined in numbered paragraphs exactly what you must do. I was aware of that as a very high standard of specification publication and would have tried to get it up to that level.

In an unpublished manuscript about his career, Henrion (1979: 9) reflected on his 'long friendship and collaboration' with Parkin, noting that: 'on very large design projects a mathematician can be an enormous help – because what you're doing is really an ordering process, and so is mathematics, breaking things down into sets and subsets'. Caution is required when evaluating Parkin's influence in the technocratization of practice at HDA as Henrion had been deliberating about holistic design principles years before Parkin joined the firm.[12] Nevertheless, it is hard to ignore the highly technical nature of the systems deployed by Parkin during his time with Henrion. Next, I will go on to analyse the article from the *DIA Yearbook* more closely to explain the role Parkin played in developing the tools mobilized as part of HDA's new systematic method.

The 'collective enabling enterprise' of design coordination as mapping

Henrion and Parkin outline four key stages in conducting a design coordination programme, with the first stage broken down into three steps:

1. **Making a survey**
   - *Analyse the present situation*
   - *Assess the present situation*
   - *Clarify the corporate aims and their relative priorities*

2. **Information storage and retrieval**
3. **Formulating a brief**
4. **Planning and estimating for design development**

Together they emphasize that such a programme is more concerned with the 'pre-design assembling of information and formulation of design requirements, and to design planning, progressing, and implementation' than it is with what they describe as the 'actual design stages'.[13] This is significant as it suggests that, in their view, the preliminary strategic work of design is both separate to 'actual design' (and so perhaps not considered by Henrion and Parkin as design at all), yet is deemed worthy of a more rigorous and scientific approach than 'actual design'. This attempt to apply scientific ways of knowing to the design process appears counter to recent trends for 'design thinking' and 'design-driven innovation' (Verganti, 2009), where 'designerly ways of knowing' (Cross, 2001) are championed as harnessing unique problem solving capabilities that are applicable beyond conventional design contexts.[14] Far from celebrating the creative potential of designerly ways of knowing, Henrion and Parkin work deliberately to mask any perceived element of risk or uncertainty implicit in their practice. According to their account, their innovation is not to be found inherent within conventional design artefacts or outputs, but rather in the technocracy and rationality of their methods.

At the very centre of their methodology lay intricate tools for data collection and mapping. As such, the second stage of their model – 'Information storage and retrieval' – dominates their overarching ideology, permeating throughout the process and having an overbearing influence on the other stages of their process. Viewed collectively, the act of mapping is central to the method of design coordination as conceptualized by Henrion and Parkin. James Corner's conceptualization of mapping as a 'collective enabling enterprise' is useful here. According to Corner (1999), mapping is commonly misunderstood as an act of tracing that replicates or mirrors the world. He argues that in fact it is concerned with the re-shaping of the worlds in which people live. Mappings are thus not the transparent, neutral or passive devices of spatial measurement and description, as commonly believed, but rather, they should be understood as extremely opaque, imaginative, operational instruments that set the stage for future work.

For Corner, then, maps are far from objective and must be understood as essentially subjective, interpretive and fictional constructs of facts. Viewed from this perspective, mapping can be interpreted as a powerful communication technique with latent agency to control and coordinate socio-technical assemblages. As Corner (1999: 213) posits, 'mapping precipitates its most productive effects through a finding that is also a founding; its agency lies in neither reproduction nor imposition but rather in uncovering realities previously unseen or unimagined'. In other words, the process of mapping is both a performative act of exploration that reveals certain hidden truths, and also a formative, foundational process upon which future decisions can be taken and acted upon.

Of the various tools that Henrion and Parkin detail in the 'Systematic methods' article many develop from performative mapping processes akin to Corner's theorization of mapping. As such, their conception of 'design coordination' can be understood as one that is akin to a collective enabling enterprise. For Henrion and Parkin, mapping enables the representation of complex power relations and spatial hierarchies. Thus, we are presented with eight different examples of how various mapping techniques can communicate or organize ideas. These are as follows: (1) a coordinate indexing system that maps client information to produce a database; (2) a diagrammatical map of the findings derived from such a database; (3) a magnetic workflow board that maps out an intended working process, charting the movement of the labour force; (4) a dynamic display stand that maps the relationships between visual references; (5) an evolutionary mapping of the development process behind a new logotype; (6) a comparative mapping of the structure behind 'old and new' logotypes; (7) a comparative mapping of the same 'old and new' logotypes under conditions of poor visibility; (8) a mapping of the 'new' logo when exposed to horizontal movement.

According to the framework of collaborative objects set out by Nicolini et al. (2012), the design coordination tools created by Henrion and Parkin can be interpreted as 'activity objects'. To consider an entity as an activity object means to emphasize its productive role and take account of its potential to motivate collaboration and direct activities. As such, activity objects are forcefully active entities with potential to bestow power on those that create them or control their future development; this means they can assume positions of power within collaborative social settings. Describing the traits of activity objects, Nicolini et al. (2012) state that such objects are, 'incomplete, emergent and expansive, which gives them their performative character'. This accords closely with Corner's contention that mapping, properly understood, is a performative process, or as Deleuze and Guattari's (2004: 13) describe, 'an experimentation in contact with the real'. In conclusion we can surmise that, HDA's practice of design coordination depended on a range of mapping tools that can be productively interpreted as activity objects. Next, I will examine these eight examples, dividing them into two distinct categories, looking firstly at those involved in what Henrion and Parkin call the 'pre-design stages', before examining those that influence what could be considered the post-design stages of work.

Pre-design stages

Of the HDA design coordination tools centred around the pre-design stages, their diagram of the Post Office survey is aesthetically most clearly aligned with conventional notions of topographic mapping, presenting itself as a kind of complex network map. By the same measure, their magnetic workflow board shares many similarities with standard flow charts. By comparison the final two examples of the coordinate indexing system and the dynamic display stand differ in as much that they are the most emergent tools, with the potential to point to new potentialities, as opposed to prescribing them; neither resembles a conventional map as such, but both are concerned with fundamental mapping principles, such as data collection and comparison, and taxonomic categorization.

(1) Coordinate indexing systems

Alan Parkin took a lead in developing the indexing tools mobilized by HDA in their work for the Post Office and Blue Circle Cement. Long before the computer had made its entry into the designers professional working context, Parkin's intricate indexing systems emerged from a form of elaborate computation (Figure 4.8). Parkin's indexes used a form of coordinate indexing, with each item stored within

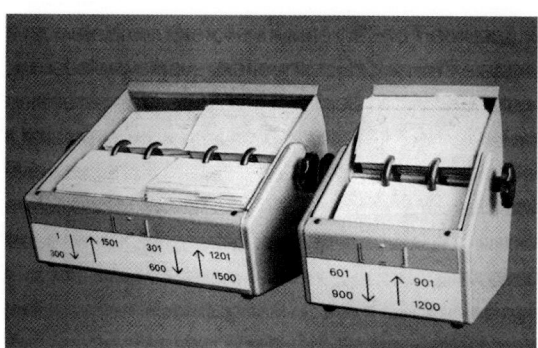

Figure 4.8 'Rotary filing system for Blue Circle Cement', *DIA Yearbook 1967/68* (Henrion and Parkin, 1968: 34). Photograph by the author. Item held by the University of Brighton Design Archives.

RECONFIGURING PRACTICE

the system broken up into elementary units of information. So, for example, within the Post Office library there were two kinds of reference cards within the system: plain white and coloured. White index cards containing keywords, or descriptors, were organized alphabetically so they could be used as reference points from which the relevant entries within the full library could be identified. So, if searching for a cross connection cabinet one would consult the white keyword cards for 'cross-connection' and 'cabinet' and note down the reference number repeated on both index cards. Consulting a library of numerically arranged blue and pink item cards one could then identify the relevant number card and isolate the card in question (Figure 4.9). The blue and pink item cards were designed as blank questionnaires, which could be completed by Post Office employees and returned to HDA for filing.

According to Henrion and Parkin, this system allowed them to access and assemble all the information they had on any Post Office subject within a matter of minutes. They were clearly proud of their achievements here, dedicating several columns of text to a detailed explanation of the inner workings of the system, illustrating the Post Office index cards alongside a further illustration of a rotary filing system used for sorting specimens within an index for another client, Blue Circle Cement (Figure 4.10).

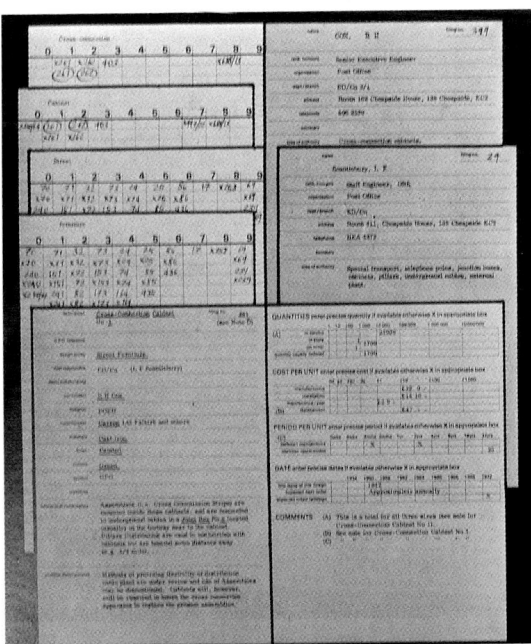

Figure 4.9 'Cards from the Post Office design library', *DIA Yearbook 1967/68* (Henrion and Parkin, 1968: 38). Photograph by the author. Item held by the University of Brighton Design Archives.

Figure 4.10 An example of the design work for Blue Circle Cement created as a result of their systematic methods, as featured in *IDEA* magazine No 114, 1972. Courtesy of the Estate of F. H. K. Henrion.

HDA's indexing tools can be understood as vacant frameworks that later became infiltrated with the relevant organizational data from the client. In this sense they reflect the expansive nature of activity objects (Nicolini et al., 2012). Whereas brand identity designers of the 1960s typically sought to deny the significance of change, developing fixed brands for a singular moment frozen in time, HDA's indexing systems had the potential to foster more dynamic approaches to design that could counter the normalized ideal of concretization. In their expansive nature these systems provided the affordance for a more dynamic approach, whereby multiple readings could be taken from an ever-changing data-set. This could in-turn inform more agile design approaches and strategies. However, this did not come to pass, and instead the deployment of these index systems appears to have followed the normal pattern, in as much that they were treated as another static, concrete entity to inform a marked strategic juncture at a specific moment in time. This line of development means that the emergent and expansive qualities of the indexing systems were restricted, and instead of being harnessed as working tools of benefit on an ongoing basis, their use was limited to the initial moment of release as the findings were reported to the client. In this scenario when the data-entry process was complete, the information contained within the index could be mobilized to inform future action. The course of action being dependent on the specific kinds of data collected by HDA and their interpretation of this data. So, although Henrion and Parkin describe their tools as if they are objective, impartial third parties in the relationship between design consultant and client, their agency in the creation and mobilization of these mapping tools must not be ignored. Counter to this, it is equally important to recognize that the new HDA mapping tools do have a type of agency in terms of the establishment of a new working model of the HDA process.

(2) Diagram of the Post Office design survey

From the findings of the Post Office library, HDA produced a diagram or map summarizing their design survey of the organization (Figure 4.11). This visual representation held potential for far-reaching action, being used to argue for the redistribution of some 5,000 design artefacts into new groupings based on design-need, as opposed to administrative convenience. For example, following HDA's proposal, Post Office items located closely together on a street pavement would now be controlled by the same department within the organization, having

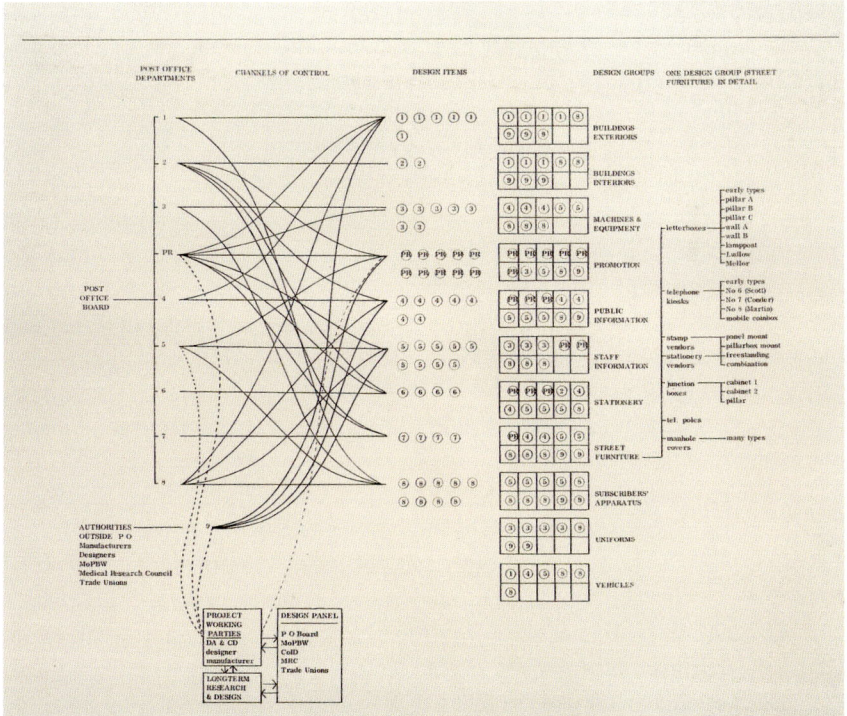

Figure 4.11 Diagram of Post Office design survey, *DIA Yearbook 1967/68* (Henrion and Parkin, 1968: 36). Photograph by the author. Item held by the University of Brighton Design Archives.

previously been grouped by what had been convenient for the administrative stakeholders involved in their operation, rather than the end-user. In aligning certain artefacts with certain administrative departments HDA sought to control not only design entities, but also the internal structure of the Post Office itself. They argued that the relative success of such a design coordination scheme was dependent on the prior coordination of the staff base, with Henrion and Parkin (1968: 39) claiming, 'it is essential that co-ordination of people should precede co-ordination of items'. They also advised on how the administration of design work should be managed across the organization to ensure successful deployment of their proposals. This 'proposal for design management' would involve appointing a permanent 'design administrator' and a 'co-ordinating designer', alongside a 'design panel', who would be required for sign-off on all major projects and policy changes.

Here we see what could be conceived of as a simple graphic design problem (to coordinate a range of corporate design assets) being reframed as a larger organizational and design management issue. In this sense we can begin to understand how individual graphic design practitioners like Henrion became implicated in more bureaucratic corporate practices of management and governance. Furthermore, we can also see that designers in 1960s Britain were already beginning to understand that programmatic identity design had far-reaching implications well beyond aesthetic values and the media's constant preoccupation with logos.

When the Post Office diagram is combined with the indexing systems from which its findings are derived, together they constitute a clear example of the ability of maps to reformulate what already exists. Following Corner then, the Post Office library should be understood as the finding, whereas the summative diagram of the survey represents the founding – i.e. the basis on which what already exists is reformulated. Another way of looking at this is that the indexed library of cards is generative and thus should be understood as a mapping (though it pretends to be an objective tracing), whereas the diagram is prescriptive and should be understood therefore as a planning (rather than a mapping).

Corner touches on the relationship between maps and plans, explaining: 'Whereas the plan leads to an end, the map provides a generative means, a suggestive vehicle that "points" but does not overly determine'; he describes the act of planning as, 'imposing a more-or-less idealized project from on high' (Corner, 1999: 228). This accords with Henrion and Parkin's vision for the Post Office, though their plan derives directly from their mapping. The Post Office diagram purports to be a summative representation of the findings from the indexing project, but it does more than merely point towards a solution, with Henrion and Parkin forcefully taking matters into their own hands and regrouping Post Office artefacts and employees into new configurations. Here in this one document it is difficult to separate processes of mapping from processes of planning, such is the convergence of these two activities.[15]

(3) Magnetic workflow board

A dramatic offshoot of the shift towards design coordination was the need for a more concerted attempt to coordinate the workforce. As Michael Middleton (1967: 82) explains in his timely book *Group Practice in Design*, the ever-increasing scope of corporate design commissions led individual designers towards group practice:

> A 'corporate identity programme' will bring, buildings, products, printed matter and all other aspects of an organisation into a common design framework. […] Clearly such large scale undertakings are beyond the capacity of the individual designer; the team is born. Different skills form new patterns of collaboration – on an ad hoc basis for specific jobs, in continuing association, or permanently in an integrated office.

Group practice became ever more prevalent in design from the 1950s onwards, with a surge of groups focused on graphic design emerging during the 1960s and 1970s.

The practice of HDA was, to some extent, restricted in scope by their premises at Pond Street, Hampstead (also Henrion's long-term home). Henrion worked initially from the drawing room at the front of the house, with his assistants working from a small back room. By 1962 a substantial studio extension had been built, designed by Team 4, an early partnership between Richard and Su Rogers, together with Norman and Sue Foster. This allowed the staff base to grow to around fourteen or fifteen members by the 1970s.

Given that Henrion liked to retain direct control of all operations in the HDA studio it would not have suited him to have grown the studio any larger. Recalling a moment in the mid-1970s when a merger had been mooted between HDA and Negus & Negus (the studio of Dick and Pam Negus), Henrion's second wife Marion Wesel (cited in Shaughnessy, 2013: 90) explains why it had been called off: 'Both Dick Negus and Henri were not used to having anyone interfere with their decisions, and their staff were more like assistants'. This evocation of the relatively dictatorial design leader clearly establishes the nature of HDA as a group practice in which Henrion directed affairs. Parkin is somewhat anomalous within this one-man team, in that he seems to have developed a more equitable working relationship with Henrion, due largely to his ability to proffer forms of knowledge and expertise beyond Henrion's own command.

As a consequence of HDA's growing labour force, the flow of work through the studio needed to be managed more purposefully. The deliberate and rational organization of group work was far removed from Henrion's earlier career where he had operated according to the master–apprentice model with the odd assistant in the back room. Initially he got by in much the same manner as the lone commercial artist of his earlier years, using assistants to take the legwork out of any arduous or repetitive labour, but as his team grew this presented new leadership and management challenges. To organize the team and their work, they mobilized visual aids in the form of workflow diagrams that enabled them to plan out their collective design process in advance, assigning members of the workforce to specific tasks and designating time allowances to specific organizational activities. These workflow diagrams set out a sequence of operations that prescribe a time-based process, as well as the workers involved in fulfilling such a process.

One of eight workflow diagrams used in the Blue Circle Cement job was illustrated within 'Systematic methods' (Figure 4.12). It is extremely unusual to see a post-war graphic design consultancy publicize a bureaucratic device such as this, with their technocratic flow diagram taking up four times the space of the creative design work illustrated on the same spread.[16] Referred to by Henrion and Parkin as 'network planning', and described as 'a network method

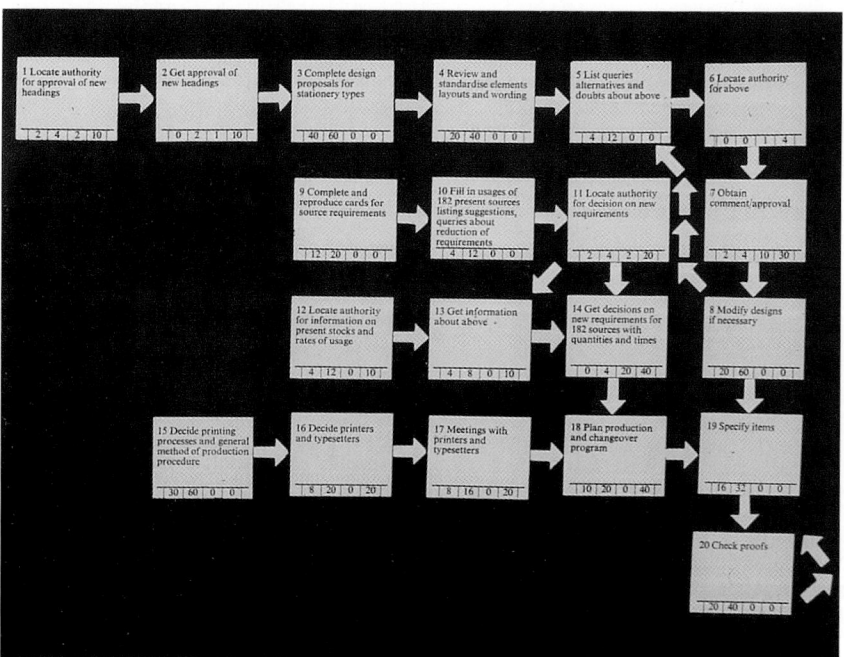

Figure 4.12 'One of eight magnetic boards used for network planning for the Blue Circle design co-ordination programme', from *DIA Yearbook 1967/68* (Henrion and Parkin, 1968: 40). Photograph by the author. Item held by the University of Brighton Design Archives.

for planning, estimating and progressing each major assignment', these work tools can be seen to derive from the fields of Operations Research and more specifically scientific management.

The notion of managing or optimizing workflow can be traced back to early twentieth century industrialists such as Frederick Taylor and Henry Gantt who are credited as important pioneers of scientific management. Using a stopwatch, Taylor (1911) developed the time-based study of work (later called 'time and motion studies'), wherein rule of thumb methods were replaced by more deliberate, rational ones that derived from a scientific study of the work tasks themselves. Gantt, who worked closely with Taylor, is remembered most clearly for the workflow planning charts he conceived, the Gantt Milestone Chart, a form of graphic schedule for planning a programme of interrelated work tasks. The Gantt chart was later built upon by researchers in the United States who sought to develop network planning and analysis by creating graphical tools that could reflect more fully the inter-relationships between distinct but connected work tasks.

As Mercier and Nunnally (1965) explain, these earlier initiatives led to the development of critical path analysis (CPA, or often called the critical path method, or CPM) by researchers at the American company duPont; while during the same period researchers working for the US Navy developed closely related hypotheses that led them to posit the concept of the Program Evaluation and Review Technique. These initiatives in the field of network planning clearly influenced the ideas of Parkin and his colleagues at HDA, with them referring to the concept of critical path five times in the 'Systematic methods' text. They carefully articulate the significance of the critical path method, explaining how it enables them to optimize the way they use their time in meeting tightly fixed client deadlines. Interestingly HDA's workflow diagrams do allow for some malleability, in that they set out a minimum and a maximum time allowance for each task. This estimate was then used to derive the probable time in which a client project would be delivered.

These workflow diagrams can be understood as a form of map-based inscription device that enabled collective action to happen. Though individual micro-practices within the overarching design coordination practice of HDA were routine and repeatable, on a macroscopic level each new client project would be unique in terms of its time scale and the issues involved. As activity objects, the magnetic workflow boards focused the minds and energies of HDA's employees, centralizing their labours around one focal point of inscription. As such they can be seen to mobilize various social and technical actors around a commonly agreed objective. ANT scholar Michel Callon (1981, 1986) refers to this as a process of 'translation' through which various diverse actors form a network or alliance in response to a particular problem.

It remains unclear to what extent the designers at HDA actually followed the plans set out in the workflow boards, or whether these devices remained in use over a longer period of time. Nevertheless, Henrion and Parkin's decision to promote this aspect of their practice is important. Though these magnetic planning boards are described as internally situated work tools, it is evident that they had ramifications for external clients too. So, although it is impossible to say how the knowledge inscribed in these diagrams was represented or communicated to clients, it is evident that decisions inscribed within these devices had wider ramifications, setting clear frameworks and expectations around which the project would unfold, thus defining the roles and responsibilities of client-actors a well as locally situated ones. The introduction of such tools within the context of graphic design practice is of great significance as it represents the emergence of a new culture of audit and measurement that rather inevitably accompanies carefully managed group practice.

(4) Dynamic display stand

Henrion and Parkin provide one illustrated example of an interactive display stand created for Blue Circle Cement (one of two stands used in total), with this device receiving less attention than the other tools dedicated to their pre-design stages – only being mentioned in the image caption and not in the main body of text (Figure 4.13). These display stands grouped together photographic references of the client's existing design collateral, with examples of their vehicles on one panel, signs on another and publications and stationery on further panels. By rotating the individual panels, HDA staff members or clients, could readily analyse the level of unification running across the various instances of the existing design collateral.

According to Henrion and Parkin the stands provided 'a fair representation' of how the public sees Blue Circle, acting as a model of the existing state of the company's house style. They served the purpose of revealing any such lack of unity across the existing designs; as Henrion and Parkin claim, 'lack of coordination, and the size and complexity of the task are immediately obvious'. In evidencing the existing issues for the client, these tools act as a collective enabling device, bringing together the various actors involved in the process (both internal and external), enfolding them around a common problem and objective.

At one level, the display stands sought to objectively trace the state of Blue Circle's existing design collateral. In practice though, HDA's agency in the construction of the stands and selection of the images would have inherently shaped the overall picture presented, giving HDA a degree of agency over how the information presented would be perceived. Assuming that they took the photographs themselves, there are the issues of framing, angle and crop

Figure 4.13 'A specially constructed display stand with rotating felt screens carrying hundreds of colour photographs of design items belonging to the Blue Circle Group', from *DIA Yearbook 1967/68* (Henrion and Parkin, 1968: 34). Photograph by the author. Item held by the University of Brighton Design Archives.

that could all impact the interpretation of the observer. But even without this consideration, the selection of certain representative entities and the omission of others was a powerful determining factor in the observer's interpretation.

Post-design stages

Though they claim that 'Systematic Methods in Design Co-ordination' is mostly concerned with 'pre-design stages', Henrion and Parkin provide three examples of 'mappings' that are mobilized to support creative design work. I have referred to these mappings as part of the post-design stages, as they concern the production of analytical props conceived after the creative work has been completed. These image references are given relatively short text captions and are not addressed at all in the main body of Henrion and Parkin's text. Given that they are rather shoe-horned in at the end of the article, it raises the possibility that they may have been a late addition to the text, perhaps at the suggestion of Henrion. This may be little more than conjecture, but there remains something anomalous about the inclusion of these images; ultimately, they are neither the tools, nor the products, of a design coordination process, and as such have little to do with the immediate subject of the article. However, it is notable that they follow a form of technical rationality that is in close alignment with the ideology of the various apparatuses described in the rest of their text.

Each of the four graphics were conceived to present the 'new' KLM logotype as the robust by-product of a technically rational, systematic process. But particularly notable here is the evolutionary representation of the emblem's development, which Wibo Bakker argues, had concealed the true development course of the design.

5) An evolutionary mapping of the logo development process

The 'evolutionary' mapping of the development process behind the new KLM logo (Figure 4.14) borrows more from the format of the timeline than the cartographic map, structuring a sequential development from old to new, whereby each increment became gradually more reductive, leaving ornamentation behind in favour of a stricter geometric form. As Bakker (2006) explains, the logo was conceived relatively early in the development of the project, but after HDA's initial design proposals were rejected for being too modern by their clients at KLM, they were forced to reconsider the proposals. Bakker argues that the resistance to the original presentation led Henrion to re-present the same materials again,

Figure 4.14 Evolutionary mapping of the KLM logo development process, from *DIA Yearbook 1967/68* (Henrion and Parkin, 1968: 41). Photograph by the author. Item held by the University of Brighton Design Archives.

only this time to present them as the product of an almost natural evolutionary development, involving no human intervention. As such, HDA looked to suggest that the authority of the design derived not from HDA's expertise as human design decision makers, but rather from the natural laws of form and vision implicit within their design approach.

In *Design Coordination and Corporate Image*, Henrion and Parkin (1967) refer to the strong 'Gestalt' of the proposed logo, recalling the efforts of mid-century scholars such as György Kepes and Rudolf Arnheim who had sought to codify universal rules of perception. Bakker (2006: 8) accords this approach with that of the engineer, explaining that: 'Where beforehand there was the impression that graphic designers would just show an emblem design as if it was the result of an artistic whim, now they showed it as an almost technical exercise, as if they were engineers.' Inherent in this approach was the notion of a more legitimate, objective method that borrowed weight from more scientific practices.

It is notable that this mapping of the logo's development featured in both the article as well as the more well-known book. The text accompanying the illustration differed quite significantly in each case though, with the book suggesting that the logo emerged directly out of this evolutionary process, whereas the article revealed more frankly that the process diagram was a by-product of the logo design, explaining how it had been created as a persuasive prop to convince the client of the legitimacy of the design:

Design Coordination and Corporate Image
The crown was progressively reduced through many stages (of which 15 are shown), to an ultimate form with very strong 'Gestalt'. (Henrion and Parkin, 1967: 24)

Systematic Methods for Design Co-ordination
One of many possible evolutionary developments from the old crown to the new, to convince KLM management of the necessity to go to an ultimate form in one step. (Henrion and Parkin, 1968: 41)

The mention of this being 'one of many possible evolutionary developments' reflects the fact that in their attempts to persuade the client, HDA had conceived multiple variations of this development graphic, with Bakker evidencing two earlier examples from 1963 and 1964 that preceded the example featured in the article. Here HDA's approach to design practice accords with some sociologists' research methods, wherein bouts of rationalization are deployed to straighten out otherwise tangled and incoherent complexes of action. As Hutheesing (1990: 10) explains, for the practising ethnographic researcher 'little did happen the way it is put down on paper, in terms of substance and sequence', thus a zig-zagging sequence of events is commonly reframed and re-construed to produce 'a well organised logical design with a beginning and a rounded-off ending'. Kaplan (1963) cites this as 'reconstructed logic', i.e. a form of sense-making that emerges after the fact; as opposed to 'logic in use', which refers to the direct application of logical principles in action. In HDA's case they seemed to have gone through several bouts of rationalization, translating their reconstructed logic into ever more persuasive graphic form.

This development represents an important shift in the driving imperatives of graphic design practitioners, with the individual case of HDA's brand identity work for KLM clearly showing how materials used to frame a client's comprehension of a design proposal can become more pivotal to designers in terms of their business success than the creative designs they produce. Clearly, there is a mutual relationship between a proposed design and how that proposal is framed, in that they are contingent on one another, yet the case of KLM suggests that, from a capitalist perspective, designers may be better placed channelling their energies into the development of compelling and persuasive presentation materials aimed at their clients, rather than concentrating their efforts on the production of engaging designs targeted at consumers or society more broadly (this persuasive element of project management arguably become only more important in the latter part of the twentieth century). The other KLM graphics illustrated within the 'Systematic Methods' article support this notion, providing further evidence of how HDA sought to purposefully prove the efficacy of their designs.

6) *A comparative mapping of the structure behind 'old and new' logotypes*

The comparative mapping of the structure behind 'old and new' KLM logotypes (Figure 4.15) takes on a more diagrammatical form and would not generally be considered a conventional map. However, reconsidered as a kind of cartographic tracing of the underlying structure behind the logotypes, the process can be interpreted as directly analogous to conventional map-making, whereby spatial territory is captured and measured, a process Corner refers to as tracing. The grid structure overlaid on top of the old and new emblems seeks, through comparison, to reinforce the simpler, reductive structure of the new design, showing how it can be constructed from fewer gridlines that are more intentionally placed and in more harmonious relationship with one another. Here the perceived rationality of the grid is deployed to imbue the proposed design with notions of rigour and precision.

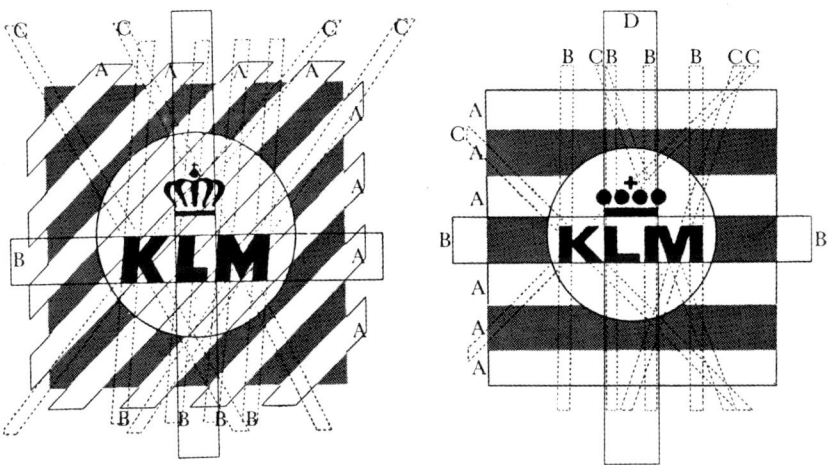

Figure 4.15 'Comparative analyses of old and new KLM symbols', from *DIA Yearbook 1967/68* (Henrion and Parkin, 1968: 40). Photograph by the author. Item held by the University of Brighton Design Archives.

(7) and (8) A comparative mapping of 'old and new' logotypes under conditions of poor visibility and horizontal movement

These final graphic illustrations from Henrion and Parkin's article render the effect of various adverse viewing conditions upon the proposed new logo design (Figure 4.16). By simulating the impact of conditions such as horizontal movement and focal range, HDA sought to illustrate how the simple Gestalt properties of their logo made it more robust and recognizable, especially in these unfavourable conditions.[17] In their book they go so far as to suggest that the logo excels more fully under such adverse conditions, claiming that: 'the worse the viewing conditions – distance, movement, sharp angle, low attention – the more "crown like" it becomes'. In stating that their design performed better within the most important contexts of use (i.e. the aeroplane livery moving across the runway), Henrion and Parkin built an ever more persuasive case of its efficacy.

In these various inscription devices for KLM, the development of a new culture of legitimacy can begin to be traced, whereby designers are increasingly aware of how the rational properties of their designs can be made evident in a persuasive manner to their clients. Where Henrion had once favoured the virtuous and intuitive originality of the individual design artefact – his beloved 'ideas poster' – the notion of originality as a driver of cultural production began to be challenged by more dogmatic notions of legitimacy and efficacy. As such the

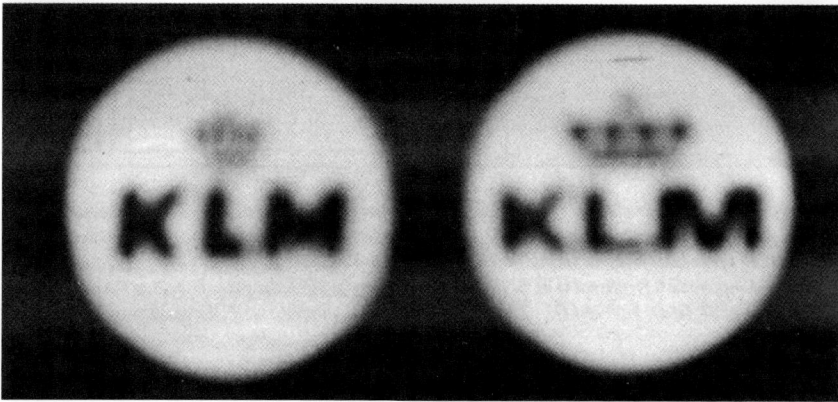

Figure 4.16 'Test of recognisability of KLM symbol when blurred by horizontal movement' and 'Comparative tests of old and new symbols when out of focus, such as in poor visibility conditions', both from *DIA Yearbook 1967/68* (Henrion and Parkin, 1968: 41). Photograph by the author. Item held by the University of Brighton Design Archives.

KLM presentation graphics should rightfully be considered as 'boundary objects' (Nicolini et al., 2012) that translate the mindset and values of the graphic design practitioner into more readily recognizable forms.[18]

Concluding remarks

The organizational history of Henrion Design Associates corresponds closely with the framing of this book in terms of the focal period which runs for twenty-five-years from 1945 to 1970. Having set up as Studio H in 1948, F. H. K. Henrion renamed his practice to become Henrion Design Associates in 1951 and by 1973 had changed it again to become HDA International, signifying the significant growth in brand identity design as a practice, as well as its increasingly globalized outlook. HDA had grown steadily since their formation in 1951, and it is notable that they repositioned their practice for a more global marketplace early in the 1970s. This business trajectory supports my argument that the period from 1945 to 1970 was one of great importance in terms of the establishment of brand identity practice. So, while the 1970s and onwards was a period of proliferation and consolidation in terms of brand identity design, the 1950s and 1960s were crucial in terms of the patterns of practice becoming established.

In terms of their client list and the scale of their branding contracts, HDA flourished most fully during the 1960s and 1970s, before slowly ceding their position as a widely influential force within the industry as competition increased. Klaus Schmidt and Chris Ludlow took over the firm in 1981, and at this time Henrion shifted his focus to his educational endeavours. He acted as a consultant to the new directors as they set up office in the West End of London as Henrion Ludlow Schmidt. Despite Henrion's limited involvement with the firm, they decided to retain his name given its eminent prestige.

The tools and apparatuses HDA developed during the 1950s and 1960s constituted a radical departure from the intuitive, rule of thumb methods that were associated with commercial art practices of earlier decades. By inscribing certain practice-based routines into material apparatus they brought increasing stability to the rituals of design work, introducing design management tools that would enable them to better understand their clients' collateral, plan their own design processes and manage the internal work force, as well as important interconnected external agents. So, whereas some designers resisted the urge to standardize or codify their practice (as we will see in the next chapter), HDA were inspired by technological developments and initiatives like the Design Methods Movement, seeking to bring a scientific rationality to their process. By codifying certain routines HDA played an important role in developing and establishing patterns of consultant graphic design practice in Britain. Though it is difficult to say with any great certainty that their methods infiltrated the wider professional community, it is evident that they influenced young design practitioners who would go on to contribute to the development of corporate design work in the following decades.

Henrion's most loyal employees remained with him over a sustained period, but given the flat structure and relatively small scale of the firm there was little room for significant career progression. As a result, there remained an inevitable ebb and flow around contributors to the studio and a number of commercially successful design groups benefitted from founders who first 'cut their teeth' with Henrion. Among these were Sampson Tyrell, founded by HDA employees Martin Sampson and Terry Tyrell in 1976. Speaking to the trade journal *Design Week*, Tyrell (*Sampson Tyrrell Enterprise*, 1998) recalled the 'incredible grounding in what was to become modern day corporate identity' that he had received working at HDA after he left art college.[19] The German Dieter Heil was another who benefitted from time with Henrion (as well as a spell with DRU), going on to found the influential design group MetaDesign with Erik Spiekermann (who also freelanced for HDA), Florian Fischer and Gerhard Doerrié in Berlin, 1979 (*Feature: Erik Spiekermann*, 2014).

The shift to a more technocratic and programmatic design approach inevitably impacted the nature of the designs produced by Henrion's studio. So, whereas his early 'ideas posters' had hinged around a witty, conceptual approach to communication, the programmatic corporate design programmes emanating from the studio from the 1960s onwards were founded on a basis of strict aesthetic unification. As such the examples of design work put forward by Henrion into the public domain privileged consistency, control and order over any sense of individual wit. Here each item of collateral worked together in harmony, with an emphasis on the sum of parts, as opposed to the power of the individual design artefact to affect change. This is exemplified by the way the studio's work for KLM was showcased in various publications. For instance, in *Design Coordination and Corporate Image* one spread shows an extensive selection of KLM artefacts all branded with the same repetitive visual elements, creating a highly homogenized and monotonous effect (Figure 4.17). To achieve this effect they developed elaborate specification manuals that sought to control and coordinate the application of their identity programmes, with the example of KLM being an important early case in point (Figure 4.18).

Although the way of practising design developed radically at HDA during the 1960s in line with profound transformations occurring across the profession more broadly, it is impossible to accurately gauge the extent to which these practices were adopted by younger practitioners of the coming generations. In terms of their working methods, the ideas set out by Henrion and Parkin in their article for the *DIA Yearbook* are significant as unique early attempts to apply the systematic rigour of the Design Methods Movement within the context of brand identity design practice. It is notable that these ideas were disseminated beyond British borders, with a similar article titled 'Designpolitik – Ziele, Kriterien, Methoden' (Design policy – Goals, Criteria, Methods) having been published in the German press (Henrion, 1968). In these efforts to scientize graphic design, they sought to codify working methods and occupational formulae specific to corporate identity practice. This meant introducing project management tools commonly used in other, more well developed professions, an approach that Spinosa, Flores and Dreyfus (1997) refer to as 'cross-appropriation', whereby practices, ideas or tools are adopted from other practices or social worlds. So, as we saw, they adopted the 'critical path method' from the field of Operations Research.

While the tools and principles HDA developed may not always have been novel, their deployment within the context of graphic design consultancy was unprecedented and significant in terms of the development of the discipline and its increasing technocratization. Inherent in these gradual changes was a shift away from design that responded to the needs of consumers, or even, for those ambitious post-war designers, the needs of society (many post-war

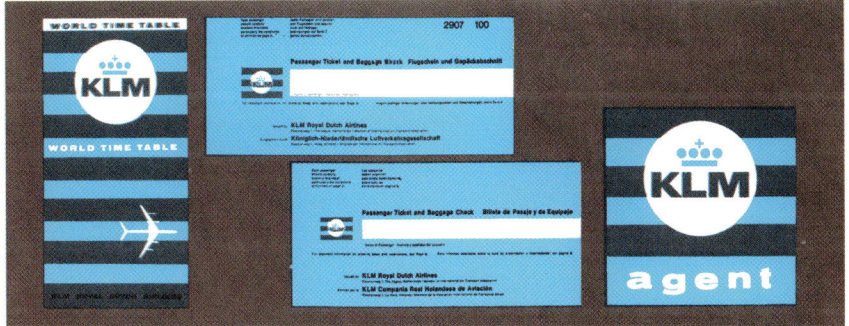

Figure 4.17 Excerpt from *Design Coordination and Corporate Image* showcasing a small selection of design applications from the KLM brand identity programme. Courtesy of the Estate of F. H. K. Henrion.

designers believed that their right to be considered professionals was dependent on their ability to serve society). Now the consumers who really mattered were the commissioning clients; for the satisfaction of end-users or the grand objective of bettering society were of scant concern if the design group could not get their ambitious proposals approved by the client. These issues were not unprecedented, with pre-war commercial artists having had similar challenges with those who commissioned their work; yet these concerns around client satisfaction accelerated rapidly as the stakes began to be raised with the

Figure 4.18 Henrion Design Associates' 'House Style Manual' for KLM, c.1967. Courtesy of the Estate of F. H. K. Henrion.

ever-increasing scope of graphic designers' work. As the size of the average corporate design job grew from the odd artefact to the comprehensive system of artefacts, the risks involved grew for both clients and designers. For the client, decisions regarding brand programmes began to take on important policy-making significance, in that their choices could have major implications across the entirety of their organization. For designers meanwhile, the success or failure of a major brand identity programme running over several years and involving multiple staff members could make or break their firm.

As the financial risks associated with brand identity design practice began to increase, the creative risks taken by practitioners can be seen to diminish. So as the client came to be considered the most important consumer of design, design labour was increasingly directed away from cultural production and the pursuit of cultural capital, towards rationalizations mobilized to support the design product and thus the accrual of economic capital. Here the practices of HDA accord closely with Michel Callon's (1986) concept of interessement, whereby efforts are made to mobilize all parties behind an idea in an attempt to get 'buy-in' for a strategic approach. Energies were thus channelled into persuading the commissioning client of the legitimacy of the design proposals and the robustness of the processes from which they had derived. Any sign of human intuition or taste were to be masked in favour of a technical rationality that accorded brand identity designers more closely with engineers than artists. Thus, HDA promoted the systematic nature of their new methods to imbue the innovation process with a sense of rigour and integrity.

The tendency for maps to be misunderstood as objective tracings that simply mirror reality played into the hands of Henrion and Parkin in their attempts to present their design process as highly rational and beyond scrutiny. That maps – along with other information graphics that lend from their geo-spatial aesthetic – often remain unquestioned as neutral, benign conveyors of information is due in part to the way their technical vernacular masks the cultural situatedness and human decision-making that is inherent in their production. As such, Henrion and Parkin conceal the human agency implicit in their process behind a technical aesthetic that promotes the supposed supremacy of technical rationality.

There is a danger that Henrion and Parkin's hyperbolic distinction between rational, systematic methods and traditional, intuitive ones presents a false separation between explicit and tacit forms of knowing (Polanyi, 1966). Far from being binary opposites, Nonaka and others (Nonaka, 1994; Nonaka and Takeuchi, 1995; Nonaka and von Krogh, 2009) show that explicit and tacit knowledge are mutually complementary and in dynamic interaction with one another, so rather than being understood in opposition to one another, they should instead be considered as elements on a continuum of knowledge. It is thus at the intersection of explicit and tacit knowledge that enhanced understandings, enhanced capacity to act and new social practices are generated.

There is an element of disingenuousness to the way HDA aimed to convince KLM of the integrity of their design proposals for their corporate emblem. In their efforts to post-rationalize or reconstruct a more fully considered argument for their work, they reframed their development processes as rational and explicit, rather than tacit and intuitive. Given that graphic design was not considered an established or even a legitimate professional activity at the time, their developmental process was reconceived as a process founded on objective reasoning, thus denying the intuitive basis of their approach. While the notion of intuition has often been greeted with scepticism due to its accordance with instinctive human feelings, scholarship from the profession of nursing shows that it is a fundamental cornerstone of the practising professional or expert across a diverse range of disciplines. Intuition should thus be understood as an irrational process with a rational basis, with Easen and Wilcockson (1996: 669) explaining that the perceived irrationality of the intuiting process 'does not make the basis of any intuitive decision itself irrational'.

For the designers at HDA practising a largely unrecognized profession, the notion of an intuitive judgement appears to have been difficult to defend to their sceptical clients. As such they constructed fictional process diagrams to persuade KLM that their proposals followed natural evolutionary progress derived from universal principles of vision (Kepes, 1944; Arnheim, 1954). Framing their proposals from this technically rational perspective made it difficult for KLM to contest the proposals. Just as Corner (1999: 251; original emphasis) explains in relation to mapping:

> [...] it is the apparent rigour of objective analysis and logical argument that possesses the greatest efficacy in a pluralistic, democratic society. Analytical research through mapping enables the designer to *construct* an argument, to embed it within the dominant practices of rational culture, and ultimately to turn those practices towards more productive and collective ends.

Henrion and Parkin's systematic methods can thus be understood to promote the idea of the designer as mapmaker, and ultimately, the mapmaker as persuader.

Viewed more favourably from Nonaka's (1994; Nonaka and Takeuchi, 1995; Nonaka and von Krogh, 2009) perspective, the complex socio-technical scenario that unfolded between KLM and HDA can be interpreted not as a deceitful one, but as a positive, dynamic interchange between tacit and explicit knowledge. From this perspective, HDA substantiated their instinctive design hunches with carefully conceived technically rational documentation and evidence, reflecting on their action to construct 'boundary objects' (Nicolini et al., 2012) that would translate their own personal tacit knowing into more readily comprehensible forms. In this sense, their working process can be understood to begin and end with technical rationality. They adopt scientific approaches to first understand the problem, and then to frame the solution. This follows Bruce Archer's (1963: 73) analogy of the 'creative sandwich', wherein the analytically framed slices of bread (the pre- and post-design reasoning) sandwich the design process, thus acting as a holding device from which the more impulsive innovation act at the centre can be interpreted. It is by these same means that HDA sought to gain support for their creative work.

These emergent practices of 'reconstructed logic' recall Corner's (1999: 251) conceptualization of mapping as:

> [...] an extremely shrewd and tactical enterprise, a practice of relational reasoning that intelligently unfolds new realities out of existing constraints,

quantities, facts and conditions. The artistry lies in the use of technique, in the way in which things are framed and set up.

HDA's tactical approach to mapping can thus be understood as a strategy to align the interests of important actors around their own proposals for innovation and to strengthen the association between these actors, thus managing economic risks associated with the new design programmes of ever-increasing scope and scale.

5
COORDINATED BUT NOT STANDARDIZED: THE PRACTICAL RATIONALITY OF HANS SCHLEGER & ASSOCIATES

The following chapter provides an example of the relationship between early British graphic designers of the 1950s and the advertising businesses that they were dependent upon. Hans Schleger, leader of the group Hans Schleger & Associates, was a recognized commercial artist who was representative of art-school-trained designers working in Britain in that he was suspicious of large corporations and their drives towards efficiency and standardization. So, whereas some designers, such as Henrion, began to be increasingly interested in systems thinking and operations research, Schleger's group privileged practical rationality over codified scientific forms of designerly knowledge. Their approach was reflective and agile, as they understood that corporate design could be made to appear coherent without becoming homogenously standardized. In the following chapter I explore how advertising agencies used Guard Books as a control mechanism to monitor the implementation of a brand identity programme and how this approach impacted the designs produced.

The development of Hans Schleger & Associates

Biographical background

Hans Schleger & Associates (HSA) was a consultant design group founded in London in 1953 by the German-born graphic designer Hans Schleger (Figure 5.1). Born in 1898 in Kempen, Prussia, Schleger (born Schlesinger) went

Figure 5.1 Photographic portrait of Hans Schleger. Courtesy of the Estate of Hans Schleger.

on to establish his reputation in the advertising industries of Germany and America in the 1920s and 1930s. Having studied painting and drawing at the Kunstgewerbeschule in Berlin (1918–21), he took on the role of Artistic Director for the film set designer Karl Hagenbeck in Berlin (1921–4). He then moved on to New York in search of new opportunities, partly in response to the economic downturn occurring in Berlin at the time, but perhaps also in response to his experiences on the front in World War One. By 1926 he had established his own studio practice on Madison Avenue, signing his work with the pseudonym Zéró (Figure 5.2). Schleger found commercial success during his short five-year spell in the US but returned to Berlin in 1929 to marry his cousin Annemarie Mendelsohn, with the Wall Street crash cited as a factor that contributed to his decision to return. Back in Germany he worked as an Art Director for the German office of British advertising firm W. S. Crawford. A feature in *Gebrauchsgraphik* magazine indicates the regard in which he was held, being introduced as he was as, 'the distinguished advertising expert and commercial artist, who has achieved so much success both in Germany and America' (Frenzel, 1931).

By 1933 Schleger was on the move again, this time to London, where he would reside for the remainder of his life. He was one of several artistic Jewish émigrés from central Europe who came to Britain to escape from repressive and intolerant European regimes (Black, 2012). In London he benefitted from

Figure 5.2 Newspaper advertisement for Schleger's services in New York, publicized under his pseudonym Zéró. Courtesy of the Estate of Hans Schleger.

the connections he had made at Crawford's in Berlin, including links with their influential Art Director, Ashley Havinden. The American-born designer Edward McKnight Kauffer was particularly supportive of him, sharing his own client contacts and helping him to organize an exhibition of his work at the leading art and design publisher Lund Humphries in 1934.[1]

Once settled in Britain Schleger relied on a series of commissions from advertising agents (e.g. John Tait and Partners Ltd and William Grant & Sons) and influential patrons of the arts (e.g. Frank Pick at London Transport, Jack Beddington at Shell and Stephen Tallents at the General Post Office). The most significant intermediary in his early British career was a US advertising agency with offices in London, Mather and Crowther (Mathers hereafter). From 1952 to 1964 he worked as a consultant for Mathers on an exclusive retainer contract which meant he was forbidden from producing press advertisements for other agencies. During their period of collaboration, HSA and Mathers embarked together on several ambitious identity schemes for a range of corporate clients. The most remarkable of these being a comprehensive identity programme for the fishmonger Mac Fisheries, which would come to impact on nearly all visual manifestations of the firm. This programme of work would prove noteworthy in the design scene due to its unusual mix of consistent and recurrent corporate imagery, combined with an unorthodox wit and dynamism that was more typical within the advertising scene than the field of brand communications. Furthermore, the programme was significant for its broad national scope, being representative of a wider post-war trend for retail organizations to move from regional to national representation as rationing gradually came to an end.

In exploring the triadic working relationship between Schleger's studio, Mather and Crowther and Mac Fisheries I will reveal the hierarchical tensions that existed between designers, advertising agencies and clients during the early post-war period. In order to understand this collaborative labour, I examine the tools of practice implicated in their collective work. This means looking closely at a pair of Guard Books compiled by Mathers to record the development of the advertising campaign for Mac Fisheries. By scrutinizing the socio-technical relationships between human and non-human actors I explicate the role of each party, thus untangling the complex interrelationships between twentieth century advertising professionals and the first British 'graphic designers' then known as commercial artists.[2] This endeavour is important in order to establish the role that advertising played in the development of graphic design, for, as Heller (1995a) explains, 'in most accounts of graphic design's origins advertising is virtually denied'.

HSA's identity work for Mac Fisheries presents an alternative model of design coordination where more varied, 'contrapuntal rhythms' (Venturi, 1966) are favoured over the homogeneous unification later typical of the field. The Mac Fisheries scheme thus demonstrates that identity programmes may be dynamic and humorous, while also retaining a coherence that binds various artefacts together in unison.

Mac Fisheries, the early years

By the time Schleger came to work for them, Mac Fisheries were already a retailer of significant repute, with William Hesketh Leverhulme, of Lever Brothers (now Unilever), having founded the chain in 1918. The first Mac Fisheries shop opened on Hill Street in Richmond, Surrey in February 1919. From its early formation the firm developed a habit of commissioning high pedigree art and design, with renowned coin designer George Kruger Gray contracted to create a symbol for the firm around 1920.[3] Other notable commercial artists were also commissioned, with advertisements commissioned from Fred Taylor in 1922 and both Gregory Brown and Kennedy North contributing poster designs in 1927.[4] Despite the pedigree of their early marketing, Mac Fisheries did not expand on a national level until after the Second World War when demand for wet fish grew significantly. Unlike meat, fish was not rationed, so Mac Fisheries stores became adept at advertising new deliveries, with display notices positioned prominently to publicize incoming deliveries, resulting in long queues of patrons waiting at store opening times.

Rationing continued until 1954, nine years after the war, but by the early 1950s the company began to plan for further expansion. As the rationing of meat began to ease and the branded goods of pre-war became available again, consumers' appetite for wet fish began to wane. To compete with other retail outlets, Mac Fisheries decided to widen their range of produce to include fruit, vegetables and dairy products, but in order to expand, existing retail units had to be sold to facilitate the larger premises required to display an ever-increasing range of produce.

As new shops started to open, newspaper advertisements were published to promote the arrival of the new, larger Mac Fisheries outlets. One advert was deployed repeatedly to publicize the new openings, with the same template adapted with the store details updated to reflect the latest location (Figure 5.3).

Figure 5.3 Uncredited press advertisement for Mac Fisheries used to announce new store openings between 1951 and 1954, from Mather and Crowther Guard Books. Photograph by the author. Item held by the History of Advertising Trust Archive.

The standard template featured an illustration with a self-contained, fully kitted-out store being lowered into place by crane onto the archetypal British high-street; the headline reading rather ominously in all capitals: 'WE ARE COMING TO …', with the village or town name inserted in place alongside the opening date. The Mathers's Guard Books show that this template was used over a period of four years, from November 1951 to January 1954 and appears to have been the last advertisement printed by Mac Fisheries before Schleger and his colleagues arrived on the scene. This advert continued to be used long after HSA's own scheme had commenced roll-out, indicating that it was common for brand identity schemes to be more multifarious and misaligned than they proclaimed to be within press releases in the design trade journals.

Defining the role of the trademark

Hans Schleger & Associates begin work

As Mac Fisheries began to expand, reusing the same adapted advertisement in the process, Hans Schleger was commissioned by the advertising agents at Mathers to begin work on a nationwide publicity campaign for the firm. As already noted, the firm had taken steps to standardize their appearance from their first beginnings in 1919, but HSA together with Mathers would go further, creating a totalizing identity programme that would impact every manifestation of the firm – at least, this was the principle. The new scheme would prove significant as an early example of a 'total' identity programme of broad national scope and its pre-eminence gained considerable attention from the international design press, as well as peers within the industry. A report prepared by Schleger (1959) about the work, listed his own duties as, 'consultant and designer, works in cooperation with Advertising Agents Mather & Crowther Ltd'. Regrettably, little evidence remains of correspondence or meetings between the two parties, but a pair of Guard Books compiled by Mathers offers a unique insight into the process of implementing such a publicity campaign.[5] Held in the archive collection of Mather and Crowther at the History of Advertising Trust (HAT), the Mac Fisheries Guard Books collate together, in chronological order, each press advertisement published by Mac Fisheries between November 1951 and December 1958. These documents chart, in minute detail, the transition from the existing design style to the adoption of Schleger and Mathers's comprehensive new scheme.

As documents, the Guard Books are unremarkable in form, with little design to speak of, aside from discreet labelling on the spine of each volume to mark their contents. They are large and heavy hard-bound volumes bound with green cartridge paper inside. The pages of the books are approximately the same height as an A4 sheet, but broader in width, allowing two small press advertisements to be composited onto a single page. Their binding, meanwhile, implies that they were pre-bound, much like a glorified hardback scrap book. These books were pre-prepared waiting to be filled with press adverts glued into place sequentially as they were released in the regional newspapers of the day. Each book is stuffed full of press advertisements and little else besides, with little to no annotation or labelling, aside from the details printed at the top of each advert about in which newspaper it appeared and on which date. The result is a chronology of a long-standing press campaign sustained over a seven-year period. What the Guard Books do not provide, is any sense of how the company's press campaign related to their wider brand communications beyond the newspaper format. In this sense they are not a comprehensive record of what was actually an omni-channel marketing campaign.

As design consultant to Mathers, HSA had significant influence over the art direction of the campaign. According to his colleague and wife, Pat Schleger, her husband Hans would be present at Mathers's headquarters during design meetings with the client and would present his design proposals directly to the client. This was not common procedure, as commercial artists like Schleger would normally be kept at arms-length by the agencies they worked for, partly to protect the agency's lucrative commercial contracts and partly because commercial artists tended to be viewed as 'hired-hands', or as artists not fit to participate directly in serious business discussions. Although early British graphic designers like Schleger had sought independence and professional integrity through organizations like the Society of Industrial Artists, in practice most remained heavily dependent on the advertising profession to provide them with work.[6] It was likely Schleger's well-founded reputation in the advertising industry that secured such an unusually close involvement with the client and a strong influence in the direction of the campaign. Still, regardless of his relative power, the day-to-day communications between client and designer continued to be channelled through the agency, Mathers.

Nestled amongst the many pages of press advertisements, two letters are found, fixed in place within the Guard Books at the relevant time at which their messages were transmitted. Addressed to Hans Schleger from Mathers's executive Ernest Arthur Lough, these letters stand out amongst the plethora of printed press adverts. From the first letter, dated 22 February 1952, it is clear to see Mathers's role as an intermediary between HSA and the client, Mac Fisheries. As Lough writes:

'OPERATION MAC FISH'

Client has just telephoned to say that a Board ruling from Mac Fisheries is that wherever we show the Mac Fisheries trade mark, it must always have the four fish shown in the appropriate places. We can still show it in symbolic form, but it must never appear without the four fish.

Existing material cannot be altered, but this ruling is to apply on all material produced from to-day.

E. A. Lough

The tone in this note is brash and dictatorial, leaving little room for HSA to respond in any way other than to follow the instructions found therein. The given directions are labelled as a 'ruling', suggesting that the client was explicitly trying to govern HSA's conduct. By comparison, Mathers act as a neutral messenger, inflecting no opinion of their own, though their allegiance to the client appears stronger than any loyalty towards the design consultancy.

Further through the first of the two Guard Books and almost two years later, on 25 of January 1954, the second letter can be found from Lough, addressed to Schleger:

'MAC FISHERIES – TRADE MARKS'

Further to my note of October 1953, we have now received a final directive from Client concerning the use of his trade mark.

It has now been laid down that wherever the trade mark is used near the word 'Mac Fisheries' it must be the official trade mark with two rings and detailed fish as shown on the letter headings. Wherever the trade mark is used other than near the word 'Mac Fisheries', variations such as we are using at the moment are permitted.

It is finally laid down by Client that we are not allowed to use any form of trade mark that is without an indication of the four fish.

E. A. Lough.

The first part of the note alludes to the existence of additional written correspondence between Mathers and HSA beyond the two notes found in the Guard Books at the HAT archive. For instance, Lough references a note of October 1953 which is not present in the Guard Books. It is unclear why certain messages were included and other correspondence excluded, but it is likely that the content of the two featured notes was felt to be of critical importance for the development of the campaign. It is important to highlight the language used in the second note from Mathers. According to Lough, new directions had been 'laid down' by Mac Fisheries, implying that the new instruction was a command of law not to be disputed (i.e. they have 'laid down the law').

It is clear from these notes that tension existed between the wishes of Schleger and those of the client, Mac Fisheries. While Schleger appears to have wanted his new, modernized 'symbolic' trademark to replace the original more

Figure 5.4 A selection of some of the logo variants deployed by Hans Schleger & Associates in their work for Mac Fisheries, with original logo design top centre. Courtesy of the Estate of Hans Schleger.

traditional symbol designed by Kruger Gray, the client was not convinced about discarding the well-established elements of their identity. Although the Mac Fisheries programme has been regarded as an early exemplar of coordinated identity design, the constraints that emerged from the client forced HSA to explore different approaches to the original trademark, which meant that the identity was less unitary than it otherwise would have been. At least five stylistic variations distinct from the original Kruger Gray logo design can be seen within the advertisements in the Guard Books at HAT (Figure 5.4) and still further variations are evident when looking beyond the realm of the Guard Books. These range from designs rendered in loose, imprecise brush strokes, to those with a more minimalist geometric approach. These variations are all stylistically different, but each one transforms the four recognizable fish into indistinct ovals, meaning the fish are no longer recognizable as fish, but rather non-specific seed-shaped lozenges.

One common approach was to combine the logo with the words 'Mac Fish – Fresh Fish' in a script lettering as one integrated design (Figure 5.5), while

Figure 5.5 Press advertisement for Mac Fisheries by HSA, 1952, from Mather and Crowther Guard Books. Photograph by the author. Item held by the History of Advertising Trust Archive. Courtesy of the Estate of Hans Schleger.

a further example is more hybrid in form, combining the reductive style of Schleger's circular holding device, with recognizable fish motifs (Figure 5.6). Here the four fish are finished with a shadow effect that gives them the impression of being three-dimensional – this echoes the more naturalistic approach of Kruger Gray's original design.

Untangling the chronological narrative behind each of these subtle trademark variations is complex. Nevertheless, examining this small aspect of the campaign can help to reveal more about personal interrelations between the client, advertising agency and designer, whilst also explicating the issues that surround the implementation of such large-scale standardization programmes. It appears from the two Guard Books at the History of Advertising Trust that Schleger's initial designs used the integrated logo which cojoined the trademark with the brand name in script lettering. This is evidenced by the fact that each of the initial advertisements are labelled with a number, for example, 'Mac Fisheries (Operation Mac Fish) Advt. No. 1'. Whoever collated these advertisements at Mathers added the date of the advertisement in pen,

Figure 5.6 Press advertisement for Mac Fisheries by HSA, c. 1953, from Mather and Crowther Guard Books. Photograph by the author. Item held by the History of Advertising Trust Archive. Courtesy of the Estate of Hans Schleger.

e.g. 'March 1952'. So, we can surmise that the first four advertisements all used the same logo-type variant.

Just days, or weeks, before these adverts had appeared in the press, Lough passed on his first note from the client (dated 22nd February), instructing that future work ' … must always have the four fish shown in the appropriate places'. In the press advertisements the four fish are included in their standard positions, suggesting that this note refers to designs that are not catalogued within the Guard Books. This raises an interesting issue about the Guard Books in terms of their ability to catalogue an ambitious multi-channel national identity programme. It is a quirk of these comprehensive campaign documents that they record only a small fraction of the whole identity scheme, focusing on press adverts, but overlooking countless other outputs produced by HSA, including instore signage and publicity, labels and packaging, van livery design, ephemera and retail bags. From further research it is evident that some instore posters and bag designs were produced that excluded the fish motifs entirely.

What happens immediately after the first note is unclear, but twenty months later the client appears to have toughened their stance, putting forward more precise instructions that assert, 'wherever the trade mark is used near the word "Mac Fisheries" it must be the official trade mark with two rings and detailed fish as shown on the letter headings'. They were seemingly not against the more illustrative and loose use of the symbol, but they insisted that it must appear as a secondary element away from the headline brand name. The effect of this decision was to banish the looser variations of the symbol to the role of illustration. An advert from 1955 demonstrates how reverting to the original trademark design had forced the loose illustrative version of the trademark to become redundant, acting merely as a secondary element that was repetitive and discordant (Figure 5.7). In this example the two trademarks are essentially in conflict given that they are of similar size, but of different graphic styles. The illustrative version is slightly larger, but the detailed original holds a more critical position in the centre of the composition, attracting the eye courtesy of its darker mass. The hierarchy between these two elements remains unclear.

Figure 5.7 1955 press advertisement for Mac Fisheries by HSA, from Mather and Crowther Guard Books. Note the combination of the detailed Kruger Gray logo at the bottom and the loose illustrative Schleger logo variant at the top. Item held by the History of Advertising Trust Archive.

The perception of the programme

A wider assessment of the material produced by HSA for Mac Fisheries reveals that the range of trademark variations in use went far beyond those found purely in the printed advertisements. For example, the icon used by HSA in their range of packaging for Mac Fisheries takes the trademark in an altogether different direction, with fish that closely resemble the Ichthys (or 'Jesus fish') used to denote the Christian faith (Figure 5.8). This lack of consistency raises questions as to whether the Mac Fisheries design programme can be considered an exemplar of coordinated branding.

The response from the design press, as well as from Schleger's peers, suggests that the campaign was undoubtedly regarded as successful at the time of its release. For example, Ashley Havinden (1953) wrote personally to Schleger to congratulate him on the quality of the coordination across the programme:

16th December 1953

Dear Hans

I am being continually struck by the excellent publicity for Mac Fisheries. I do congratulate you on this. Not only is all the designing first class, but I think more important still is the co-ordination of your work which is brilliant. That is to say, the advertisements, posters, delivery vans and the shops, all echo the same theme.

As the theme is a brilliant one, I imagine your work is proving a great success to Mac Fisheries. Congratulations on this great contribution you are making to keep good design going in advertising.

As ever yours

Ashley

It is notable that Havinden points to the coordination of the work as being more important than the quality of the individual designs themselves. This shows that it is the successful alignment of the parts that aroused his interest, prompting him to compliment work. Havinden's note implies that the work was extraordinary, for if such coordination were the norm, it would be unlikely he would have taken the time to convey his opinion in such a way.

It is worth noting Havinden's early use of the word 'co-ordination', which was not commonly employed in design circles at this time but found popularity over the coming decades. As we have already seen, Havinden took an active interest in the practice of brand identity design, writing on 'company handwriting' for the *Penrose Annual*.

Figure 5.8 HSA's packaging scheme for Mac Fisheries, late 1950s. Courtesy of the Estate of Hans Schleger.

Whereas Havinden was explicit about the role of coordination in Schleger's work, British Transport Commission's Chief Publicity Officer, Christian Barman (1954) sent his own more general praise in a letter of appreciation:

My dear Jack [a personal nickname for Schleger]

The more I see of it the more I enjoy and admire your wonderful MACFICIENCY

Yours

Chris

21.11.54

Although less directly complimenting the coherence of the scheme, Barman's note could be considered a reaction to the cumulative power of the campaign, as he seems to imply that with each new manifestation seen, a further appreciation is gained. Adding to this, the final pun used by Barman to combine 'Mac Fisheries' and 'efficiency', could be read as a compliment on the coordination of the scheme. In other words, there is an efficiency in each design element, as each part comes together to contribute to the impression of a whole.

Aside from these personal letters, the coverage in the advertising, design and marketing press was predominantly positive, complimenting the coherence and ambition of the scheme. For example, *Printing World* (*Graphic Art Annuals*, 1954) were explicit in their praise for the coherence of the scheme:

The recent, perfectly conceived and executed campaign of the Mac Fisheries, with posters, showcards, price tags, wrappers and leaflets, planned in a perfectly interrelated fashion, each of them indicative of the style and characteristics of the others.

Whilst editor of the German magazine *Graphik*, Heinrich Maiwald (1953b: 2), wrote:

> It is from the conviction that the various branches of applied art are not things apart, that Zero derives his capacity to introduce continuity of thought and design into his publicity designs; this impresses itself on the public's mind as a pictorial translation of what is, in fact, thought association. Colour and form create a unified total picture based on the words 'Mac Fish – Fresh Fish'. Through repetition this concept, the symbol 'Fresh …' plus the trade mark, becomes synonymous with the name and trade mark of Mac Fisheries. Zero has for example, fitted the 'fish symbol' shown on these pages – into a large diverse series of advertisements without ever losing his characteristic spontaneity of line and conception.

Moreover, Maiwald (1953b: 2) lauded the way that the campaign refused to force 'a sales-success formula' upon the consumer, arguing that Schleger, with his 'imagination, the sophistication of humour of his drawings, typographic wit and, most important, with his firm base of common sense, is authoritative yet disarming and persuasive'.

In the pages of *Art & Industry*, Mary Gowing (1956: 206–7), who had collaborated with Schleger on the ATS campaign, wrote as follows:

> Seen numerically the job is a big one. Some five hundred items, most of them complex in themselves, have already been completed. But this is not a job to look at in terms of quantity, or even in terms of its truly impeccable detail. It is a job to assess for its bold and beautifully related over-all plan, for the way each item is a consistent piece of public relations work for the whole Mac Fisheries enterprise, for the continuous consistent repetition of the unique selling point … and for the way the items are grouped for immediate identification and memorisation.

When interviewed by *Sales Appeal* in 1952, Schleger himself claimed that the work was a 'complete campaign', but the broad inconsistencies in the application of the trademark seem to counter this idea of complete coherence. The inconsistent use of the company trademark can be traced to two major factors. Firstly, and perhaps most importantly, the conflict between Schleger and the client proved a major factor in the quirks and idiosyncrasies evident in the scheme as a whole. The notes passed on by the advertising agency in their role as an intermediary show how Schleger had favoured the reductive and modern approach, whilst the firm preferred to stick with the established design of the trademark. This resulted in a to-and-fro between client, intermediary and designer, and an ever-increasing number of variations emerging because of this uncertainty. Here we get a sense of a brand identity in permanent transition, adapting and evolving over time in relation to the directives of the client. There is also some sense of the designer as a creative deviant whose urge to push and pull the brand in different directions must be controlled. This feeds into the second factor, which relates to Schleger's own beliefs and philosophies about design. From his time in New York he had begun to explore the notion of a flexible brand identity, treating the trademark as a malleable device that could be manipulated and mutated to create visual interest without losing its unique recognizability. A key example of this approach was his early work from 1925–9 for clothing and haberdashery chain, Weber and Heilbroner, to which I will now turn.

The trademark as illustrative device

Advertising manager Silas Spitzer was responsible for commissioning Schleger to work for Weber and Heilbroner and was, according to *Gebrauchsgraphik* magazine (cited in Schleger, 2001: 118): 'the first to replace the usual realistic American advertising by more modern methods'. This reference to 'modern methods' refers to the idea that instead of just depicting the product within an advert, more creative, distinctive and unexpected visualizations could be employed. At the heart of Weber and Heilbroner's campaigns lay Schleger's Fabric Group trademark, which comprised three men in fedoras standing side-by-side. This trademark shared the reductive simplicity of Schleger's modernized and geometric Mac Fisheries symbol and was unusual for the way it was used in the organization's publicity. For example, their 'Looming up' advert (Figure 5.9) shows how the trademark could be repeated as part of a larger illustrative component of a design, so we see the logo towards the bottom, as well as being depicted much larger in the background, bleeding off the edges of the page. In other advertisements, the trademark was used purely as an illustrative element and not as a static trademark at all. This can be seen in the 'Mills! Mills! Mills!' (Figure 5.10) design where the trademark is adapted with the addition of new elements, such as canes in the first instance, and a geometric, decorative graphic in the second instance. In other examples the trademark is neglected altogether, with the three figures remaining, but becoming far more naturalistic. In this case, the audience may or may not perceive the connection between the trademark and the illustration of the three figures. The connection is based on decoding the meaning of the content, rather than a perception of pure form.

Figure 5.9 Schleger's 'Looming Up' advertisement for Weber and Heilbroner, c. 1925. Item held by the V&A Museum, Archive of Art and Design. Courtesy of the Estate of Hans Schleger.

Alongside Schleger's publicity campaign ran another series of advertisements with photographs by Anton Bruehl. Spitzer was again credited with commissioning the work, acting as copywriter in this instance and providing captions for the advertisements. Each featured scene is constructed with model-making tools, with the three figures comprised simply of a paper cut-out of the trademark added to each scene. It is unclear whether Schleger was involved in this campaign beyond the use of his trademark, but it is clear to see the extension of the same strategy within both sets of work; this strategy being the use of the trademark as an illustrative device. Furthermore, we can clearly see in Schleger's work for Weber and Heilbroner a precedent for the Mac Fisheries campaign that came later. There is a light-handed approach to coordination with rigorous consistency put aside in favour of a coordination that is complex and varied, but clear to the eye. In this sense, Schleger refused to patronize his audience by placing the trademark in the same place in a formulaic fashion. There was a formula in use, but it was never overly prescriptive or prosaic.

Figures 5.10 Schleger's 'Mills! Mills! Mills!' advertisement for Weber and Heilbroner, c. 1925. Item held by the V&A Museum, Archive of Art and Design. Courtesy of the Estate of Hans Schleger.

Schleger's friend Paul Rand (1952: 61), who is one of the most highly regarded protagonists in the development of brand identity in the US, wrote of the potential for trademarks to be used as more than just monotonous and repetitive clichés:

> A trademark is not merely a device to adorn a letterhead, to stamp on a product or to insert at the base of an advertisement; nor one whose sole prerogative is to imprint itself by dint of constant repetition on the mind of the consumer public. The trademark is a potential illustrative feature of unappreciated vigor and efficacy; and when used as such escapes its customary fate of being a boring restatement of the identity of the product's maker.

Rand's viewpoint conflicted with the dominant mindset of most successful designers during the 1950s and 1960s, whose stance tended to favour rigorous and unequivocal coordination over expression or vigour. As clients were increasingly sold on the concept of visual coherence, it was common for trademarks to be repetitively badged across multiple design outputs to make this coherence explicit. But Rand and Schleger advocated a different path, where it would be possible to 'repeat without being repetitious' to 'actively stimulate interest in the product or brand' (Rand, 1952: 61). Schleger built on this premise throughout his career, firstly with Weber and Heilbroner in New York, then later in the late 1940s with family firm W. Raven & Company based in Leicester, England. Next came a brand identity for Finmar Furniture Limited, around the same time as Mac Fisheries. Before long, a raft of other schemes followed, including those for Edinburgh International Festival, British Sugar Corporation and Manchester Polytechnic.

The scheme for Edinburgh International Festival was particularly poetic in the way that it evolved over several years. A trademark was created featuring two birds positioned inside a depiction of Edinburgh castle. During the first few years of their campaigns the trademark was applied with restraint, so a recognizable visual impression could be built up across a range of applications (Figure 5.11). Over subsequent years they began to employ the trademark in increasingly diverse ways; so the birds that had originally been depicted within the confines of the castle were now used in more open and dynamic illustrative compositions. In the words of Pat Schleger (2001: 200), 'after a

Figure 5.11 HSA poster for Edinburgh International Festival, 1970, showing how the trademark was initially deployed in a restrained manner. Courtesy of the Estate of Hans Schleger.

number of years we began to let the birds out of the castle, as it were'. This is a resonant metaphor for HSA's approach to branding, whereby they gradually moved away from the point at which they had started, albeit generally with a sense of great care and deftness. The moment at which the birds began to leave the castle was caught rather aptly in a poster from the 1973 campaign (Figure 5.12). In subsequent designs, the castle is removed entirely from the central image, making way for ever looser configurations of the bird motifs (Figure 5.13).

Another example of the ability to 'repeat without being repetitious' is HSA's work for homeware store Finmar (1953–63). This was initiated with flexibility in mind, with three different weights of the trademark being created from the outset to ensure maximum adaptability without compromising consistency. Even this multi-weight trademark was not sufficient for Schleger, as he continued to manipulate the blueprint, rendering it in increasingly diverse treatments. The most divergent of which was composed of various cutlery, including knives, forks and spoons.

Figure 5.12 HSA poster for Edinburgh International Festival, 1973, showing how the trademark was deployed with greater fluidity, with the birds now leaving the castle. Courtesy of the Estate of Hans Schleger.

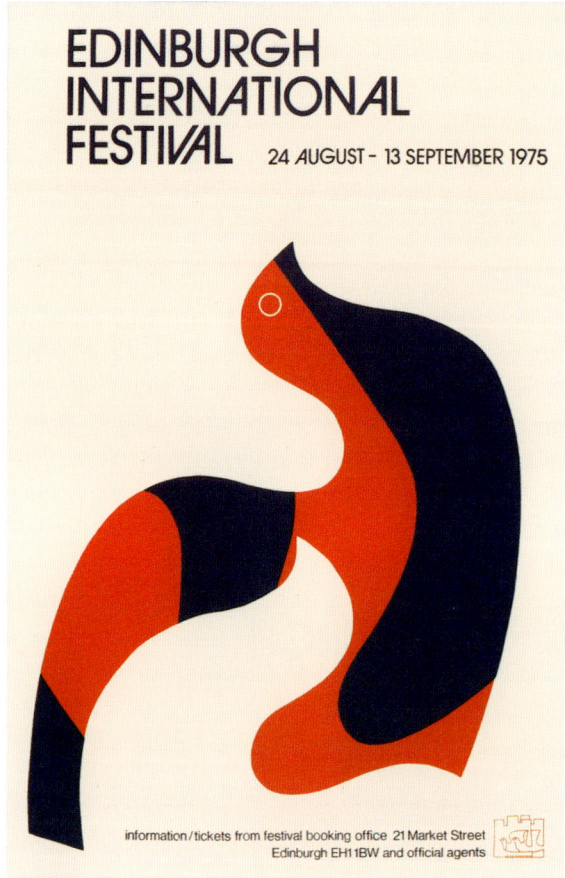

Figure 5.13 HSA poster for Edinburgh International Festival, 1975, showing how the trademark was increasingly abstracted over subsequent iterations of the campaign. Courtesy of the Estate of Hans Schleger.

Control systems at Hans Schleger & Associates

Hans Schleger as Art Director

Despite his penchant for design flexibility and vigour, organizational consistency and control remained important for Schleger in the implementation of the Mac Fisheries campaign. In making the transition from individual commercial artist (with the occasional assistant) to consultant design group, Schleger attempted to retain ultimate creative control of the studio. Studio numbers never swelled significantly beyond seven or eight members, but this represented a significant operational shift from Schleger's earlier days working in relative isolation (Schleger, 2011).

Describing the Mac Fisheries account, wife and colleague Pat Schleger recalls how her husband would oversee and sign-off on all work emanating from the studio. Where other consultancies developed scientific management tools to ensure good-and-proper working standards, Schleger preferred to be the all-seeing eye. The management structure of HSA was very shallow in hierarchical terms, with two core levels of importance: first Schleger, and then the rest of his team of employees working under his guidance. They did have a full-time secretary, but the lack of formal job titles left some ambiguity about remaining levels of staff seniority. As Pat Schleger (2011) recalls, employee Hermann Hecht was 'the studio manager, I suppose', explaining that 'we never gave ourselves titles'. But despite Hecht's slight seniority, it was Hans Schleger who remained the manager and art director of all work, organizing everyone, including Hecht. As Pat Schleger (2011) explains:

> You had something practical to do – I did all the curls on the AOA [American Overseas Airlines] things – but then also at the same time you were allowed to experiment with something else and then he would come as an art director and say: 'oh yes I like that, continue doing that', so he was a very good art director and you got a bit of freedom.

The reference here to 'a bit of freedom', suggests that Schleger did keep on top of his staff, allowing them just a little leeway, but not too much. According to Pat Schleger, Hans had wanted to keep an eye on everything in the studio and did not want anything to go out that was not as good as it could have been.

The atelier style set up of HSA could be likened to the master and apprentice model in the manner that staff were trained up by Schleger, but one of the problems of this approach was the lack of development opportunities for staff, with ambitious employees having been known to leave the studio to develop their own consultant practice. The limited capacity of the studio premises also restricted the scale of the operation and as a result they did not expand beyond seven or eight staff members. Given that Schleger treated the studio much like a family and his employees like his children, or '*kinder*', it seems unlikely that he would have wanted to expand the operation further. This is not to say that HSA were a family business in the typical sense, for intergenerational interaction was not a core element of the business. Rather, their ethos embraced the spirit of the family in that they looked after one another, with Hans Schleger a patriarchal father figure to his employees.

Regarding Hans Schleger's responsibilities in the Mac Fisheries campaign, it is clear that the illustrative fish characters were his domain, with many of the early advertisements carrying his own personal signature, Zéró. Pat Schleger confirms that her husband had been the original author of these characters, but he was not able to produce all the creative work emanating from the business, hence the need to hire a supporting staff team. Sooner or later, other staff members were required to fill in for him and complete work that he may have ideally liked to have authored himself. This is evident in the artwork for the Mac Fish characters, some of which Pat Schleger was required to render. It is probable that other workers in the studio contributed here too, as the client apparently required new artwork on a weekly basis over a period of many years.

The difference between Hans Schleger's Mac Fish characters and his wife Pat's versions can be seen when comparing two similar menu cards. The contrast between Hans's fluent Mac Fish character (Figure 5.14) and Pat's attempt to emulate his style (Figure 5.15) is noticeable when called attention to. The brush work in Hans's design is highly fluent, with a consistent quality of line that gives the impression that the artwork was confidently dashed-off, without too much self-awareness. By comparison, Pat's artwork seems laboured and inconsistent.

Figure 5.14 Mac Fisheries leaflet design illustrated by Hans Schleger. Courtesy of the Estate of Hans Schleger.

COORDINATED BUT NOT STANDARDIZED 141

Figure 5.15 Mac Fisheries leaflet design illustrated by Pat Schleger. Courtesy of the Estate of Hans Schleger.

This example highlights one interesting aspect of standardizing complex identity programmes, that is the unenviable task of trying to standardize illustrative work. The idea of aligning multiple illustrators' work under one specific style runs counter to the long-entrenched conception of the illustrator or commercial artist as one who cultivates their own unique individual style.[7]

Illustration can be standardized with relative ease if the same artist can be ensured to fulfil the entire programme, with Max Hof's fashion illustrations for Simpson department store being one such example (Havinden, 1955). In any other scenario, the idiosyncrasy of many hands must attempt to give the impression of just one, and in this instance a happy compromise must be reached, as in the case of the Mac Fish characters, which were rendered by different members of the practice. This collaborative spirit is central to group practice, as it is inevitable that a client's project may need to be passed between different hands, just as we have seen in this case. These issues are only heightened as the complexity of design programmes and the relative size of design groups increase in scale and geographical reach.

The individual and the programme

Concerns around the standardization of multifarious illustration work highlight the difficulties involved when seeking to homogenize work made by many hands. As discussed in the preceding chapters, some early brand identity programmes had taken more mechanistic approaches to this problem. For example, to eliminate the imprecision of the individual, LNER used typography as a modular component that could be readily specified and repeated. Still, one way or another the individual hand would normally impose itself onto the process. In the case of the LNER, lettering artists were required to render large-scale train name-plates by hand that could not be printed via the mechanistic letterpress process; meanwhile, poster artists would deviate from the mechanistic standard, rendering their own lettering as part of holistic poster compositions that included text and image within one visual construct.

As brand identity programmes grew in scope, designers often began to set down rules and guidelines that could be shared amongst those working on implementing a programme. An early example of this can be seen in the planning of the Festival of Britain, where Charles Hasler and his typographic advisory panel produced a style guide for lettering in order to coordinate the typographic appearance on the Festival (Rennie, 2001). The Festival had been the first time most designers had worked in such large collaborative teams, and as such, it was one of the first occasions that design guidelines had been required to coordinate the work of the many designers involved. The Festival typographic specimen document set out examples of the kinds of lettering that should be used throughout the Festival site. Though it was neither strict, nor formal in its guidance, the specimen book attempted to outline a stylistic spirit that was to be closely adhered to. For some reason, Schleger was not involved in preparations for the Festival. He had proposed a logo for the event as one of eight pre-selected designers asked to do so (along with Robin Day, Tom Eckersley, Abram Games, Milner Gray, F. H. K. Henrion, Theyre Lee-Elliott and Peter Ray), but his proposal was overlooked in favour of Abram Games's logo (Massey, 1996). He may not have been well-suited to the Festival's spirit of collaboration, coming across as a more introverted character, slightly less keen to compete, collaborate or fraternize with his peers. Unlike many fellow designers he was against standardization manuals, preferring a personal, humanistic design approach to a programmatic one, and believing that specification documents were likely to be outdated by the time they were put into practice. Others who worked on the Festival project did not share the same view, and later went on to develop more prescriptive, detailed design manuals for their own clients (F. H.K. Henrion, H. A. Rothholz and Milner Gray of Design Research Unit being key examples).

Beyond the official programme

According to Pat Schleger, all work for Mac Fisheries during Hans Schleger's time as consultant was completed in-house at HSA on behalf of Mather and

Crowther, yet the Mac Fisheries Guard Books suggest that some adverts fell outside their domain. It is impossible to attribute every advertisement in the Guard Books accurately, but there are clearly those that reside outside of Schleger's 'official' scheme, despite being published during the same period. These range from the purely typographic (Figure 5.16), to those that include incongruous photographic imagery. Those of the typographic variety make no attempt to emulate the typographic approach used in HSA's scheme, with even the 'Mac Fisheries' name rendered in nondescript, inconsistent fonts. These typographic adverts would most likely have been constructed by the compositors who put together the newspapers they were contained within. Some adverts sought to emulate the script lettering used in HSA's design with mechanized typefaces replacing the hand lettering, others including photographs often jarred with the lively illustrations of the HSA campaign.

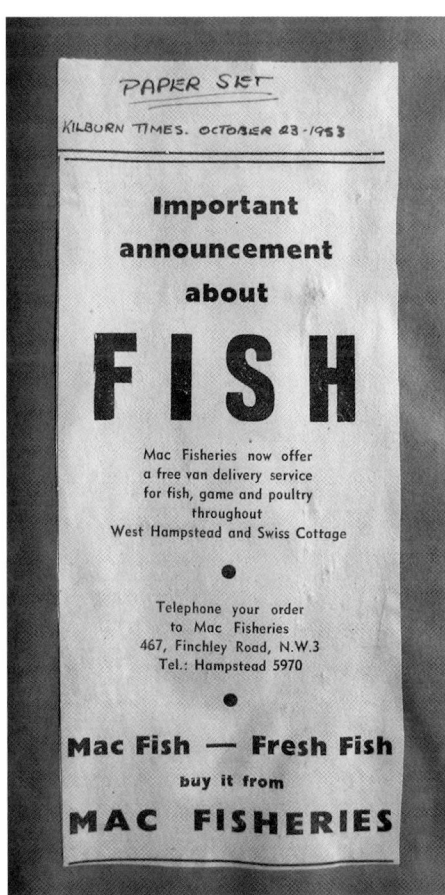

Figure 5.16 Typographic advertisement for Mac Fisheries from *Kilburn Times*, 23 October 1953, from Mather and Crowther Guard Books. Photograph by the author. Item held by the History of Advertising Trust Archive.

Beyond the domain of the Mathers Guard Books can be found examples of other graphic ephemera for Mac Fisheries that lie outside of Schleger's varied but controlled design scheme. One of the practitioners responsible for working on such ephemera was lettering artist Leslie Edward Watson (1919–77). Watson contributed lettering art and occasionally illustrations to various advertisements for Mac Fisheries, though he is not known to have worked directly for, or with HSA. Watson was a freelance artist who commonly worked from his home on commissions for London-based studios such as Max Rayner Studios and Phoenix Studios. These firms focused more on the jobbing side of advertising work, such as the preparation of artwork, as opposed to the creative art direction that HSA was involved in. Amongst the Mac Fisheries adverts Watson was involved in were those publicizing specific produce, such as quick-frozen cod steaks and oven-ready chickens. According to Watson's daughter, Elaine Rushin (2011), her father contributed lettering and illustrations to advertisements, with one such creation being a Schleger-esque 'Mac Chicken' character (Figure 5.17). It is interesting to see how jobbing designers working outside the Schleger studio

Figure 5.17 A Mac Fisheries advertisement featuring a Mac Chicken character created by Leslie Watson in the style of the HSA scheme. Item held by the Estate of Leslie Watson. Courtesy of Elaine Rushin.

Figure 5.18 An example of the photo-realistic product packaging style as featured in a Mac Fisheries advertisement created by lettering artist Leslie Watson. Item held by the Estate of Leslie Watson. Courtesy of Elaine Rushin.

helped to build and extend the wider brand identity for the client. In this case the available evidence suggests that this practice was conducted on a purely tacit basis, depending on the intuitive aesthetic mimicry of the commercial artist in question, as opposed to any inscribed design standards or specifications. Some of the adverts Watson created incorporated photo-realistic illustrations of product packs which are thought to have been produced by another artist specializing in this specific practice (Figure 5.18). The photorealism of these product illustrations jars with the playful approach of the HSA scheme, and it is unlikely that the Schleger studio had oversight of these designs given the dissimilarity with their own designs. What we see here is the difficulty of maintaining a consistent brand image given the need to mobilize a wide range of practitioners including design consultants, commercial art studios, typographers and print specialists.

Regarding the lettering used throughout the scheme, Pat Schleger suggests that it was an intentional decision to avoid standardizing the script style. As the lettering was meant to represent a fishmonger's traditional chalked-up blackboard, no handwriting typeface was constructed or used, giving the impression of lettering that had been created afresh each time. This decision fitted well with the need for artwork to be produced by a range of practitioners, including those operating away from the HSA studio, such as independent commercial artists like Leslie Watson.

In the design press of the 1950s HSA gained extensive publicity for their work with Mac Fisheries. The most significant example being the January edition of German magazine *Graphik*, which gave over twelve pages to the Mac Fisheries campaign, including thirty illustrations. The editor of *Graphik* wrote to Schleger to confirm acceptance of the feature: 'Just the stuff to suit Graphik, cast in one, a clear approach and yet colourful and manyfold, just what, in our opinion, advertising should be' (Maiwald, 1952).

Within the pages of the magazine, a harmonious vision of design coordination emerges through the presentation of a range of designs that are united in visual style and spirit (Figures 5.19 and 5.20). Within these designs there is a consistent treatment of illustration, typography and colour, yet there remains a vitality and vigour. This visual coordination may not be dogmatically standardized, but its coherence is evident. This construction of a coordination that repeats without

Figure 5.19 Double-page spread from *Graphik* magazine (Maiwald, 1953a: 22–3). Photograph by the author. Item held by the V&A Museum, Archive of Art and Design. Courtesy of the Estate of Hans Schleger.

COORDINATED BUT NOT STANDARDIZED 147

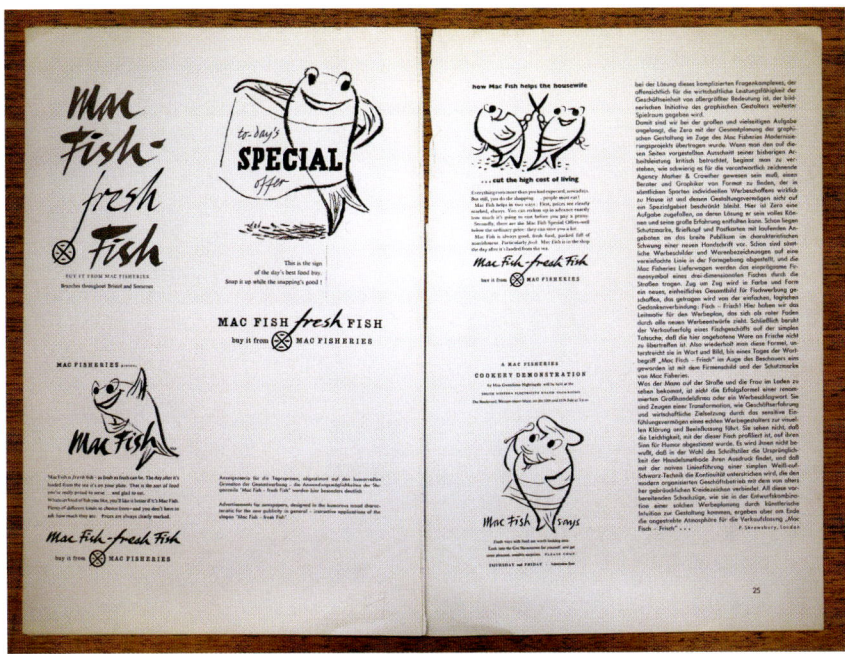

Figure 5.20 Double-page spread from *Graphik* magazine (Maiwald, 1953a: 24–5). Photograph by the author. Item held by the V&A Museum, Archive of Art and Design. Courtesy of the Estate of Hans Schleger.

being repetitious conflicts with the reality presented by the Mathers Guard Books and the work of individual artists such as Leslie Watson. This leads to the impression that Schleger constructed the image of coordination, perhaps not with an intent to deceive, but rather to present the most impactful, pure articulation of his brand identity programme. In many respects he simply shows the work that he had directed, preferring to overlook other jobbing work that may have fallen outside of his command and that he may even have been unaware of. This can be justified given that the work presented in *Graphik* is shown under his own pseudonym, Zéró.[8] It is interesting to note that the work is presented as the efforts of a single man, as opposed to a design studio comprised of several individuals.

Specification and deviations in quality

There is one further issue that the Guard Books allude to and that is the difficulty HSA had in matching the final printed advertisements with the designs that had been planned. This refers to design discrepancies between advertisements Schleger put forward in the design press and those that were published in newspapers and recorded in the Mathers Guard Books.

Figure 5.21 'Mac Fisheries present Mac Fish', advertisement from *Graphik* magazine article (Maiwald, 1953a: 24). Photograph by the author. Item held by the V&A Museum, Archive of Art and Design. Courtesy of the Estate of Hans Schleger.

Comparing specific advertisements reveals what is essentially the same design in two distinct formulations. The first shows Schleger's blueprint, the standard set by him as the campaign's Art Director, as published in issue one of *Graphik* magazine in 1953 (Figure 5.21). I will refer to this as the Schleger version. The second version shows the same design, but a printed variation that appeared in the Mathers's Guard Books (Figure 5.22). I shall refer to this as the Mathers version. There are several deviations between these designs which warrant further consideration. From the annotated record inscribed in the Guard Book it is possible to deduce that the Mathers design appeared in at least one newspaper within the Bristol area during March 1952. Unfortunately, it is less clear to discern the full usage of the other design; or indeed, whether it appeared in usage at all outside *Graphik*. It is possible that it could have been an early proof, as there is no evidence of this configuration in the Guard Books. As the Mathers advert is labelled as the first design of the campaign, 'Advt. No. 1. Prov. Press – Bristol Test Area', this could imply that the Schleger version may have been unused.

COORDINATED BUT NOT STANDARDIZED

Figure 5.22 'Mac Fisheries present Mac Fish', advertisement, Bristol test area, 1952, from Mather and Crowther Guard Books. Photograph by the author. Courtesy of the Estate of Hans Schleger.

The most obvious difference between the two versions is the additional fish character with two lines of text beside it. But aside from this extra content there are other discrepancies between the two. Most significantly, the printed name of the company appears in two very different typefaces. While the Schleger version from *Graphik* has a heavier, more robust type that holds its place next to the assertive illustration and graphic script lettering, in the Mathers design the typeface used for 'Mac Fisheries' is too light-weight to counterbalance with the other elements in the composition. In this instance at the very top of the design it is overpowered by the strength of the illustration, whilst in the second instance lower down, it is too weak to hold its place within the construct of the lettering and trademark lock-up device, fading into hierarchical obscurity. Thus, within the criterion of functionality, Schleger's version is more effective.

The typeface Schleger chose to adopt for the titling in the *Graphik* variant was in line with the typographic zeitgeist of the 1950s, being of the Clarendon category of typefaces that gained significant popularity following their revivalist usage in the Festival of Britain (Rennie, 2001). The type in the Mathers advert meanwhile, is a far more elegant and refined Roman style, inspired by the inscriptional lettering that appears on the Trajan column in Rome. Schleger's version again takes precedence, presenting the more appropriate and up-to-date aesthetic to appeal to the everyday consumer.

There are other discrepancies in the presentation of text within the two advertisements, not least the 'buy it from' titling text, which is inconsistently treated in each instance, with the text in all lowercase in one version, and all capitals in the other. The inter-linear spacing between the various segments of the design also demonstrates deviation between the two examples. The Schleger version has a balance and rhythm to the use of negative or white space. In the alternate Mathers version there is more spacing between the bottom of the main fish illustration and the top of the text block. Although this may be viewed as a minor detailing issue, it does contribute to the lack of cohesion presented in this published version of the advert. The lack of finesse in how negative space is used proves significant, as the design simply does not ring true as the work of Schleger. As Pat Schleger (2011) argues in relation to her husband's work for Fisons: 'it's the detailing that Hans was so good at, the space between the lines, all the subtleties of good typography'.

Yet, even if this spacing issue is regarded as a minor detail, then the additional content placed between the main body text and the company strapline is a more major one, destabilizing any sense of compositional harmony. This added content throws the delicate spacing and hierarchical balance of dark and light into disarray. The second Mac Fish character is certainly eye-catching, but its prominence is a distraction. Whereas the rest of the design is positioned around a central axis, this fish, positioned far left, draws the eye in a conflicting direction.

It is feasible that Schleger, or one of his associates at least, was responsible for the design of the additional component placed in the Mathers advert. Alternatively, it could have been a late instruction from the client that was fed directly to the production house where the artwork was being prepared for print. Either way, this extra component presents itself as a late addition. Given that the Schleger design from *Graphik* is aesthetically resolved (being the one Schleger was keen to disseminate), whilst the Mathers version is fragmented, it appears that this extra component was added to the Mathers design, rather than being removed from Schleger's. With this in mind, it is surprising that the Mathers's advert is labelled as 'Advt. No. 1'. One assumes that all parties would have been keen to ensure that their very first advertisement was of the highest standard, but as I have shown, there are a spate of discrepancies that exist between what we know Schleger had approved of, and what then appeared in the mainstream press. These discrepancies fall within Schleger's remit as art director, as it would typically be his responsibility to liaise with the printer and specify precisely what was required. This act of 'specification' was of great significance in the graphic designer's role, with typographic scholar, Paul Stiff (1996: 27) claiming that it was 'the means by which typographers sought to achieve "quality"'. Stiff explains how a specification would set down a designer's intention, in order that another actor, most likely a printer, could realize this intention:

> What designers make is a specification: its implementation, and so the realisation of the designer's intention, has normally been done by other people. When design is practised in an industrial process, specification is the end product of the designer's work: it is what leads to manufacture.

Stiff goes on to describe the relationship between the printer and designer as a complex nexus of communication, with a designer's instructional language ranging from the declarative to the commanding. He suggests that designers 'have always relied on printers to fill the gaps in their knowledge: to secure quality they have needed printers' consent and co-operation' (Stiff, 1996: 27).

Judging by the discrepancies between the two instances of the Mac Fisheries design, it is hard to believe that Schleger had a close working relationship with the printer of the Mathers version. It is possible that he was not in contact with the printer at all, for it seems unlikely he would have approved of the newspaper version of the design, which suggests that, perhaps, he was not given the chance to approve of it. This would appear to be the most likely reason for these discrepancies, but there could be a few other possible explanations. It is possible that Mac Fisheries demanded – against Schleger's wishes – that their advertisements retained some of the Roman style lettering used on their shop fascias – this fascia lettering was one prominent anomaly in Schleger's programme, remaining in the Roman style, which was in distinct contrast to the rest of the scheme. It is also feasible that the printer simply did not have the typeface that Schleger had specified; as such, a compromise would have had to have been reached, which would explain an alternate typeface being used.

The end of a working relationship

As an outside consultant employed by Mather and Crowther to work on the Mac Fisheries account, Schleger retained a relatively free, creative hand in the direction of the work. He was not simply offering a straightforward production service, but was a more forceful influence, steering the direction and planning of the campaign. As Mary Gowing (1956: 206) puts it:

> Most people who are interested in the planning side of advertising will know that Hans Schleger, in co-operation with Mather and Crowther and with Mac Fisheries themselves, has carried heavy responsibilities in the creative planning and development of that highly successful campaign.

Yet it was Schleger's unusual level of power and responsibility in the planning of this, and other campaigns for Mathers, that eventually led to the demise of their working relationship. New executives rising through the hierarchy of Mathers in the post-war period are said to have become uncomfortable with Schleger's level of governance as an outside consultant. As Pat Schleger (2011) recalls:

> [...] there were people coming up who didn't like the arrangement, and so Gordon Bogan, who was the chairman of Mathers, said to Hans, 'you know Hans, I think you should quit, because I think one or two of the new people coming up would rather not keep this arrangement going because it's too much trouble to have somebody from outside'. It was a bit awkward, Fisons wanted to keep Hans, they came to an amicable agreement, and it was transferred to Service Advertising in Knightsbridge.

Perhaps it was the fallout from the relationship with Mathers that prompted Hans to seek greater independence from the advertising business. Not to suggest that he immediately stopped working for advertising agents (clearly, he did not, for the work for Fisons continued though the company Service Advertising), but rather that a gradual shift began to take place. A shift away from a financial dependency upon the advertising business and towards a more independent professional stance where work would be done predominantly direct-to-client, without the aid of advertising agencies acting as intermediaries.[9]

It wasn't until March 1957 that Hans Schleger and Associates were registered as a private company, as announced by *World's Press News* on the 5th April (*Art designer forms own firm*, 1957):

> World-known graphic arts designer Hans Schleger, design-consultant to advertising agents Mather and Crowther Ltd, has founded his own private company. Registered on March 14 was Hans Schleger and Associates Ltd, with a capital of £100 in £1 shares.

The reference to Schleger's consultancy work for Mathers within this short press announcement is noteworthy, seemingly implying the grave significance of this particular contract to his business. Schleger did have other clients of note during this time, including Finmar and The Design Centre, yet the reference to Mathers seems to largely define his company. Aside from Mac Fisheries, Fisons was another prodigious client commissioned through Mathers. Regrettably no financial records exist to demonstrate the ratio of Schleger's income coming from the agency, but it seems reasonable to deduce that without Mathers, HSA may have been a very different design studio in the 1950s and 1960s.

Concluding remarks

To coordinate and control the design process and its contingent labour force, some design practitioners had, by the 1960s, begun to grapple with more systematic and scientific understandings of design. Inspired by the Design Methods Movement, they attempted to translate the act of design into a kind of mechanistic universal formula that could produce more predictable, risk-free outcomes. By adopting the tools of scientific management and applying the 'hard' knowledge of science and scholarship to practical design projects, these individuals sought to rationalize and manage creativity, seeking to legitimize design as more a respectable, profitable form of labour. Such efforts worked to counter the commonly held belief that minor professions, like design, were hopelessly non-rigorous by their very nature.

As we saw in the previous chapter, some graphic designers were heavily influenced and inspired by these developments, but Schleger was not among them. Instead, he operated his group on a largely intuitive basis, with fluid and ambiguous organizational structures in place and relatively low levels of cost efficiency. In terms of their business operations, HSA employee Pat Schleger (2011) describes how, 'we always worked far longer than we could possibly have charged for', adding, 'we were certainly not cost effective'. Despite the use of timecards to keep track of the number of hours spent on each studio project, her husband Hans would apparently go to work on Sundays to decide how much time they could realistically charge for. As she explains, 'he [Hans] had to make a decision about what we would charge, he couldn't really charge by the hour' (Schleger, 2011). This apparent disregard for cost effectiveness gives the impression of Schleger as a commercial artist committed to the pursuit of his art above all else, with the accrual of profit being less of a motivating factor. The suggestion that the hours worked at the studio outweighed the number of hours charged to the client may appear like a kind of false modesty, but Guy Julier (2017) lends weight to the idea that design professionals were not especially business-like during the post-war years, claiming that designers in general failed to take issues of cost efficiency and the accountancy of their businesses particularly seriously until well into the 1980s.

Fiona MacCarthy (2001: 17) supports the notion that Schleger conformed to this expectation of the commercial artist, writing that:

> If Schleger's early supremacy in corporate identity was to be eclipsed as the profession of design management expanded over the next decades, this was because he regarded himself primarily as an artist, refusing to transform himself into a businessman.

Meanwhile, in her review of Schleger for the journal *Art & Industry*, one-time collaborator Mary Gowing (1956: 204) argues that he was able, 'to enter the rough and tumble of commercial life without selling the pass to his own conscience'; thus, reiterating the creative, rather than financial, imperatives that underlay his practice.

Schleger can be seen to value practical rationality over its technical or scientific counterpart. In this sense the practice of HSA can be understood with reference to Donald Schön's (1983) conceptualization of the 'reflective practitioner', relying as it did upon more improvisational skills learned in practice, than on prescriptive formulas or techniques. So, by contrast to those attempting to codify design methods, HSA relied upon the 'intuition, artistry and unvarnished' opinion that Schön (1983: vii) termed soft knowledge. There was a dexterity to HSA's creative practice in the way that they would approach each new project afresh, devoid of pre-conceived ideas, styles or methods. Pierre Bourdieu (1990: 66) describes this as a 'feel for the game', which can be understood as an approach concerned with doing the right or best thing under the circumstances. This instinctive approach being thought of by HSA as preferential to any such desire to standardize or codify the practice of graphic design.

Schleger believed that each design should speak for itself, so when called upon by clients to explain or justify his reasoning, he is reported to have responded as follows:

> Your clients in a newspaper won't have a long report about why we have done it like this, and nor will I give you one. If it doesn't work when it's in the paper, then it's no good. Wait till you get the sales report.
>
> (Schleger, 2011)

This suspicion of formal design reports was in direct contrast to many of his peers, who used such forms of specified inscription to stake out the merits of their own design proposals and ensure they were applied consistently by external practitioners and producers.

It would be easy to underestimate the intelligence of Schleger's approach on the basis that it was seemingly less robust than more techno-scientifically framed methods of coordinating a brand, such as those of Henrion and Parkin, whose methods were conceived to persuade. Yet the HSA approach demonstrates a keen sensitivity for human factors as well as a consideration of audience need. Schleger was conscious of how large organizations could be rather daunting environments for consumers in 1950s Britain and as a result he was wary of standardization, being sensitive to the homogenizing effects of corporate consumerism. Commenting on the complexities of working for large organizations, he (cited in Gowing, 1956: 207) suggests that: 'The difficulty of interpreting a large organisation to the public is its impersonal character. People are understandably afraid of the large organisation. Everybody wants to be treated in a personal way.' The fact that HSA's approach was less mechanistic made it more complex in some ways, due to the nuance and subtleties applied to each unique individual design output. In this sense their approach can be seen to bridge between the individualistic virtuosity of earlier ideas-based commercial art and the later unified corporate design programmes that Henrion and others brought to the fore in Britain.

Schleger's preference for the personal touch is exemplified in his studio's work for Mac Fisheries, where the non-standardized script lettering gave each store an impression of individuality and the produce sold an impression of freshness that was implied by the haphazard hand lettering reminiscent of traditional fishmonger's chalkboards. As Schleger (cited in Barmas, 1952) explained in a magazine interview:

> Mac Fisheries have an enormous number of branches, but I want to give each branch a personal note. So I am putting myself in the place of the fishmonger and I'm designing as if the fishmonger himself had quickly chalked up a notice on his blackboard.

Schleger understood that a coordinated brand did not have to mean a standardized or homogenized brand identity. So, while Henrion and Parkin scientifically catalogued hundreds or thousands of design assets, Schleger's team took a more ad-hoc, piece-by-piece approach that prioritized a 'feel for the game', rejecting the dominant model of technical rationality generally demanded by business professionals. Schleger was known to dislike specification manuals, believing instead in the value of the individual one-off design, yet with his associates they managed to align a range of virtuoso one-off artefacts into coordinated multifarious systems. To do so they relied upon an unspoken tacit knowledge, the kind of knowledge that can only be revealed in the way that we carry out tasks and approach problems. Schön (1983: 49) refers to this as 'knowing-in-action', explaining that: 'Our knowing is ordinarily tacit, implicit in our patterns of action and in our feel for the stuff with which we are dealing. It seems right to say that our knowing is in our action'. Knowing-in-action is dependent upon our own research, experience and reflections, but to respond amid action when the scenario is beyond one's current knowledge base, practitioners must 'reflect-in-action'. This is a more active cognitive process, in which practitioners reflect within the 'action-present', rather than after the action has ended (this is described as 'reflection-on-action').[10]

It is important to acknowledge that some aspects of reflective practice can be tacit in the truest sense and that they may not be revealed through traditional forms of inscription. In this sense they may be understood as ineffable. This is not to say that they are necessarily irrational, but rather that they cannot be expressed verbally or through language, often due to the embodied or performative nature of such knowledge. Reflective practice such as this can be underestimated on the basis that its rational logic remains unclear. This leads some to believe that an intuitive approach to practice is irrational by default. But as we saw in the previous chapter, intuitive decisions can be either rational or irrational, but are not irrational by their very nature. As such, an intuitive approach to design may result in rational design outputs that lack an explicated logic. This can be explained by the fact that the logic of such work is not imposed from the outset, but rather emerges through the practice itself (or if not explicated, can remain embedded in the work itself). Robert Chia and Robin Holt (2009) refer to this as emergent strategy, arguing that strategies that emerge during a project tend to be more effective than those pre-planned and imposed in advance which tend to be inflexible and unresponsive to unanticipated and unpredictable problems and opportunities.

The Mac Fisheries identity campaign can be understood as an example of an emergent, non-linear marketing strategy, with the Bristol test demonstrating how the Schleger studio tested and trialled ideas before rolling them out on a wider basis. This approach to testing and iterating the campaign shows how reflection-in and on-action was built into the long-term development of the brand identity, with Mathers and HSA reviewing the effectiveness of the initial design proposals outside the immediate action-present. As *Advertiser's Weekly* (*How Operation Mac Fish was planned*, 1954) explained about the Bristol test:

> A strict eye was kept on all promotion. A weekly shop by shop sales analysis was made so that, at a glance, it could be seen where sales were falling or where they were rising. From these figures could be gauged the effect of specific items of publicity.

What was learnt in the trials was used to inform future marketing efforts, with Schleger revising some of the display ideas before they were rolled out on a national basis. This step-by-step operation goes some way to explain the imperfect visual synergy found between the items designed for Mac Fisheries. As the client changed the goals and criteria of the work, the designs themselves were adapted accordingly. This could be viewed as a quite natural process, though it is in direct conflict with the standardizing nature of much brand identity design, which is sold on the premise of consistency and recognition, as we saw in the journalism of Alec Davis who routinely linked consistency of style with audience recognition.

HSA did not conform to this typical ideal of brand unification, for Schleger refused to believe in corporate design manuals, or the idea of strict standardization and control. As Pat Schleger (2011) explains: 'He was always for moving on, he wouldn't want anything set in stone. He thought why not change it, why not go on developing something you started, instead of saying this is it'. Schleger understood that consistency and standardization were ideals that only really exist in an imaginary or ideal state where time stands still and all around is static. So, having recognized that strict uniformity was an unattainable ideal, Schleger sought to embrace a more practical balance between consistent and variable elements. Rather than trying to control everything, he decided what would remain stable and what would have a certain agility and dynamism. Schleger's rejection of standardization and scientific rationality can be seen to reflect the natural resistance of a certain generation of British-based graphic designers who were accustomed to their work being understood in relation to the paradigms of art, rather than science, medicine or law. In this sense the practical ethos of HSA should be understood as typical rather than exceptional.

6
SETTING STANDARDS: DESIGN RESEARCH UNIT AND THE DESIGN MANUAL AS AN INSTRUMENT OF CONTROL

In this chapter we will move away from a focus on the design group as led by one man (as per Hans Schleger at Hans Schleger & Associates and F. H. K. Henrion at Henrion Design Associates), turning our attention instead to a group fronted by two men, a diarchy, Misha Black and Milner Gray. Having two men at the helm, as opposed to one, may not sound especially significant, but the Design Research Unit (DRU) were a very different proposition to either of the groups examined previously. Perhaps most significant is the fact that they set out to provide a multidisciplinary offering that combined Misha Black's architectural expertise with Milner Gray's prowess in graphic design – ultimately this meant a more expansive operation that balanced the ideals, interests and concerns of multiple partners. It is revealing to see how the DRU reoriented themselves from a socially motivated design organization, suspicious of corporate homogenization, to one who came to embrace the flourishing corporate identity scene of the 1960s, developing corporate manuals that championed strict standardization. Furthermore, the nature of the 'texts' circulated by DRU in the performance of their practice changed radically during this period too, gradually moving away from soft, or sometimes hesitant forms of guidance, to more authoritarian forms of inscription conceived to govern the behaviours of clients and other designers.

The development of the Design Research Unit

Early antecedents in group practice

Founded in London in 1942, the DRU was initially conceived by art historian and critic Herbert Read and advertising executive Marcus Brumwell in response to what they saw as the necessity for comprehensive design services in the coming era of post-war reconstruction. Designers Milner Gray and Misha Black were enlisted in the formation of the group and became central to its future development. Gray had been asked to put forward a proposal for the firm by Cecil Notley, a friend of Brumwell's from the advertising scene, and he set out his objective as follows: 'The final aim is to present a service so complete that it could undertake any design case which might confront the State, Municipal Authorities, Industry or Commerce' (Gray, cited in Brumwell, 2010: 50). Gray's proposition developed with the financial support of several heavy weights from the advertising scene who were all members of the Advertising Service Guild, of which Brumwell was a central figure. These included: Cecil Notley (Notley Advertising), Albert Everett Jones (Everetts Advertising) and Rupert Casson (Casson Advertising). Marcus Brumwell later became financial controller of the DRU, buying out all company shares in 1956, with Read continuing to act as director and later president of the group.

The DRU had important antecedents in two earlier design groups, Bassett Gray and the Industrial Design Partnership (IDP). Bassett Gray were among the first practising design groups in Britain, having been founded in 1920 by Milner Gray and brothers Charles and Henry Bassett. Gray met Charles Bassett while studying Commercial Art at Goldsmiths College and together they set up office in Ludgate Circus, describing themselves as a Group of Artists and Writers whose aim was to 'steer a middle course between the stultifying influence of the commercial art factory on the one hand and the limited opportunities of complete isolation on the other' (*The Work of the Bassett Gray Studio*, 1927: 282).

The group soon grew in number to contain several other designers and artists, including the renowned painter, Graham Sutherland. Together they shared the cost of rent, utility bills, stationery and the office boy's wages. It was an unusual arrangement, which proclaimed to champion 'team spirit and co-operative effort' (Cotton, 2012: 12), yet paradoxically, each practitioner was encouraged to channel their own signature style and working methods. As they explained in the pages of *Commercial Art*, 'each member of the Bassett Gray group is an individual craftsman, drawing inspiration from his own sources, working on his own individual lines and freely developing his individual style' (*The Work of the*

Bassett Gray Studio, 1927: 282).[1] This clash between the cooperative ideals of the group and the individualism expressed through their personal work made them comparable to a latter-day illustration, or graphic art agency.

Designer Misha Black joined Bassett Gray in 1933, signalling the beginning of a long association with Milner Gray that lasted for the rest of their careers (their time working together amounted to 44 years up to the point of Black's death in 1977). By 1935 the Bassett brothers had left and the group was reorganized to become the IDP. Six members of Bassett Gray became legally bound partners of the new group, including Black and Gray, as well as James de Holden Stone, Thomas Gray, Walter Landauer (the German émigré who would go on to become a key figure in the rise of branding in the US with his firm Landor) and influential educator Jesse Collins (a future principal at the Central School). In an announcement to mark their formation they set out their intention to move from being 'an agency distributing the work of a group of free-lances' to one who would work more proactively together to solve complex multidisciplinary design problems, thus claiming themselves to be 'a group of experts working in collaboration' (Gray, 1935).

Though only relatively short lived, dissolving soon after the onset of war, the group was notable as it acted as a form of prototype for the DRU. Packaging, both graphic and structural, was a central tenet of their offering and a significant specialism of Gray's, but they were keen to assert their ability to handle a broad range of problems, with *The Boxmakers' Journal and Packaging Review* reporting that: 'The group handle complete schemes of presentation, from the styling of goods to the press advertising' (cited in Blake, 1984: 15). In this sense they can be seen to present themselves as a forerunner of the total design ethos that emerged with 'house style' in the 1950s, wherein comprehensive systems of artefacts came to be considered under the rubric of a single design project. The report continued:

> The complete approach has been built up: materials, designs, construction and costs are studied. The group is equipped, through its research and the specialised knowledge of one or several of its members, to give intelligent assistance and a guidance to any firm that sees the value of a good pack in the selling scheme.
>
> (cited in Blake, 1986: 15)

The reference to 'research' is especially noteworthy given the centrality of the term within the name of their later group, the Design Research Unit. It is unusual to find British commercial artists of the 1930s referencing research in relation to their work, suggesting that Gray and Black had more interest in the methods of design practice than was typical for designers of the period.[2] Gray is noted to have taken an interest in the client-facing duties of designers, such as managing client expectations and organizing the design process more broadly, developing an ever-growing checklist of questions over his career, which helped to aid him in his interactions with clients. Equally Gray acknowledged the relationship between the personal/intuitive and the analytical/objective facets of the design process, concluding that 'data alone will not provide the answer, but data is still necessary' (Gray, cited in Blake, 1986: 16).

Born in London in 1899, Gray was a central figure in the development of design as a recognized profession in Britain. In 1930 he was involved in the formation of the Society of Industrial Artists (SIA, later the Society of Industrial Artists and Designers, or SIAD, now known as the Chartered Society of Designers, CSD), and worked persistently throughout his career to promote the organization, serving as Honorary Secretary from 1932 to 1940 and as President twice, from 1943 to 1949 and again from 1966 to 1967.[3] Furthermore, he was closely involved with design education, especially early in his career, having taught at Goldsmiths College, the Royal College of Art, Central School of Art, as well as serving as Principal of the Sir John Cass School of Arts and Crafts from 1937 to 1940. In discussing Gray's contribution, designer Dick Negus (1997) makes note of the lack of recognition accorded to commercial artists of the early twentieth century:

> In a calling commonly thought, in its early days, at best to be a refuge of the less intelligent, Gray was unique. With a clear understanding of the future importance of design to Britain, he had a vision of establishing design as a profession and was largely responsible for forming, in 1930, the Society of Industrial Artists.

Black, meanwhile, was born in Baku, Azerbaijan in 1910 and was brought to England by his parents, Lionel and Sophia Tcherny, at the age of eighteen months.[4] He received little training, taking drawing classes at the Central School in the evenings, but by the age of seventeen had begun to design posters and exhibition stands, mainly for the advertising agent J. Arundell-Clark. At eighteen years of age he travelled to Seville to supervise an exhibition stand he had designed for the Rio Tinto Company, travelling home via a long stopover in Paris, during which he sought opportunities to further his studies in art. On his return he continued his work on exhibition stands, but decided more money could be made working independently, so in 1930 set up 'Studio Z' with Lucy Rossetti. They operated from a small design office in Seven Dials, London, designing bookplates, letter headings, window displays, exhibition stands and a bedside table. Rossetti soon retired from the business due to illness and in 1933 Black joined Gray at Bassett Gray.

While Gray made his name in graphic design and packaging, Black was mostly known for industrial design, interior architecture and exhibition work.

At IDP he designed exhibition stands, radios and a television cabinet, as well as writing for the trade journal *Shelf Appeal*. His interest in architecture led him to become secretary of the Modern Architecture Research Group (MARS), which had been formed early in the 1930s. He was also a founder member of the Artists' International Association, as well as an active member of the SIA and the International Council of Societies of Industrial Design. Through these social networks Black and Gray established strong connections that helped them to flourish throughout their careers. During the Second World War they worked together at the Ministry of Information (MoI) developing government propaganda exhibitions, going on to make significant contributions to the Festival of Britain.[5] Like Gray, Black was heavily involved in education, serving as Professor of Industrial Design at the Royal College of Art from 1959 until his retirement in 1975.

Establishing a 'general consultant' design group

In 1953 the notion of the design group conceived to offer a total design service to industry (an idea that had been trialled by the IDP in the 1930s) was further concretized when the SIA established the 'General Consultant Designer' as a distinct categorization of design practitioner. Drawing on the Society's private archive, Armstrong (2014) explains how members of the General Consultant Designers' Group were granted elite status within the SIA, taking a leading role in the organization and administration of the Society. Furthermore, she explains that Misha Black had been instrumental in the establishment of this influential new collective.

According to design historian Penny Sparke (1983), the notion of the consultant designer had developed in Britain in the late 1940s, partly in response to developments in America, where the role of the industrial design consultant was already well established. Sparke explains that the role of the consultant designer was to synthesize elements of numerous existing specialisms, bringing together elements of the fine artist, the architect, the craftsman, the engineer and the technician. The establishment of the General Consultant Design Group was significant as it implied a move away from consultancy services founded on the deep-rooted knowledge of a single design craft. So instead of emphasizing their schooling in a single discipline, the general consultant sought to bring to market a more coordinated service that focused on the concerns of a company's collective design policy. As Bendixson (1963: 30) reported in a feature on consultant practice for *Design* magazine: 'The general consultants offer a service distinguished by its comprehensiveness. This enables them to offer advice on design policy as well as on designing'. Linking the development of the general consultant designer to the emergence of brand identity design,

Bendixson claimed that general consultants were needed to coordinate house style programmes that incorporated a diverse range of creative artefacts.

By 1963, when Bendixson published his report, a total of twenty-one individuals are recorded as members of the General Consultant Designers' Group. Membership was by application only, with applicants having to present work covering a seven-year period to demonstrate their experience along with their dexterity as design polymaths. As Bendixson noted: 'qualification for the group depends on the ability of the individual, not on the collective ability of the team he leads' (Bendixson, 1963: 31). By vetting applicants based on their individual design skillsets the General Consultant Designers' Group appears to have penalized those whose talents lay in the leadership, management or administrative duties surrounding design.

Though a central tenet of the membership process was to demonstrate expertise in multiple fields – five categories were presented as core competencies: graphic design, constructional design, product design, product design engineering and miscellaneous skills – most members of the group were actually masters of one or two fields at most, with Bendixson (1963: 31) conceding that membership was 'as much an indication of organisational ability and experience as of design skill'. This is telling, as it raises questions around the tenability of the General Consultant Designer as a fundamental concept. Some commentators also questioned the viability of the concept at the time. For instance, responding to an exhibition mounted at the ICA in 1960 to celebrate F. H. K. Henrion's work, Bruce Archer (1960: 65, original emphasis) writes:

> The inference of the exhibition appears to be that the general consultant designer is a special kind of designer who can turn his hand equally to designing a firm's letterheads, products, trade marks, exhibitions and packaging. Is this *really* possible? If one is to go by the evidence of the exhibition, the answer is 'no'.

Archer highlights the uneven nature of the exhibition and the strong predominance of graphic design work to counter the idea of a designer who could 'turn his hand equally to all kinds of design'. He argues that the whole concept is a fallacy that few industrialists would accept. Instead, he backs the idea of the General Consultant Designer as a kind of design policy maker with expertise in a specific design field, as well as a competence in broader marketing and brand imagery principles, thus suggesting, 'while specialising in one field of design, [the general consultant designer] is capable of guiding other designers in the projection of a consistent image of a firm through its products, literature, advertising and show room design' (Archer, 1960: 65).[6] This seems to have been the practical reality for most members of the SIA's General Consultant Design Group.

Though Herbert Read and Marcus Brumwell had identified the potential for a general design consultancy as early as 1942, there was little immediate scope for such an enterprise. Read became Design Research Unit's first active employee, working as director from a base in Kingsway two days a week. He co-opted a small team of associates that included designers Misha Black, Milner Gray, Kenneth Bayes and Norbert Dutton (all still employed by the MoI), the architects Frederick Gibberd and Sadie Speight, as well as the structural engineer Felix Samuely. It was not until 1946 that the founder partners were released from their war-time jobs and the unit became fully operational.

They initially acquired a temporary home at Bedford Square in the premises of the art printer Lund Humphries (whose Director, E. C. Gregory, became chairman of DRU) and by the summer of 1946, twelve full-time employees are on record. By the autumn of the same year they had moved to permanent premises at Park Street, London W1 and the team soon grew to thirty in number. In the early years staff numbers fluctuated in relation to workflow, so once contracts had been signed for work on the Festival of Britain due to take place in 1951 (and with which DRU were heavily involved), the firm briefly moved to new offices and grew to forty in number, but they soon reduced in size again after the Festival, returning to their previous office base. After the Festival, identity design became a core driving force at the heart of business development for the DRU, with the graphics department shaping the development of the business as a whole during this period. Important work was initiated to develop house style programmes for Ilford, Tate & Lyle, Gilbey's, Watneys and British Railways. Some of these programmes of work lasted more than a decade, with long-term associations developed with Gilbey (over fifteen years) and British Railways (ten years), for example. By 1958 the team had moved premises again and grown in number to fifty, and by 1960 they also had two external offices, in Dublin (founded 1954) and Newcastle (founded 1959). By the late 1960s they averaged around sixty employees, which represented a radical departure from the days of the IDP, yet still relatively small in scale by comparison to the multi-national conglomerates that dominate corporate design today (Figure 6.1).

Given the collective expertise of the partners of the firm, DRU were well poised to deliver on the comprehensive service promised by the idea of the general consultant designer. For a decade or more after the war they held the unique advantage that they were a truly multidisciplinary group supported by the broad expertise and specialist skills of a range of senior practitioners from different fields.[7] By comparison, their main competitors for brand identity work had emerged from the practices of successful individuals who specialized in graphic design. This included Hans Schleger, F. H. K. Henrion, Willy de Majo and to a lesser extent, H. A. Rothholz.[8] It was common for lone practitioners, such as these, to develop group practices of their own after the war, as we have seen with the preceding chapters on Henrion and Schleger. However, it took

SETTING STANDARDS

Figure 6.1 The employees of DRU photographed together in 1968. Courtesy of Scott Brownrigg.

these individuals time to build impetus and establish themselves as tenable, independent commercial entities, with many practitioners continuing to be reliant on the printing and advertising trades for work, just as they had been before the war.

By the mid to late 1950s, when groups such as Henrion's and Schleger's had gradually built up their roster of clients as well as their base of employees, DRU were already flourishing as a more substantial, fully operational and well-drilled group, offering a breadth of specialist expertise across graphic, industrial and product design. In this sense they fit with Ken Garland's (1996) characterization of the *medium sized design group* whose work is based on 'craftsmanlike concerns' and reliant on 'close personal relationships'. By comparison, based on what we have saw in the previous chapter, Schleger's group aligned more to Garland's depiction of the *small design studio*, which exhibits an individualist mindset, with a 'reluctance to parade its wares in the market place' and a 'casual disregard for its own cost-effectiveness and profit margins'.[9] While this supports my findings in regards to Schleger's less pushy commercial attitude, my research suggests that Henrion had been rather more commercially minded and thus constitutes a less typical representation of Garland's *small design studio*.

The power-structure that underlay the operation of the DRU thus singled them out from their competitors. While their rivals commonly operated as

Figure 6.2 The DRU directorate in a meeting, with Misha Black far left, Milner Gray third from left, and Dorothy Goslett third from right. Courtesy of Scott Brownrigg.

one-man teams, with a known figure at the head of the firm directing a small group of assistants (as in the case of Henrion and Schleger), DRU were more egalitarian in the sense that the strategic direction of the firm was distributed across the two senior design partners, with further steering coming from Read and Brumwell who remained heavily involved in the early decades (Figure 6.2). As such, decision-making within the organization was more broadly distributed, with the ongoing collaborative exchange between Black and Gray encouraging a wider socialization of ideals to filter down through the group. DRU recognized their potential as a progressive, socially minded group and actively sought to promulgate this idea, claiming that they were a non-hierarchical company who advocated transparency and collaboration. Within *Design*, Bendixson (1963: 33) introduced them as, 'almost certainly the best known design office in the country', going on to report on their firm adherence to, 'a belief in horizontal or rakehead organisation'. In reference to this non-bureaucratic structure of the firm, one DRU employee is said to have claimed, 'there is no mandarinism in this office'.

Bendixson (1963: 33) refers to the DRU's design discussion meetings – held at regular six-week intervals – as the most characteristic expression of this non-hierarchical horizontal structure, claiming that 'comparable talks undoubtedly go on in other offices, but nowhere else are they so clearly built into the constitution'. Ostensibly, all staff members, no matter their status, were encouraged to take a view on matters discussed at the meetings, with a broad range of participants invited, including architects, designers, research library staff and 'even secretaries'. Bendixson (1963: 33) explains further:

> Each designer or architect who is in charge of a job on the agenda pins his sketches on the wall, justifies them to the assembly, and then waits for all hell to break loose. The object is not to force individuals to break down and confess their errors, but to provide them with food for thought. Occasionally a problem gets discussed at these meetings before any solution has been proposed. These forums seem likely to be a proving ground for exactly those qualities of experience and judgement that Professor Black thinks are at the root of design consultancy.

It is worth noting that the picture projected by the DRU of their own practice is not beyond critique. Long-term DRU employee, Chris Timings (2012) posits a rather different picture in which architects and designers worked in relative isolation from one another, segregated by distinct workspaces split across separate office floors.[10] According to Timings it was ultimately the senior partners, Black and Gray, who directed events on a day-to-day basis, which is unsurprising given that the venerated design discussion meetings – where Brumwell and Read were usually present – only happened eight or nine times a year (Black, 1964–76).

Given that they operated with Herbert Read and Marcus Brumwell acting in support of Black and Gray, structurally speaking the group can be understood in relation to design management pioneer Peter Gorb's model of a partnership – for Gorb (1978), a partnership usually comprises three or more equal people at the top of the structure. However, as Timings (2012) reminds us, Black and Gray were the dominant forces managing the group on a day-to-day basis, and as such the structure can also be interpreted according to Gorb's model of a *diarchy*. As Gorb explains, a diarchy is run by two people with equal, different but complementary skills and relies upon the reaction between opposites. It does seem that Black and Gray were complementary opposites, with Gray having reflected on their contrasting personalities in a letter to Henrion after Black's death (Gray, 1977).

Herbert Read passed away in 1968, while Marcus Brumwell ceased involvement with the firm by 1974, leaving Black and Gray free to shape the development and operation of the business. This led them to become recognized as the dominant personalities at the forefront of the business. Indeed, such was their stature as co-joined figureheads of the firm that Black and Gray were affectionately referred to by some of their peers as the halftone boys.[11] This supports the idea that they were understood by their colleagues, collaborators and peers as more of a *diarchy*, than a strict *partnership*.

By comparison to the projected horizontal 'rakehead' structure DRU claimed to operate under, the one-man teams of Henrion and Schleger were more akin to very shallow pyramids, with one central figure at the summit and various assistants working directly under them. Gorb (1978: 286) identifies this as a traditional authoritarian organizational structure, where 'one man is the moving spirit'.[12] The generation of designers that emerged from art school after the Second World War provided a different competitive proposition, in that they appear to have been more inclined to go into partnership with one another. Thus, businesses such as Negus & Sharland, 1951; Banks & Miles, 1958; BDMW Associates, 1959; Fletcher/Forbes/Gill, 1962; Main Wolff & Partners, 1963; and Minale Tattersfield, 1964 all emerged between 1951 and 1964.[13] Given the shared status inherent in such partnerships, DRU gradually began to face more equitable competition from groups in which the leadership of the company was more evenly distributed.

From practising design to practising leadership

In his 1956 address to the International Design Conference in Aspen, Misha Black acknowledged the significant proportion of time the practising designer dedicated to design management duties, explaining that the designer in industry is, 'predisposed to compromise and is willing to occupy at least part of his life with problems of persuasion, diplomacy, and administration' (Black, 1974: 67). He clearly found frustration in the client–designer relationship, lamenting what he called the 'soul-destroying battle of persuading the philistine'. The client's powerful agency in the development of design work was a cause for concern too, leading Black (1974: 64) to posit that: 'the client exercises so important an influence on the job as to make him almost equal to the designer in determining its final form'.

In Black's view, designers entering the industry needed to be wary of becoming all-consumed by the challenge of managing their clients through the necessary 'talking, writing and administering' practices that supported their creative work. His suggested solution was for the designer to advance his career and become a design leader with design protégés working under his command. For Black, this trajectory from creative labourer to design leader was a natural progression, which could enable the design consultant to take on a role more akin to that of the client. So natural was this transition for Black (1974: 64), that he described it as 'the inevitable lot of all but the most resolute artist'. This new role of the 'client/designer' would involve managing the creative practices of those less experienced designers working under their command. Black (1974: 67) described the transition as follows:

> The erstwhile designer himself becomes the client; if memories of his own travail on the drawing board have not been completely buried under the avalanche

of business lunches, he turns, by slow metamorphosis, into the client who is the more able to draw from younger designers on his staff that enthusiastic, dedicated endeavour essential to the production of outstanding work.

Whereas the figureheads of one man teams had been largely able to dictate the operations of their assistants, simultaneously 'keeping their hand-in' and continuing to practice their own individual design craft,[14] by comparison the relatively rapid growth of DRU led Black and Gray to work in a more open and discursive fashion, gradually ceding control of the creative design act to allow their younger colleagues to take on greater responsibility. One such staff member moving through the ranks was Chris Timings, a young graduate of the Graphic Design course at the Royal College of Art (RCA), who had joined DRU in 1954 immediately after finishing his studies. Gray had visited the RCA on the look-out for talent six months earlier, with Timings presenting his folio of work for assessment. Timings was a relatively early recruit to Gray's team of graphic designers who stayed with the firm for several years, progressing to become manager of the graphics department in 1969. Recalling his early years at DRU, he says: 'design groups as we know them now, didn't exist in those days, DRU was really a very small organisation' (Timings, 2012). He continues:

> It started off with Misha Black and a group of young architects, recently qualified, and Milner Gray, on his own at first. There was a woman called Dorothy Goslett who was their business manager, who was very important in that her job was specifically to manage the business. The business of design management was put on the map at the same time as the business of design. What was terribly important in those days was being seen to be a reliable, efficient and organised graphic designer, not a sort of ex-art student who wouldn't know how to invoice you.
>
> (Timings, 2012)

During the war Dorothy Goslett had worked closely alongside Black and Gray at the MoI, joining as an administrator in 1941 (Middleton, 1967). She became a partner of DRU in 1946 and was referred to as 'Business Manager' in company records. Her book on the administrative aspects of running a design business, *Professional Practice for the Designer* (Goslett, 1960), became a popular reference point for aspiring design professionals who sought to run their own companies, being republished through a number of editions over many decades, later as *The Professional Practice of Design* – the most recent reissue of which came as recently as 1999, some forty years after the original release.[15] It is notable that Timings accords business manager Goslett comparable status to Black and Gray, citing her significance in terms of the development of design management. According to Timings (2012), Goslett's text presents an extremely accurate account of the how the DRU was run from a financial and business point of view.

Evolving instruments of control: from recommendations to standards

To evidence the shifting patterns of ruling relations within DRU's design consultancy I will now draw attention to two important forms of inscription mobilized within their practice. These are, first, the written reports created for numerous clients to summarize DRU's project work, and second, the design standards manuals conceived to specify and control the design policies they developed for their clients. Though these two forms of documents are in essence quite different in tone and intent, I will demonstrate how these material articulations of practice are in fact interlinked, with the sophisticated and finely tuned corporate standards manual being a direct descendant of more suggestive and propositional written reports.

The design standards manual as an instrument of control

It is challenging to pinpoint the specific moment that the corporate identity manual was 'born', so to speak. As mentioned earlier, the Nazi Organisational Handbook of 1936 is understood by some as a precursor to the contemporary brand manual, but does not cover many of the concerns typical within the modern identity manuals, such as how to construct the logo, its measurements, or guidelines on correct and incorrect usage across various applications. According to Klevgaard (Barbieri et al., 2014: 66) the Norwegian Labour Party's (Det Norske Arbeiderparti) Handbook for Agitation and Propaganda (Håndbok i agitasjon og propaganda) does share many traits with the manuals we recognize today. Given the probability that there are further examples of early guideline documents waiting to be identified, I suggest that the emergence of the manual is best understood as the result of a gradual sequence of developments, as opposed to a symbolic birthing. This is certainly the case in terms of the DRU, as I will go on to show in the subsequent section of this case study.

For DRU, the development of the standards manual came about through incremental adjustments wherein the specification of brand identity programmes came to be treated as a matter of ever greater concern. So, whereas their first design specification documents consisted of bureaucratic A4 files with typewritten recommendations inside, by the mid-to-late 1960s these files had progressed

SETTING STANDARDS

to become lavish and extensive publications with meticulous attention to detail in terms of their design layout, materiality and production values (as well as a greater concern for notions of usability). In the following section I will examine a range of these documents to trace the emergence of the corporate standards manual.

In recent times, there has been unprecedented interest in the corporate identity manual as a design object. Publishing house Unit Editions have released two popular tomes cataloguing a total of forty different manuals conceived between 1960 and 2008. Furthermore, crowdfunding websites such as Kickstarter have empowered several successful campaigns to republish old manuals, including those for the New York City Transit Authority, NASA, US Environmental Protection Agency, the Canadian Broadcasting Corporation and, most significantly for this project, the British Rail Corporate Identity Manual designed by the DRU. These essentially bureaucratic objects, which have often been the subject of derision from those designers tasked with either creating them or implementing them, have become an obsession for certain connoisseurs of design, as evidenced by the unprecedented interest in these newly republished documents.

The basic premise of the design standards manual is to inscribe a set of specifications that seeks to control and govern how a design programme is to be implemented. Central to this pursuit is the corporate logo – or what Whitbread (2009) calls 'corporate identifiers' – around which several other specifications unfold, such as directions around the use of colour and typography, for example. As Naylor (1966) explains, the identity manual has a duty to both instruct and persuade, with the intended audience of the manual including senior stakeholders on the client side (who may see such a document as a form of legislation that supports and reifies their new design scheme), as well as designers, managers and administrators tasked with implementing the scheme (these could be from the client side, or from within the design team who conceived the manual, or as is often the case, from external design agencies tasked with the more jobbing operation of implementing the guidelines).

A key principle underlying the success of the manual is the codifying impetus of inscription (Latour, 1986), whereby certain information is concretized in written or visual form, thereby becoming more durable and transferable between actors and scenarios. The manual can thus be interpreted as a supreme example of what Latour calls the 'immutable mobile', in that it is a communication tool that is relatively concrete and stable (i.e., immutable) and readily shareable across different contexts (i.e., mobile). Latour explains that the power of the immutable mobile comes from its ability to enable coalition building around an idea. Thus, the publication of the manual can be seen as an indication that certain actors (in this case the design group) are winning the struggle to create order within a given network, that is, the broader context in which the programme is to be implemented including all the stakeholders implicated in its deployment.

One could interpret the manual as the foremost actor asserting agency across the broader contextual network. Alternatively, following traces of influence, one might suggest that the designers responsible for the conception of the manual are most important, in that they have inscribed certain affordances into the manual as a technical entity, and as such, they are governing other actors in the network (including the manual itself). Your stance here depends on whether you follow a more humanistic approach to theorizing practice, which privileges human agency, as per Bourdieu (1990) or Schatzki's (2002) agential humanism; or the post-humanist perspective that recognizes the agency of non-human actors as equal to humans, as per scholars of Actor-Network Theory like Latour (1983, 1986, 1992), Callon (1981, 1986) and Akrich (1992).[16] Laidlaw (2010) clearly sets out the merits of these different approaches, arguing for a pragmatic middle ground that recognizes the potential agency of non-humans, but also takes account of humans' responsibility for political–ethical values – described by Schatzki (2002) as 'value humanism'.

The notion that the manual forms an alliance around emergent knowledge suggests it can be productively interpreted as an 'epistemic object', though it could equally be considered a 'boundary object' in that it translates complex information into forms that are transferable across disciplines (Nicolini et al., 2012). Khazraee and Gasson (2015) explain that epistemic objects embed emergent knowledge into material form, citing objects such as categorization schemes and representational models as examples – this idea of the materialization of emerging knowledge provides a most apt definition of the corporate standards manual. Nicolini et al. (2012: 8) explain that objects 'become epistemic when they embody what one does not yet know'. Thus, it is precisely the emergent nature of the standards manual that creates motivation around it, becoming the focal point of a developing new community of practice centred around the deployment of the new programme (Lave and Wenger, 1991). According to Nicolini et al.'s (2012: 21) exposition of collaborative objects: 'The emergence of an epistemic object introduces a form of a collective obligation towards it – an emotional affiliation that becomes a morally binding force'. As such, infractions against the epistemic object – that is the edicts of the manual – can be held up as infringements.

'Report on proposed design policy for Courage', 1950

The first comprehensive brand identity programme DRU completed was for the photographic company Ilford in 1946 (Figure 6.3). The scheme was revisited and redeveloped some twenty years later, resulting in an extensive 'Design Standards Manual' that specified how the elements of the Ilford visual identity should be

SETTING STANDARDS

deployed. This manual released in 1966 was not the first created by DRU, with Naylor (1966) suggesting that they had created a corporate manual for the brewer Watneys as early as 1956. However, I have not identified any clear empirical evidence to support this view. The design report DRU produced for Watneys in 1956 does not resemble a manual in form and lacks the cohesion between visual and textual elements to be directly considered as such. The earliest manual in evidence from the archives of Black and Gray at the V&A Archive of Art & Design was produced for The Civic Trust around 1958 – this document is titled as a manual. However, having studied the archives at the V&A, it is evident that they had deployed various forms of specification document in their practice before the manual emerged fully fledged, and it is with an investigation of these more primitive specification documents that I begin.

DRU produced project reports for their clients as early as 1950, setting out their findings and the key points of their proposals – it is possible that reports were mobilized prior to this point, though there is no evidence to support this at the V&A archives. A notable example of this type was the project report produced for the brewer Courage on 1 February 1950 (Gray, 1950). Typewritten on plain A4 paper, stapled and enclosed within a modest cardboard cover, the title reads

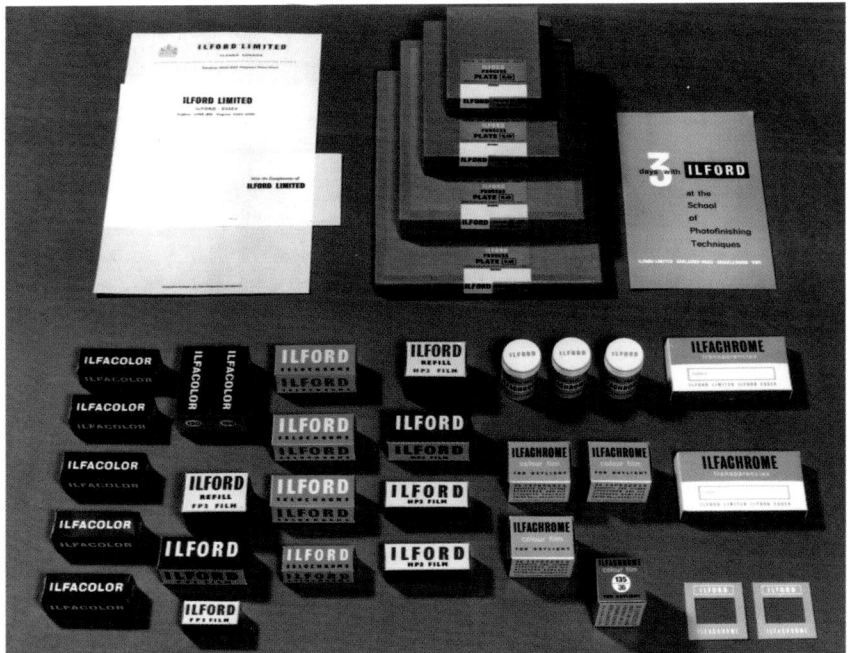

Figure 6.3 An early identity programme for the photographic company Ilford, created by DRU in 1946. Courtesy of Scott Brownrigg.

as follows: 'Report on proposed design policy and estimated expenditure on sales promotion equipment and material for 1950'. Set across sixteen pages, the report was structured into fourteen separate sections, as follows:

- Introductory
- Review of Sales Aids for 1949
- House Identification
- Cockerel Symbol
- Main Objects of Proposed Schemes
- Estimate of Present Consumer Market
- Working Men's Clubs
- Sales Promotion Media
- Method of Establishing a House Style
- Houses in The Festival of Britain Area
- Analysed Estimate of Proposed Expenditure for 1951
- Priorities
- Summary of Principal Recommendations
- Conclusion

Beneath the list of contents, a small note to Milner Gray has been made commending the quality of the report: 'Mr. Milner Gray. Congratulations – a really excellent report' (Figure 6.4). Though it is unclear who the note was from, it seems likely that it can be accredited to a contact on the client side. Assuming this was the case, it provides a reminder of the novelty of graphic designers' work at this time. Although such practices of report writing were well established in the worlds of advertising and market research (which were more well developed as professional disciplines), in terms of the typical output of graphic designers in the 1950s, a 'rational' design report founded on consumer research, such as this, was far from commonplace.

Precisely how the Courage report was deployed within DRU's brand identity practice remains uncertain, though it appears to have been used as a summative document, wherein meetings with the client resulted in typewritten proposals being finalized and submitted for approval. The introductory section of the report describes the intent of the document as follows:

> A brief report indicating the broad lines of a policy which in our view should be pursued in respect of sales promotion equipment and material supplied by Courage & Company to their tied hotels and licensed houses and to working

SETTING STANDARDS

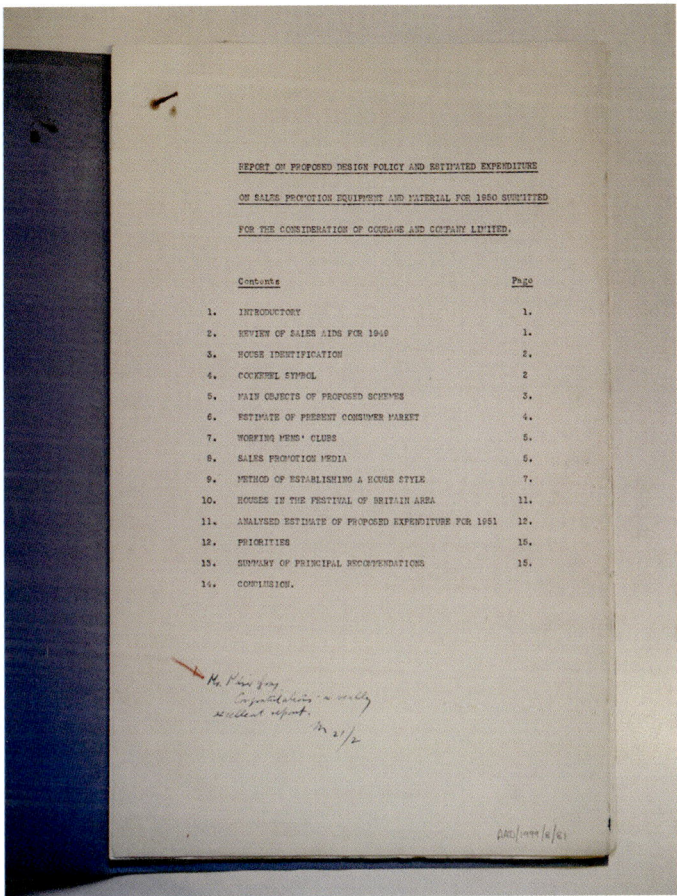

Figure 6.4 The opening page of DRU's report for Courage (Gray, 1950: 1). Photograph by the author. Item held by the V&A Museum, Archive of Art and Design.

men's clubs. These recommendations are made as a result of our experience of the Company's requirements gained over the past year, and especially in the light of the design and sales promotion policies discussed at the meetings of the Design Committee during the latter part of last year.

The reference to the significance of the design committee meetings is notable, as it implies that the report had a codifying effect, whereby the issues discussed during the meetings were reflected upon, before specific proposals were agreed and inscribed with the aid of the typewriter, setting out a clear course of action.

At the heart of the report the driving impetus was to develop a more distinctive, coherent and recognizable brand identity for Courage (Figure 6.5). Though they

Figure 6.5 Beer labels for Courage, designed by DRU, c. 1950. Courtesy of Scott Brownrigg.

referred to the idea of 'house style' in the document, this seemed to be linked more to the appearance of public houses than to the burgeoning field of brand identity design where the term was still coming to be established. So, when they spoke of 'house identification', they referred to the strong aesthetic pattern they sought to develop, emphasizing the need for their designs to aid in the ready identification of Courage public houses, thus explaining:

> It is essential, in our submission, that – always without submerging the individual character of each house – all this design material should conform to a regulated pattern, and so be designed as to be immediately recognisable as belonging to the House of Courage.

Here they were critical of Courage's earlier efforts, deriding their poor design standard as well as the lack of consistency in planning. In drawing attention to the idea that a consistent design pattern produces consumer recognition, they recall the arguments of authors such as Alec Davis, who had promoted the idea that brand identity programmes should produce readily recognizable aesthetic elements that promote brand loyalty and fundamentally result in consumer uptake and sales.

DRU methodically dismiss what they call the 'stereotyped' approach of chain stores like Woolworth's and Lyons', where the external architecture and interior furnishing was, in their opinion, overly homogenous. Instead, they propose that the brand identity programme for Courage needs agility to be malleable enough to engage with a wide range of different establishments set in diverse locales. In this respect the report suggests a class-based identity, with one design approach for the working-class establishments and another for the higher-class public houses, road houses and hotels. A budget of £42,717 was proposed for works to be completed in 1950, of which £2,085 was set aside for design fees (a substantial amount in today's money). In defending the fees, they emphasized the long-term value of the investment, claiming:

> Much of the actual design expenditure should be spread over a considerably longer period, inasmuch as a large part represents the cost of establishing basic principles of design policy of a long-term nature. Even so it will be noted that in round figures the ratio of the cost of planning and preparing designs is only a fraction over five per cent of the production costs.

Within the report it is significant that they give direct business advice to their client that goes beyond a concern for the aesthetics of design, advising on how product distribution could be extended into different contexts. For example, they suggest that redesigned Courage beer bottles could be used as a basis from which to develop a healthy new off-license trade, and further, that Courage may want to consider introducing their products into more upper and middle-class sport and social clubs of various kinds. This inherently strategic element of their consultancy service suggests that design groups had applied 'design thinking' approaches to business problems very early in their operation, confounding the idea that this tendency only emerged later in the century, as might be assumed from the heightened popularity the concept has received in recent times (Brown, 2009).

It is noteworthy that the project report is attributed in two separate places as the work of Gray alone, with the front cover and the final page stating: 'Milner Gray, R.D.I., F.S.I.A., Design Research Unit', implying that Gray was the pivotal client contact for the project and the author of the report. Given the collaborative ethos projected by DRU, it is surprising to see such a focus on a single individual within the team context (later reports clearly list several employees, as well as their job role, emphasizing the multidisciplinary team ethos of the group).

Though it is unclear how much collaboration was involved between DRU employees on the Courage work, it is apparent that the project involved considerable collaboration with agents outside the immediate DRU studio context. Gray notes that printed advertising material would continue to be handled by Cecil D. Notley Advertising (Notley had been an early backer of DRU), emphasizing the need to keep up 'many points of contact' with them to enable a successful collaboration. Likewise, he addresses the need to maintain clear communications with the internal Architectural Department at Courage, recommending that 'steps be taken and any necessary machinery set up to effect the closest co-operation between these parties'. A further agent implicated in the project was Mass Observation, the social research organization, turned market research company – of which Marcus Brumwell had been a key financial backer – who had been commissioned to carry out qualitative research for Courage that consisted of two comparatively small pilot investigations. Surveying 200 customers at fifty-six public houses Mass Observation sought to gauge the extent to which customers could identify Courage houses from the existing trade signs and symbols present on their premises, furthermore, they surveyed 100 customers at fifty public houses to monitor consumers reactions to new showcards introduced by Courage.

DRU discuss the evidence from Mass Observation's research in their report, using the given research findings to substantiate their own position as and when it suits their own ends, but contesting the relevance of Mass Observation's findings when it conflicts with their own arguments. Mass Observation's first survey indicates that several of the surveyed customers had failed to identify that they were drinking Courage beer, or in some cases, that they were even in a Courage public houses. DRU used this insight as a means to push for a more concerted attempt towards a holistic brand identity, claiming that, 'a principal plank in any sales promotion policy for 1950 should be to find means of emphasizing the ready identification of all Courage houses'.

When the second research survey by Mass Observation suggested that the recognition value of the corporate symbol – Courage's cockerel – was diminished by the fact that too many variants of the symbol were in evidence, DRU strongly contested this assertion, arguing that the number of different cockerels in use was of little significance, for what was really important was that 'the whole idea of "the cockerel for Courage" be emphasised and stimulated'. They argue:

> In our view the cockerel motif, whilst having an accepted form for trademark use, should be as widely used as possible in as wide a range of variants as expediency demands, so that in the final result the idea will be instilled in the minds of all that whenever you see a cockerel you think of Courage.

Here their approach to the cockerel as a loosely deployed design motif mimics Paul Rand and Hans Schleger's strategy of the trademark as an illustrative device that is used to add colour and variation to communication outputs.

In the report, DRU went on to restate the intent behind a series of three cockerels they had created for the company in the previous year. Explaining that:

> One of the most important steps taken in 1949 has been, therefore, the establishment of the new form of fighting cockerel as the Company's symbol.

SETTING STANDARDS

This design has been carried out in three somewhat varying treatments, – a simple one colour treatment, almost silhouette in form, for use in small sizes, such as on your bottle labels; a full colour version of the same bird in a formal rather heraldic manner; and a full colour representational or purely naturalistic treatment. These three versions of the cockerel should establish the form of the bird for all general trade-mark purposes. A complete portfolio of these three versions in a variety of sizes and different treatments has been prepared and submitted for future guidance.

Although their proposals were put forward merely as 'recommendations', DRU sought to gain authority in the tone of their document, ofttimes veering towards more dogmatic prose, particularly in their summary, where they advised:

(a) the widest use to be made of the revised cockerel motif, (b) the adoption of a standard house colours and letter forms, chosen to differentiate these from those of competitors, (c) the use in appropriate cases of flags, door and window awnings, umbrellas and other trimmings in standard house colours and treatments, (d) to increase the amenities of Courage houses by paying especial attention to their interior decoration, colour schemes and furnishings, and to provide a decorating service to tenants with this object, (e) to offer to provide similar services to working men's clubs, (f) the provision, either free or on special terms, of equipment and accessories designed to an established Courage pattern (g) a list is made of such three dimensional sales promotion media.

The report concluded with a final note re-emphasizing the nature of the collaboration with the client, restating their willingness to converse further around the given recommendations: 'the above proposals are submitted as a basis for further discussion on your whole design policy, in order that an agreed target may be set and the appropriation needed to reach it estimated and approved'.

'Report and recommendations' for Watneys, 1956

Some six years after the Courage document, DRU produced a further report for another brewer, Watney, Combe, Reid & Company Limited (Watneys hereafter), which was distributed in September 1956 (Gray, 1956) (Figure 6.6). Taking in a broad range of applications (including exterior signing and graphics, interiors, stationery and other printed material, advertising, labels and the Watneys' transport fleet), the report sought to initiate the development of a corporate 'house style'. Although the formal qualities of the report share many similarities with the Courage document – particularly in the A4 scale, modest card cover and typewritten content – the tone of voice has progressed to become more dogmatic,

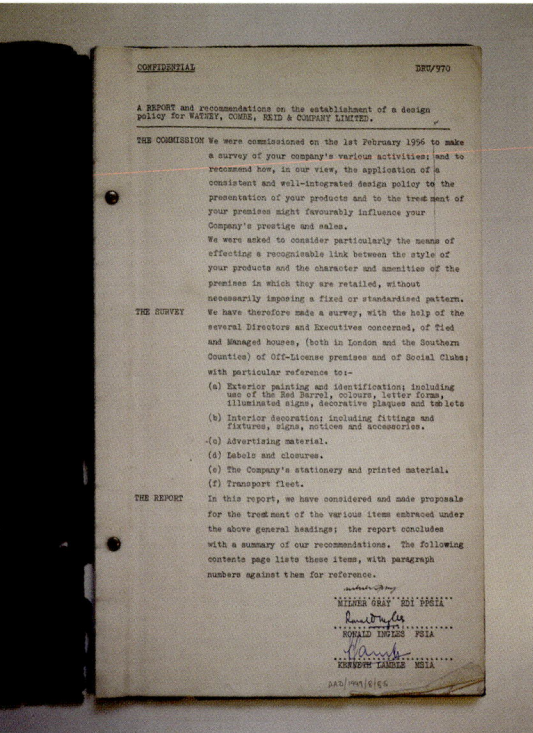

Figure 6.6 Opening page of DRU's report for Watneys (Gray, 1956: 1). Photograph by the author. Item held by the V&A Museum, Archive of Art and Design.

setting down clear proposals for the deployment of the proposed design policy. In this sense the report begins to resemble more closely the standards manuals of the 1960s, detailing certain guidelines – albeit still 'recommended' – around the deployment of standardized colours and lettering for the brand identity. These policies were set out in relative detail in the document and summarized as a series of recommendations at the conclusion of the report.

To provide an example of the documents authoritative tone, I present here a sample of the first ten points (of a total of forty-one) presented in their 'Summary of conclusions' with the original emphasis included:

> The Company's policy to avoid over-standardisation <u>recognised</u>.
>
> It is <u>recommended</u> that the individual character of house should be maintained, limiting common characteristics to certain proposed features.
>
> <u>Recommended</u> that the name WATNEY and the Red Barrel may be secondary in prominence to the name of the house, but should be more prominent than other advertising.

SETTING STANDARDS

<blockquote>

<u>Recommend</u> that the word WATNEY should normally appear in a standard letter form.

Over emphasis on Coca-Cola signs <u>deprecated</u>.

Standard house colours for fascias and signs <u>proposed</u>; employment of a group of basic colours for exterior painting <u>suggested</u>.

Other means of achieving house identification <u>listed</u>.

<u>Proposals made</u> for the uses, size, siting and for the lettering on the Red Barrel symbol. Illustration accompanies report.

<u>Suggestion made</u> for fitting clock into barrel ends.

The adoption of five selected letterforms <u>recommended</u> for use on fascias and signs to a regulated but flexible scheme. Illustrations accompany report.

</blockquote>

Of the forty-one points presented, seven were apparently accompanied by illustrations or samples to support and materialize the recommendations made. Regrettably the images were not contained as a part of the bound report, and as such, have not survived in the archives of either Black or Gray. It is worth consideration as to why these were not integrated with the text into the final bound project report. On the one hand, this may have been linked to the availability of appropriate print technology that could produce such a document in a timely and cost-effective fashion (as print technology developed through the 1960s project reports and manuals certainly became more lavish in their production values); but images could have been glued or 'tipped-in' within the report easily enough, or simply bound into the one document, with picture sheets interleaved with text sheets. On the other hand, a consideration of size and format may have been a concern, with some design proposals perhaps benefitting from a greater sense of scale and materiality, and thus presented independent of any smaller scale A4 documentation such as this. Most likely, the separation of design rationale from design visuals reflected the nature of the production process, in that the rationale was seen as secondary, or at least, separate to the production of the creative work.

Apparent from the first page of the Watneys report is the impression of a more collaborative process, with Gray's name now supplemented by the addition of Ronald Ingles and Kenneth Lamble of DRU, all of whom have signed the first page of the report. The report is also more extensive, progressing from the sixteen pages of the Courage document to thirty-eight pages for Watneys, including the addition of two appendices referencing their initial primary research around competitor practices. We are presented with numerous references to the idea of 'house style' (a concept not evident in the Courage report) though this is not fully explicated here. They also refer to the idea of the 'all embracing design policy', demonstrating a certain level of clarity and sophistication around the objectives of the project that were lacking in the Courage example.

Though the word 'recommendation' was used repeatedly throughout the report, the points they put forward represented more than just speculative propositions; for the detail, rigour and nuance of the document suggest a comprehensive and coherent design policy that was fully conceptualized and ready to be activated. In essence, the strategy they presented in their report had already been mobilized, for to contest any one of the forty-one detailed points would be to unravel the cascading, interlinked inscriptions embedded within the work presented. The report should thus be understood as a concrete proposition from DRU to their client for the work they sought to undertake for them over the coming years. Bearing in mind that there were few, if any, design companies who could compete with the heft of DRU's assets (human and non-human) and fulfil the recommendations of such a document, in effect it became a kind of contract waiting to be fulfilled.

The working relationship between Watneys and DRU appears to have prospered, with the principles inherent in this report being implemented over the coming decade (Figure 6.7). By 1966, ten years after the inception of the project,

Figure 6.7 The exterior of a Watneys public house designed according to DRU's identity principles. Courtesy of Scott Brownrigg.

SETTING STANDARDS

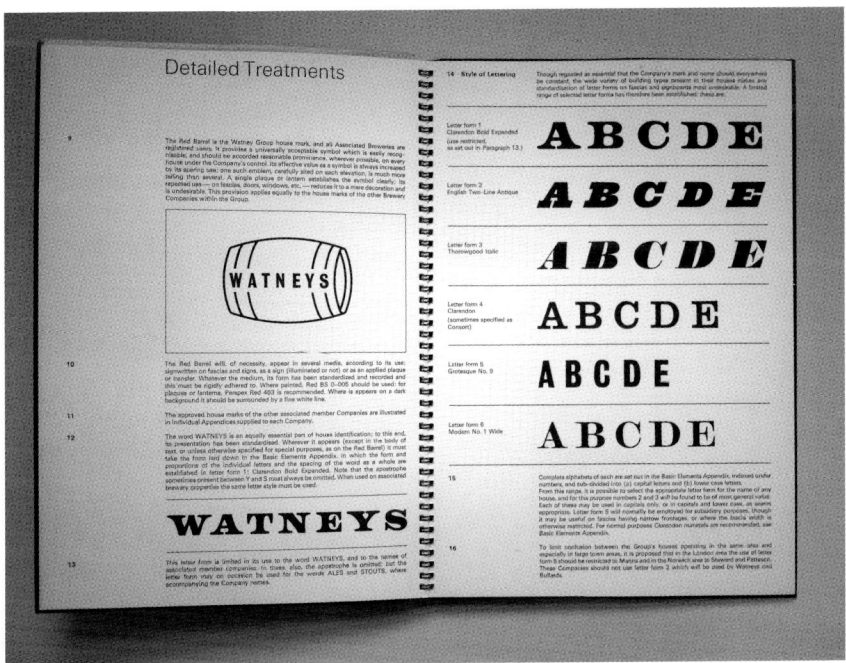

Figure 6.8 Watneys corporate identity manual, produced by DRU in 1966. Photograph by the author. Courtesy of Scott Brownrigg.

the policy was fully concretized within a rather more lavish 'House Identification Manual' produced by DRU at that time (Figure 6.8).

'Manual for Magdalen Street', 1958

During the late 1950s DRU were commissioned by The Civic Trust to lead a project that sought to coordinate the appearance of a street in the city centre of Norwich. One of the key outputs of the commission was a relatively modest A4 file, enclosed in an orange card cover and titled: 'Manual for Magdalen Street, Norwich' (Figures 6.9 and 6.10). Produced in 1958, it appears that this modest document was DRU's first de facto design manual that integrated visual and textual elements into a specification of brand standards.

One of the most significant aspects of this document was that it was targeted not only at their client, The Civic Trust, but more critically at external agents who were commissioned to implement the design vision as set out by DRU. This point about external agents is particularly important to account for, as it makes explicit the transition towards a more public application of design specifications. In other words, DRU were no longer codifying design principles solely for the benefit of their clients or their own design team, for now the specifications they

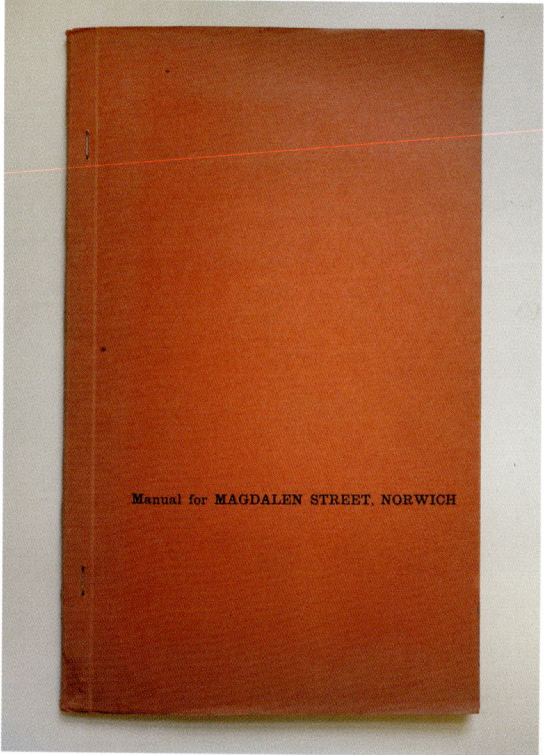

Figure 6.9 Front cover of 'Manual for Magdalen Street' (Black, 1958). Photograph by the author. Item held by the V&A Museum, Archive of Art and Design.

set out were inscribed for the benefit of those working outside the traditional client–designer relationship. It is no coincidence that their first integrated manual arrived in alliance with this more public conception of standards, wherein the agreed policy needed to be both more mobile and less contestable. The sense in which DRU's specification document needed to assert control over actors beyond their own immediate locale, mirrors the Latourian sense in which the immutable mobile acts at a distance, impacting upon distant events, objects and people (Latour, 1986).

In allowing the control of design implementation to transfer outside the immediate context of their studio, new pressures would emerge around the specification and communication of design principles. DRU could no longer rely on the tacit knowledge and understanding of its employees to ensure the smooth implementation of their policies. Instead the architects, designers and manufacturers tasked with realizing their vision would be practising in some distant context; they would almost certainly never meet and would not be in regular communication with one another either. In this sense, the guidance given in such reports needed to be more explicit and rule-based, leading to increasing

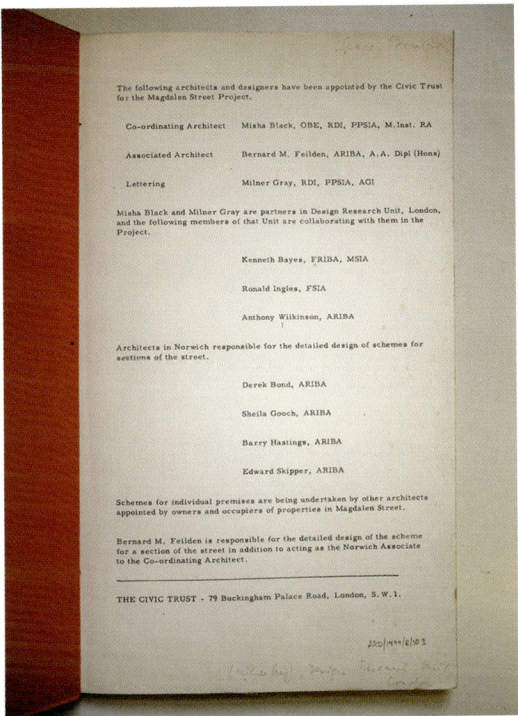

Figure 6.10 Opening page of Magdalen Street manual (Black, 1958: 1). Photograph by the author. Item held by the V&A Museum, Archive of Art and Design.

specificity and precision. Yet surprisingly the general policy put forward for Magdalen Street retained a great deal of openness and leeway for interpretation, as I will now show.

The programme of work on this project was led by Misha Black, who took on the role of 'Co-ordinating Architect' in collaboration with Milner Gray who was responsible for the scheme's lettering design. A further three DRU employees were directly involved in the scheme, with Kenneth Bayes, Ronald Ingles and Anthony Wilkinson all credited on the first page of the manual. There was also an Associated Architect, Bernard M. Feilden, situated externally and seemingly contracted either by Norwich Council or The Civic Trust.

Black introduced the manual by setting out the purpose of the scheme as follows:

> This experiment in civic design has the objective of bringing still greater vitality to this street, which already enjoys the advantages of good shops, important historical associations, and many buildings of considerable character. Unfortunately the development of individual properties without relation to any collective plan for the street as a whole has tended to reduce the street's

unity, visual impact, and air of importance. The scheme aims to restore the character of the street, without minimising the individuality of each shop or other property. It is not desired to encourage monotonous conformity and stultifying 'good taste', but to retain the advantages of diversity within a wide general framework of colour and lettering which will provide cohesion to the whole street.

Black's response to the design problem he had set out was to propose that:

By the careful painting of buildings above street level; by the grouping of properties within related decorative schemes; by selecting shop window awnings from agreed alternatives; by the careful consideration of all fascias, signs and posters; by the curtaining of upper story windows; by the removal of unused wall brackets and similar impediments, a new harmony can be created.

Covering some twenty pages, the manual went into further detail by outlining the principles of the scheme. A precise schedule of works was put forward, staggered over a nine-month period, from submission of drawings to completion of works, leading up to the launch date on the 14th of May 1959. External architects working on the scheme were 'invited' to submit their drawings to Misha Black in his capacity as the Co-ordinating Architect. Acting in a consultative capacity, Black would prepare comments on the submitted drawings, returning these to the external architects who would be tasked with developing the proposals in a manner 'satisfactory to their clients and themselves'.

Although Black acted as a kind of control mechanism within the scheme, there appears to have been no punitive consequence for those who failed to submit their drawings to him, or for those who failed to uphold the standards set out within the manual itself. Therefore, the scheme relied upon the good will of collaborators and the assumption that any wilful infraction of the programme would have been obvious to the public. Bearing this in mind, Black was careful to adopt an empathetic and enthusiastic tone, managing the expectations of those involved and calling for 'patient collaboration'. He commended the willingness and enthusiasm of those collaborators involved to date, reminding all involved that they held the opportunity to produce something of 'great credit and benefit to all, and an exemplar for other towns in Great Britain'.[17] Given that the project relied on the goodwill of all participants, this could explain why the DRU avoided an overly prescriptive approach to the manual as a series of commands.

Two areas of guidance that *were* more prescriptive were the standards set out for colour and lettering styles. In this sense the staid typewritten report now developed to include visual elements that supported the given specifications and norms. The user of the manual was presented with two interleaved pages of

SETTING STANDARDS

colour swatches (Figure 6.11) and thirteen pages of typographic samples (Figure 6.12), thus edging the document away from its earlier staid and bureaucratic form, making it into a more useful visual working aid. Also notable was the addition of two pages of coloured paper stock used to act as dividers before the lettering section (Figure 6.13) and the final page with contact details and a timetable of work. Although subtle, these small modifications to the form of the report helped to make the document feel like a carefully considered, designed document.

Within the manual eighteen colour options were set out, divided into two groups. The first group of seven colours being assigned for use on external rendered walls and above shop fronts, and the second group of eleven colours being put forward for fascias, window frames, doors and other woodwork. DRU were not insistent about the deployment of the two colour-groups they set out, literally underlining their assertion that: 'These colours need not, however, be strictly relegated to their two separate groups'. In this sense, they actively

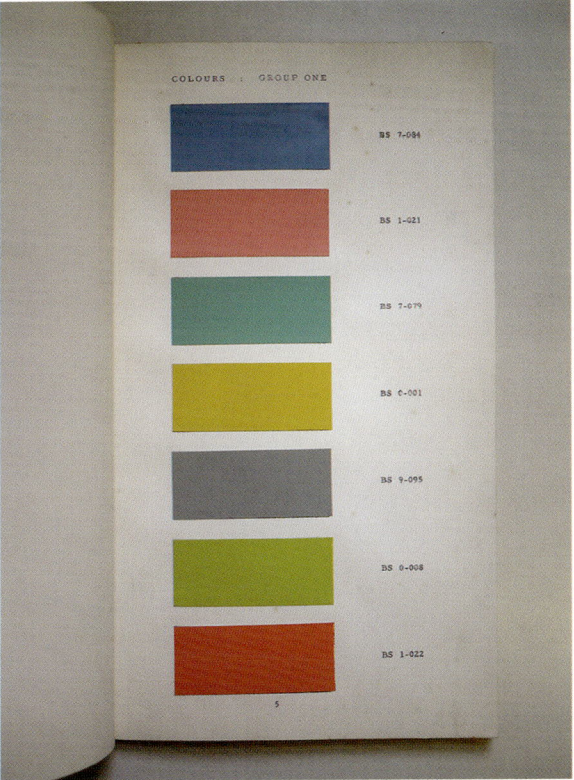

Figure 6.11 Page of colour swatches from the Magdalen Street manual, 'Colours: Group One' (Black, 1958: 5). Photograph by the author. Item held by the V&A Museum, Archive of Art and Design.

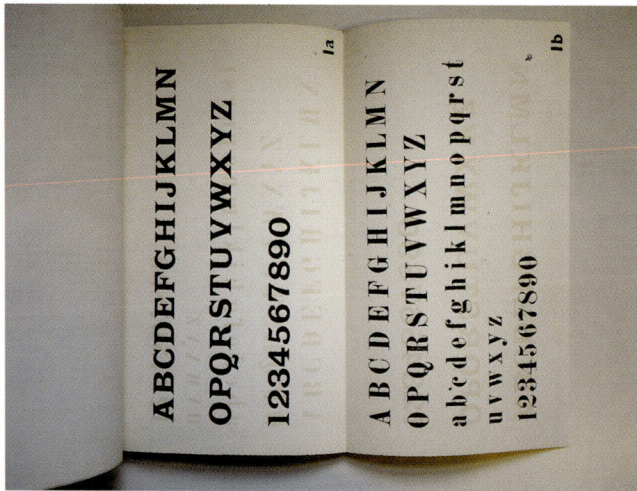

Figure 6.12 One of several fold-out spreads with sample lettering, Magdalen Street manual (Black, 1958: 1a–1b). Photograph by the author. Item held by the V&A Museum, Archive of Art and Design.

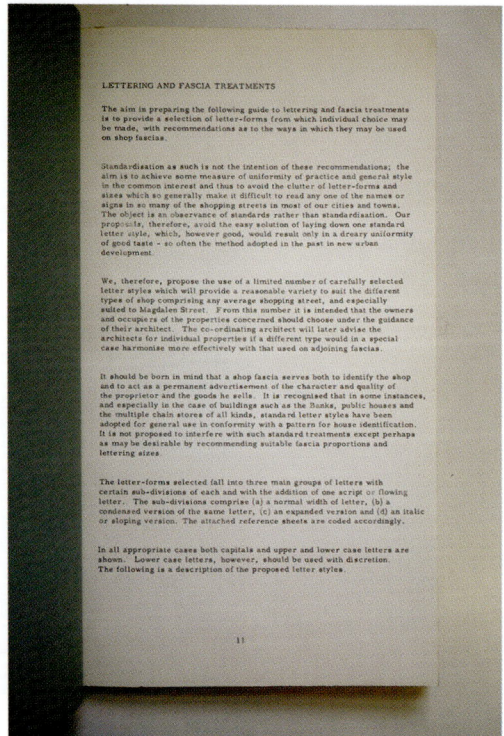

Figure 6.13 'Lettering and Fascia Treatments', Magdalen Street manual (Black, 1958: 11). Photograph by the author. Item held by the V&A Museum, Archive of Art and Design.

encouraged users of the manual to take their categories as suggestions, rather than norms to be followed.

The language of the manual sought to follow this apparent spirit of openness, so we are presented with polite requests to action, as opposed to direct commands. They explain that certain things are 'preferable', 'hoped' for, or 'can be useful', whereas others 'should be discouraged' or 'would be inappropriate'. Close analysis shows that the language of this instruction is relatively dynamic, taking on various forms, as opposed to adopting one strict and consistent code. The first part of the manual refers to what 'is', or is 'not recommended', and here the word 'not' is consistently given an underline treatment. But elsewhere we have repeated reference to what 'is' or 'isn't appropriate' and what 'should' or 'shouldn't' be done. Here the tone becomes dogmatic in places, with the user instructed that they 'should always', 'should never', or 'should not in any circumstances'.

When it came to the suggested lettering, thirteen different fonts were presented, divided into three groups of four, with one script typeface provided as an alternative option. Apparently, the idea here was to provide a 'reasonable variety' from which owners and occupiers of the properties concerned could 'choose under the guidance of their architect'. Here the typographic strategy mirrored the strategy of the project as a whole, with the introduction to this section stating: 'The object is an observance of standards rather than standardization. Our proposals, therefore, avoid the easy solution of laying down one standard letter style, which, however good, would result only in dreary uniformity of good taste'. Rather curiously the given samples were not named, but merely described by generic terms such as 'Serif letter' or 'Square or slab serif letter', this is odd given that the printed samples in the manual appear to be comprised of recognizable movable type, rather than hand-rendered lettering, as might be the case for signwriting.[18]

Contrary to the cascading inscription of rules that is the contemporary brand identity manual, DRU were notable for the openness of the design strategies that underpinned their early corporate design schemes. Their work for Courage, Watneys and Magdalen Street all rebelled against what they viewed as the homogenization of chains such as Woolworth's, Marks and Spencer and Lyon's. Instead, they sought to strike a balance between homogeneity and heterogeneity, promoting coherence rather than strict consistency and arguing for the need to retain the charm and values of individual entities (such as a public house's unique architectural details) rather than eradicating any anomalies in the spirit of total unification. This constituted a very different approach to that of international modernism, or even art nouveau.

One early precedent to the corporate manual is worthy of mention here for its likely influence on DRU's approach. That is the lettering guide created for architects and designers working on the Festival of Britain. Conceived by the Typographical Panel of the Festival, led by typographer Charles Hasler, this document sought to control and coordinate the deployment of lettering across the various Festival sites. By specifying a wide range of lettering styles all belonging to a vernacular variety referred to as 'Fat Faces', the policy sought to propagate an eclectic range of typographic content that was lively and dynamic, while exhibiting an undeniable intrinsic family likeness (Rennie, 2001).

The style of the Festival typography was considered retrogressive by some given that it sought to revive Victorian types, partly a reaction to the popularity of new sans-serif typefaces that were becoming ever-more ubiquitous (of which Gill Sans was the most omnipresent). Given the tinge of pastiche that surrounded the scheme it proved to be divisive within the design community too, perhaps in part because it represented British tradition, with its Victorian origins being in stark contrast to the developments of international modernism happening abroad. Nevertheless, the team of designers at DRU seem to have been greatly inspired by both the spirit and style of the lettering scheme for the Festival. In their capacity as coordinating designers central to the development of the Festival, the key partners at the DRU would all have engaged with the Festival specimen document and it is apparent that their projects for Courage, Watneys and Magdalen Street each took some level of influence from the Festival lettering scheme. The Watneys and Magdalen Street projects seem to have borrowed heavily from the vernacular lettering style of the Festival, capitalizing on the popular zeitgeist. So, just as the Festival had revived a wide range of 'fat face' lettering styles, DRU chose to do the same with their stylistic response for these two clients. For example, in the case of Watneys, they moved them away from what was perceived as the 'mechanical' typeface Gill Sans, towards a range of type styles thought to be 'rather richer in form and more traditional in character' (Gray, 1956).

More significant still, was the way DRU sought to mirror the inherent strategy that lay behind the Festival's typographic style. So as the Festival had trialled the idea of a loose pool of typestyles and colours (as opposed to a single corporate logo, typeface and colour), DRU adopted the same strategy, applying the method with great fervour to their work for Courage, Watneys and Magdalen Street. But as I will now go on to show, things were different for DRU when it came to their subsequent work for British Rail initiated in 1963.

'Design Manual' for British Rail, 1964

Perhaps the most noteworthy standards document created by DRU was their Corporate Identity Manual for the British Railways Board, which was first published as a three-edition volume in 1965 and subsequently expanded over the following years. Given its tightly controlled technical manner, it set itself apart from their earlier schemes that had played on eclecticism and cohesion,

SETTING STANDARDS

Figure 6.14 Photograph of 'The new face of British Railways' exhibition held at The Design Centre, London, 1964. Courtesy of Scott Brownrigg.

rather than strict consistency. Such was the cultural significance of the British Rail manual that it was released to much fanfare at an exhibition titled: 'The New Face of British Railways' at the Design Council in London, later touring to Liverpool and Dublin (Figure 6.14 and 6.15). Shortly after, its significance within the design scene was concretized through its appearance as a case study in the book *Design Coordination and Corporate Image* (Henrion and Parkin, 1967).

More surprisingly this document has continued to be a subject of considerable cultural interest up to the present day and was republished in full in 2016 following a successful crowdfunding campaign (Henning, 2016). Given the attention directed to this manual I will not go into detail about it. The vast scale and scope of the document makes it is difficult to do it justice here, so for these reasons I will focus on a less known precursor to this often-celebrated manual. In the archives of Milner Gray held at the Victoria & Albert Museum I have identified an early corporate manual for British Rail, which constitutes a soft launch of the design policy that was later fully concretized in the three-edition manual of 1965.[19] This document is significant as it helps to bridge the gap between the relatively crude manual DRU created for Magdalen Street and their more sophisticated and much-celebrated multi-volume document for British Rail. In this sense the interim manual examined here can be considered an important historical document representing a key stepping-stone in the development of the fully fledged identity design manual.

Figure 6.15 'The new face of British Railways', wall sheet explaining aspects of the British Railways 'house style'. Courtesy of Scott Brownrigg.

Labelled as a 'Preliminary Issue' and released in November 1964, the first DRU manual for British Rail was enclosed in a modest A4 black card cover, much like the very earliest reports they had produced for their clients (Figure 6.16). On the first page someone added a hand-written note discreetly at the top of the page, labelling the document as an 'Interim Manual' (Figure 6.17). This document was given added allure by the purposeful cover design, complete with corporate logo and sans-serif type. The choice of typeface is significant here given that DRU had previously been so reliant on vernacular

SETTING STANDARDS

Figure 6.16 DRU's preliminary design manual for the British Railways Board, November 1964 (Gray, 1964). Photograph by the author. Item held by the V&A Museum, Archive of Art and Design.

British typefaces in their work for Watneys and Magdalen Street. This shift from serif to sans-serif typography can be seen to reflect developmental changes in the zeitgeist between the 1950s and 1960s, with international modernism and, especially, 'Swiss style', coming to have an increasing influence on the British design scene.

The text and logo are printed in a stark white and set on a black card, with the following titling arranged in a designerly fashion:

British
Railways
Board

Corporate Identity Programme

Design
Manual

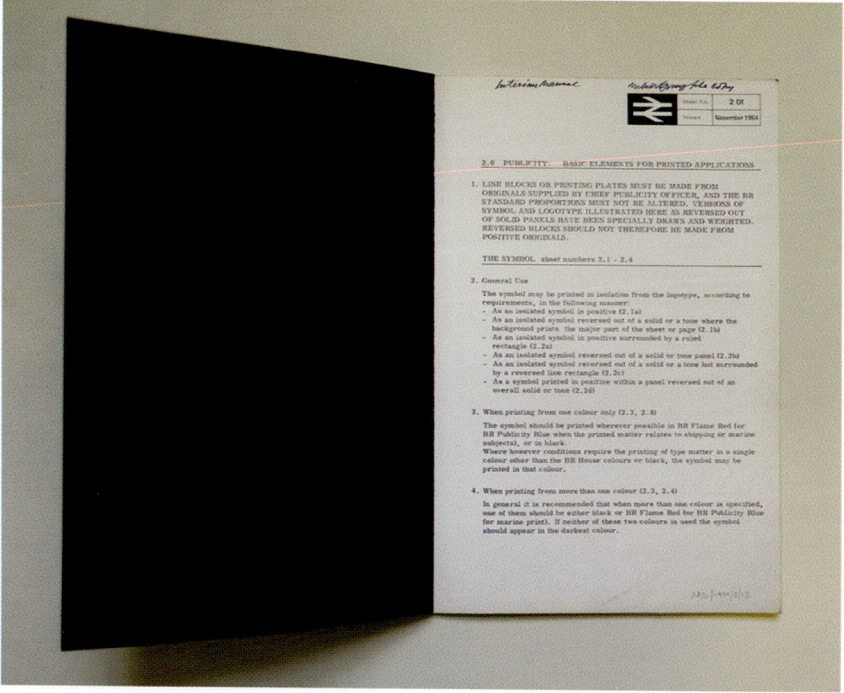

Figure 6.17 Opening page of the preliminary Design Manual for the British Railways Board (Gray, 1964: 2.01). Photograph by the author. Item held by the V&A Museum, Archive of Art and Design.

The reference to 'corporate identity' is significant, given that usage of this term was not yet commonplace. When Henrion and Parkin released their seminal text on the subject, they referred to innumerable different terms, including design coordination, corporate image, house style and corporate identity, thus highlighting the multiplicity of discourses that surrounded the discipline.[20]

Inside, the document displays many similarities with earlier reports and manuals produced by DRU, so although the typography is now printed rather than typewritten, the layout of the text continues to adopt the rather perfunctory fill-the-page typographic aesthetic of their earlier reports, with designerly notions of 'white space' not having come to bear on the manual yet. We also find the tendency for underlining the word 'not' persists. Elsewhere pages continue to be broken down into numbered points, with further delineation between sections now provided by a rule across the page, a treatment not used in their earlier typewritten reports. Here we see a process of simplification occurring in terms of the typographic presentation of the manual – this is a subject that typographic scholar Paul Luna (2011) has covered well with reference to the historical development of the dictionary. While the style of titling is consistent with earlier volumes produced by the DRU, here each page is given a unique reference code rather than a page number, with this code contained in a block of standardized information positioned at the top-right corner of every page. Within this information block is the British Rail logo, the sheet number and a reference to when the document was issued. This system of consistent labelling and attribution was a significant development that carried through into the three-volume manual released the following year. While in the 'Preliminary' manual the coded sheets were bound firmly together by two staples that went through all the sheets, in the subsequent manuals (Figure 6.18) sheets would be punched and ring-bound, a development that allowed the manual to become a dynamic and expansive entity, which could be amended or added to quickly and inexpensively. A further change afforded by technological advancements was the closer integration of text and image components, so although some pages remained purely text based, most now combined illustrations and specification diagrams with detailed textual content and description.

The tone of voice within the interim British Rail manual is notably more dictatorial than previous documents, emphasizing the shift towards a more authoritarian approach to brand identity standards. This provides a stark contrast with their initial position, which had led them, fourteen years earlier, to advise Courage away from what they called the 'stereotyped' approach

Figure 6.18 Covers from two of the ring-bound editions of the later British Rail manuals, together with a sample spread with fold-out page feature, c. 1965. Courtesy of Scott Brownrigg.

of Woolworth's and Lyons' (Gray, 1950: 11). Elsewhere they had warned Watney's of 'over-standardisation', explaining how an all embracing design policy 'can be both dignified and unobtrusive' and 'need not imply an inflexible standardization' (Gray, 1956: 6). Similarly, they claimed that the aim of the Magdalen Street project was about 'an observance of standards rather than standardization' per se, leading them to admonish the 'dreary uniformity' that resulted from taking 'the easy solution of laying down one standard letter style' (Black, 1958: 11).

Contrary to this initial stance, they now adopted a tone that mirrored a more totalitarian form of design governance. So, although we see mention of the softer 'should' and 'shouldn't' again, we now find reference to what is, or is not 'permissible', what 'must appear', or 'must not be altered'. Most powerfully we find several references to 'the rules' that are 'to be followed'. It is remarkable that the group had shifted their stance to the idea of uniformity quite so dramatically. Whereas earlier they had followed the coordinated but not standardized approach that we saw from Hans Schleger's group, now standardization and control became their raison d'être.

The typographic language of the DRU's work for British Rail echoed the overarching change in their approach. Whereas their earlier brand identity programmes for Magdalen Street and Watney's had championed an eclectic mix of revivalist typefaces in a nod to British history, their work now came to embrace the sans-serif type and grid structures of the Swiss Style (also known as the 'International Typographic Style' or 'die neue Grafik'), with cutting edge design and innovation in Britain increasingly influenced by developments on the continent. According to American design pioneer Paul Rand, the rationality and logic of the Swiss approach was well suited to the instructional impetus of the corporate design manual. As he explains, 'there is no counterpart to Swiss design, in terms of something that you can describe, that you can follow, that you can systematically understand' (Rand, cited in Heller, 1995b: 58). Evidence of the Swiss approach is clear to see in the design components specified in the interim manual (Figures 6.19 and 6.20), however this early interim version remains a relatively undesigned artefact by comparison to the ultimate set of manuals, which in their design approach can be viewed as an homage to the International Typographic Style (Figure 6.21).

One effect of the DRU's more dictatorial approach to the manual was the need to rationalize why particular rules had to be followed – albeit some more strictly than others. By explaining the reason why particular rules were in place they appealed to the users' sense of logic. So, on the first page a paragraph of text set in capital letters is presented to the reader, setting a very different tone to the enthusiastic and welcoming one Black had earlier established in his document for the Magdalen Street project:

SETTING STANDARDS

LINE BLOCKS OR PRINTING PLATES MUST BE MADE FROM ORIGINALS SUPPLIED BY CHIEF PUBLICITY OFFICER, AND THE BR STANDARD PROPORTIONS MUST NOT BE ALTERED. VERSIONS OF SYMBOL AND LOGOTYPE ILLUSTRATED HERE AS REVERSED OUT OF SOLID PANELS HAVE BEEN SPECIALLY DRAWN AND WEIGHTED. REVERSED BLOCKS SHOULD NOT THEREFORE BE MADE FROM POSITIVE ORIGINALS.

(Gray, 1964: 2.01, original emphasis)

There is a sense in this introductory paragraph that the user of the manual is not granted any great sense of intelligence or agency. Here we see the emergence of what Latour (1990) refers to as an 'anti-program', in that individual creative practitioners are understood to be a potential threat to the programme, in as much that they are considered likely to act out against the scripted programme of action inscribed within the manual. As a result, we can see the beginning of an aggressive trend towards evermore complex and detailed design manuals

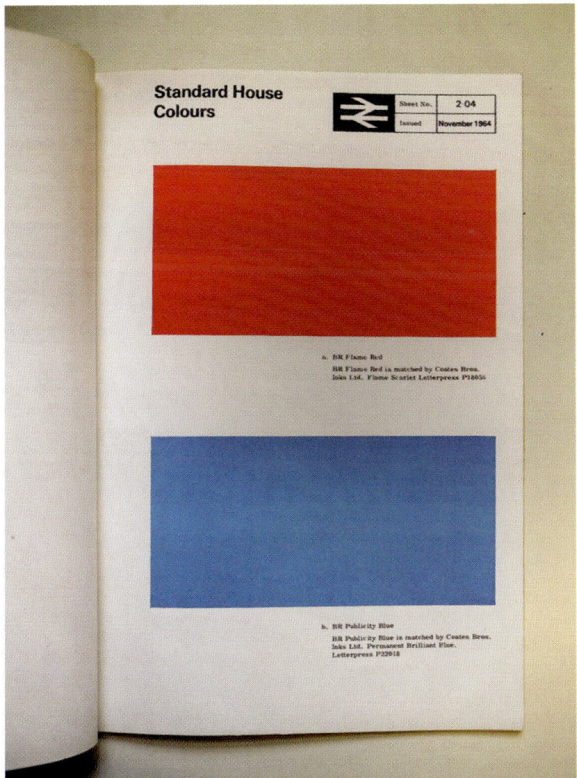

Figure 6.19 Sample page from the preliminary manual on 'Standard House Colours' (Gray, 1964: 2.04). Photograph by the author. Item held by the V&A Museum, Archive of Art and Design.

Figure 6.20 Sample page from the preliminary manual focused on the symbol (Gray, 1964: 2.1). Photograph by the author. Item held by the V&A Museum, Archive of Art and Design.

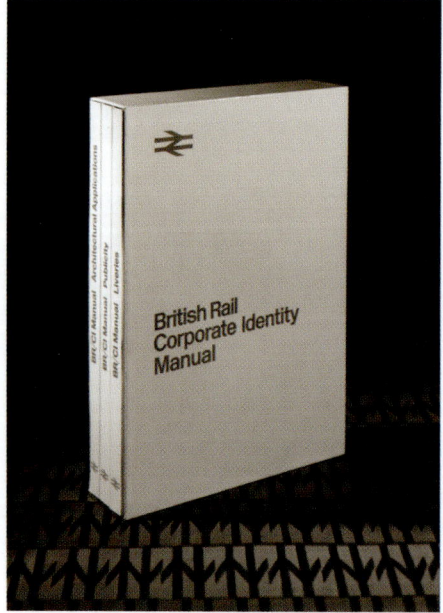

Figure 6.21 Set of three design manuals housed in a cardboard sleeve, c. 1965. Courtesy of Scott Brownrigg.

conceived to tightly control those responsible for implementing the brand identity schemes set out within them. Unlike the Magdalen Street guidance, which allowed its users the liberty to take decisions from a palette of options, the interim manual for British Rail regards its users with distrust and assumes they need to be controlled. In the relatively short space of six years, the DRU manual thus progresses from a discursive tool of collaboration in aid of a form of social progress, to a powerful part of the capitalist machine ensemble, a technocratic tool to control others.

Concluding remarks

The technocratic nature of DRU's manual for British Rail is surprising given the utopian idealism on which the group had first been founded. From their position as a non-hierarchical group who had prized sensitivity, nuance and horizontality in their design approach, the move towards a more hierarchical, controlling and homogenized form of corporate design culture is pronounced. Whereas they had earlier admonished what they called the 'stereotyped' approach of chain stores, which supressed individual virtuosity, now they embraced a more autocratic approach to brand identity design that prized strict consistency, coordination and control above all.

Here I wish to 'zoom out' to contextualize the development of the group and their shifting imperatives. Profitability had been a major concern in their first decade of business, with their first profit on record posted in 1957, twelve years after the formation of the group and a year into the consultancy work for Watneys. Nevertheless, they continued to grow their workforce steadily over the decades, becoming more profitable with time. In 1957 they returned a net profit of £10,983 (19 per cent of their turnover), but although turnover showed strong growth, records suggest that their profits peaked at 22 per cent in 1961, dropping back down to 17 per cent by 1965 and projected at 18 per cent for 1969. By the late 1960s operational problems began to arise, with the design discussion meetings lapsing in frequency and internal communications becoming increasingly strained, partly due to the staff base being split across multiple premises. By this point the two senior design partners were progressing towards the latter stages of their careers and attempts would soon be made to hand over the reins to a younger generation.

This idea of ceding control contrasts with the desire for control I noted in relation to Henrion and his employees. This links back to my argument about how coordinated practice was impacting organizational ontology in different ways. So, whereas in a firm of five to fifteen employees, as per Schleger's or Henrion's groups, one person can maintain control – or rule relations – over the day-to-day operations of their business; in an organization of sixty-plus employees like the

DRU, leadership duties inevitably become more stratified in order to delegate the wider range of managerial duties to a broader range of individuals. Yet, as I will go on to show, Milner Gray was more inclined to the hierarchical model of the one-man team, as per Henrion or Schleger. By comparison Misha Black understood that by relinquishing control of some of the day-to-day operations of the firm they could keep the business competitive in an increasingly contested marketplace.

Black had aired many concerns around the long-term viability of group work in his concluding chapter to Michael Middleton's (1967) book, *Group Practice in Design*, a book which Black had originally conceived of and would go on to champion. Here he contemplated the means by which group practices could sustain over the long term, questioning whether groups should always attempt to adapt to their circumstances, or whether in certain scenarios it was necessary for them to acknowledge that they had entered a new historical period in which they were no longer fit to serve. Ultimately, Black gave the impression that he was resigned to the idea that design groups ought to be dissolved before their innovation processes became routine and the practices of the group institutionalized; his argument being that a design practice without the dynamic vitality of innovation was unfit to be considered a design group at all. As he explains:

> In the end the group will outlive its usefulness and should dissolve. There is comfort in long-established practices, and convenience in the sturdy administrative structures which build up around them, but the function of design is to find formal relationships which simultaneously serve the needs of society and symbolise the emotional forces which motivate it. When the design group is no longer expressive and becomes content to reiterate forms which have only archaic interest, then its life is ended.
>
> (Black, cited in Middleton, 1967: 290)

Despite this strong ideological position, Black was evidently torn between a will to accept what he saw as the inevitable decline of DRU as a group and a need to adapt to sustain. The notion of ageing was touched on in some detail in Middleton's book, with Black (cited in Middleton, 1967: 86) noting that 'no organism can live without growth and group organisations are as susceptible to the laws of ageing and death as are all other biological systems'. He also warned against the complacency of middle age and the regurgitation of long-past victories, suggesting that at some time the reins of leadership would need to be passed on to younger practitioners within the group if it were to persist as a viable business operation:

> If the leader insists on retaining creative leadership when he no longer has the capacity to do so, then the group will dissolve or become yet another

humdrum design organization with a reputation for experienced practicability as partial compensation for its lack of creativity.

(Black, cited in Middleton, 1967: 289)

Although Black was seemingly keen to organize the succession of leadership within the group, Gray was less assured on the matter. By 1968 an external management consultant had been commissioned by the DRU to compile a review of the organization and management of the firm. Urwick Orr and Partners Ltd had been founded in 1934 by Lyndall Urwick and John Orr, both proponents of scientific management, with Urwick considered an important pioneer of management consultancy (Brech, Thomson and Wilson, 2010). The consultant from Urwick Orr and Partners concluded that DRU's non-hierarchical collective decision-making principles were no longer fit for purpose, as they made it difficult to 'arrive at correct decisions rapidly', they also identified that parts of the organization were operating independently from one another without 'formal unified command' (Schweizer, 1968). It is interesting to note that the consultant recommended a more mechanistic form of governance, going against what organization scholars Burns and Stalker (1961) had identified as the trend towards more organic organizational structures within the emerging technology industry of the era. It is also notable that a design group had sought the expertise of an independent management consultant as early as 1968, at a time when group practice in design was still in its relative infancy. The value of management consultancy and corporate strategy was clearly coming to the fore during this period, not just in Britain, but also the US, where in 1963 Bruce Henderson founded the influential Boston Consulting Group, credited with launching the corporate strategy revolution (Kiechel, 2010).

Following the advice of the consultant from Urwick Orr and Partners, DRU took on new premises at Aybrook Street and went through a restructuring process, with new departmental divisions introduced that were to be headed by younger managing partners. Problems persisted though, with divisions emerging between the two main partners. Although Black had plans to gradually cede control of day-to-day operations, Gray, who was eleven years his senior, had no intention of retiring. By 1973 Black complained to Brumwell that Gray was 'an increasing problem', being 'counter-productive' and a depressive presence in the graphic design group that he led – the designer Dieter Heil is reported to have handed in his notice as he could 'no longer tolerate an old man peering over his shoulder' (Black, 1973). By this time Gray was seventy-four years of age and still closely involved in the day-to-day operation of the group, by comparison Black was sixty-three and lamenting Gray's unwillingness to retire.

By 1977, three of the four founder partners had ceased to be involved with the group, Herbert Read having passed away in 1968, Marcus Brumwell resigning in 1974 and Misha Black passing away in 1977. After the early to mid

1970s the endeavours of the group are less well recorded, not having been archived or celebrated to the same extent as their earlier work.[21] As a result, a particular uncertainty remains around their operation between the mid 1970s up to 2004 when they were acquired by the architectural practice Scott Brownrigg. As Cotton (2012: 101) explains, by the 1980s the group's name dropped out of currency. During this period, they began to be written about in terms of what they had achieved in the past, as opposed to what they were achieving in the present. So, for example, in Jane Lott's (1982) feature for *Design* magazine we now find a retrospective profile of Milner Gray's career.

Gray lived on to the age of ninety-eight, passing away in 1997, and is said to have continued to serve on various SIA committees until 1984. After the loss of three of the founder partners DRU appear to have entered a period of gradual decline, being superseded by pushier, more aggressive hard-sell tactics of emergent consultant groups like Fitch and Company (160 employees by 1985), Michael Peters (around ninety employees by 1985), Conran Associates and Allied International Designers (the first design group to float on the stock exchange in 1980). Although DRU struggled to sustain success into the latter part of the twentieth century, for several decades during their heyday they set a precedent that showed how a strong ideological approach to group work could provide an antidote to the perils of overly routinized institutionalism. Black (1967: 290) thus recognized that business pressures could easily lead to overly hierarchical and rigid work structures, urging design leaders to 'be constantly aware of the need to retain the essential elements of the group concept while the pressures of time schedules and expediency concert to turn it into a master-and-servant establishment'.

As designers who had progressed into their design management roles, Black and Gray were highly sensitive to the needs of designers, recognizing that creative practitioners needed to be accorded creative agency in order to feel actively engaged within the practice, and thus to self-identify as veritable members of the group.[22] As organization theorists Peter Merholz and Kristin Skinner (2016: 129) explain, 'designers work best when they can bring their whole selves to their work, and not just behave as employees'. Paulus and Nijstad (2003) echo this sentiment, arguing that a culture of autonomy and openness can lead practitioners towards a preferred state of intrinsic motivation. DRU believed, accordingly, that affording their own designers such conditions it would be in the interests of the group as a whole, as the individual group members would be just as concerned by the well-being of the collective as they would with any sense of personal glory. In so doing they sought to avoid what Chris Argyris (1957) describes as the inevitable conflict between individuals and the organizational systems in which they work.

Aligned to these concerns, Black (cited in Middleton, 1967: 290) suggests that individual members of design groups must be placed in a position to 'accept that their salaries properly reflect their individual contributions to the group and that, when profits are made, these are fairly distributed'. Furthermore, he argues that leadership within the group must be fairly assumed, rather than imposed, and flexible enough to change when necessary. The issues that Black raises align clearly with what design management scholars have understood as the central importance of trust and transparency in fostering a productive group working climate. Paulus and Nijstad (2003) suggest that harmony is especially important in creative organizations where divergent viewpoints and 'wild' ideas can be particularly fundamental to success. Although Black understood the need for a certain organizational agility, later called 'organizational ambidexterity', his partner Gray was more closely wedded to his own role as a patriarchal leader figure and was reluctant to cede power.

Black's ideal of the highly transparent, socially motivated design organization could easily be dismissed as the product of a bygone era, but he had no illusions about the need to compromise, recognizing that idealism must be balanced with a more rigorous business ethos. In this sense he mirrored many of the traits of the ambidextrous organization (Tushman and O'Reilly, 1996) in that he sought to find an equitable balance between creative and economic success – what scholars of the subject refer to as the dual function of *exploration* (or conquering uncertainty) and *exploitation* (maximizing performance).[23] Black identified that those groups for whom creativity was their raison d'être would find difficulties in reconciling this creative leaning with the problems of daily work and efficient organization, and as such, the DRU thus naturally sided towards an emphasis on creative rather than economic performance.

Much like organization theorist Mary Parker Follett (1940), Black understood leadership not as an authoritarian bending of will, but rather as a sensitive interpretation of the needs of the group as a set of individuals.[24] As such he sought to strike a balance between the ideal of serving society and the need to accrue capital:

> Idealism is the essential bone structure of the group, but sentimentality is a disease which will quickly debilitate and finally destroy it. The working pattern of the group must be tough and fair. Wages must be adjusted to the value of work done, bonuses distributed with reasonable relation to the profits earned, slackers dismissed, financial reserves accumulated, business affairs efficiently conducted. No group achieves perfection in its business and administrative organization, but the closer it approaches that goal, the longer will be its productive life.
>
> (Black, cited in Middleton, 1967: 290)

Between the poles of the 'individual genius' designer and the fully institutionalized neoliberal design agency, Black (cited in Middleton, 1967: 287) set out his vision for the group of 'mature authority', founded on idealism, but operating with a sense of economic pragmatism:

> When the group has jettisoned immaculate ideas of equality, when it has thrown up its leader, when a hierarchy of creative talent has been recognized, then the group will be at the height of its power. It will have lost the capacity for producing the completely integrated statement which was the prerogative of its youth, but it will be able to design with that mature authority which serves well all conditions which do not require the nobility of individual genius.

This ideal state of multidisciplinary group practice was one that DRU sought to embody for much of the 1950s and 1960s, setting a progressive example for many groups that followed. As the founder partners ceased their involvement with the firm the practice gradually lost its way, being overtaken by more commercially minded enterprises that saw their contribution to society in economic rather than socio-cultural terms. In this sense the organizational development of the DRU is an interesting reflection of economic developments in Britain, as well as being indicative of the rapidly shifting imperatives of design practitioners of the era.

Next, I will go on to draw my conclusions from the three case studies investigated here. In so doing I will seek to 'zoom out' from the detailed accounts of practice detailed in the preceding chapters to draw connections between these three cases and link the changing patterns of practice that are evident with broader developments across the British design scene.

PART THREE
THEMES, THREADS AND LEGACIES

7
RECURRENT THEMES AND THREADS

In Part Two of this book, I adopted a collective case study model, or joint study, with three consultant design groups presented that together represented the phenomenon of programmatic brand identity design and its gradual emergence. As such, though each case had its own intrinsic value explored within the relevant chapters, they were chosen as part of a collective that would enable generalizations to be made from these microscopic cases to the wider macroscopic phenomenon. Here I seek to 'zoom out' to explore themes and threads that recur across the cases as a whole.

Graphic design professionalism and the fight for jurisdiction

Through the three consultant groups presented here we saw how early design practitioners schooled in the arts had sought to develop design into a more respected, tenable activity of work independent of the advertising business and associated marketing and public relations professionals. In the first instance, ambitious individual design practitioners set out to establish their own group consultancies, but during the initial operation of these groups in the late 1940s and early 1950s many remained reliant on commissions from the advertising industry. So, for example, between 1951 and 1962, Hans Schleger was contracted to the advertising agency Mather and Crowther, while F. H. K. Henrion took on the part-time post of Director of Visual Planning for Erwin Wasey between 1954 and 1958.[1] In both these cases, positions of stability within advertising were utilized as a basis from which to pivot off in order to gain greater independence from the very same industry and to move towards independent group practice in graphic design. So, as we have seen in the case of Henrion, his brand identity work for KLM developed directly from the client contacts he made working at the advertising agency Erwin Wasey.

Although Schleger and Henrion both sought to move away from the isolation of freelance commercial artwork by establishing group consultancies, they did so in their own particular ways. So, while Schleger rejected the formalization of design, preferring a more fluid, reflexive approach, Henrion embraced attempts to scientize design, adopting a Taylorist approach to the design process, wherein rationalization was taken to extreme levels in a quest for efficiency, calculability, predictability and control; what Ritzer (1992) calls the four dimensions of 'McDonaldization'. The divergence between those committed to the established idea of design as an artistic practice, and those keen to distance themselves from art (at least in certain business focused contexts) is especially pronounced here.

By comparison, the DRU developed from the initiative of Herbert Read and Marcus Brumwell, who had used the funding from their advertising contacts to persist with their own unique model of group consultancy. In this respect DRU were different from other design groups of the era who existed on a less stable footing. The role of Read and Brumwell is especially unusual, given that their involvement in the venture does not appear to have been purely economically motivated, being driven, at least in part, by a sense of social duty. Given the relative scale of DRU, they were able to take on sizable commissions beyond the capacity of those smaller one-man teams they competed against. These factors helped to set them apart, with questions of cost efficiency seemingly a less pressing factor in the day-to-day operations of the firm. In this sense the designers at the head of DRU were shielded from – or at the very least supported in – the business aspects of their practice. Where Schleger and Henrion had needed to tackle financial viability as a primary and ongoing concern, choosing to operate from studios in their homes, DRU were more ambitious and freer in spirit, striving to question the commercial orthodoxy and asserting their ethical business principles.

Each of the three consultant design groups had a distinct approach to brand identity design and this was reflected in the material apparatus deployed as part of their collaborative working practice. These material apparatuses were used to rule relations between designers, intermediaries and clients, with the circulation of these technical entities between different parties showing how governing relationships functioned over time. Whereas HDA and DRU developed and deployed such apparatus to manage and control the design process and seek agency over its outputs, HSA were controlled by the client, with material apparatus deployed to set out rulings and thus rule relations over them and their work.

In the case of HDA, numerous tools were developed and mobilized by the design consultancy to display their command over the working relationship with their clients, be they the Post Office, Blue Circle Cement or KLM. For the most part these apparatuses are conceived to materialize and evidence the group's

RECURRENT THEMES AND THREADS

control over certain scenarios and issues. So, for example, tools, diagrams and maps of different kinds are produced to make arguments for strategic design approaches that HDA favour. These tools are oriented around the efficacy and value of the design process and are designed to persuade the client, thus minimizing time-wasting and risk for the design consultants, ensuring financial prosperity for the firm.

By comparison, in the case of HSA, the intermediary Mather and Crowther used Guard Books to assert their position of power over the design consultants on behalf of their client. A chain of command thus existed here, running directly from the client, through the advertising agent, to the consultant design group, with this ruling relationship clearly inscribed within the advertising agent's Guard Books. In this case the advertising agency does not get involved in negotiations between the client and designer, but rather sets out guidance to be followed on behalf of their client. The given guidance is not presented as arguments that need to be justified, but rather rulings to be followed without question.

With the DRU case there is a certain mirroring of the HDA case, in that material apparatuses are deployed by the design group to evidence their own control over work scenarios. In the case of the DRU, some of the tools produced come to have a greater sense of power over a more expansive territory. So, for example, their corporate design standards manuals are used to inscribe programmes of action that are to be achieved by a range of actors outside the confines of their own organization.[2] The interesting aspect here is how the DRU came to rule relationships over other designers and producers working outside their own organization. In this sense the designer now acted as a kind of intermediary between the client and other designers tasked with implementation duties. A separation begins to emerge here between those more powerful designers working at a strategic planning level (and thus applying designerly ways of knowing to business problems), and those tasked more simply with the role of implementing others' instructions or ideas. In simple terms we see a divergence in power between design practitioners, with some moving closer to the boardroom, and some fixed ever more firmly to the drawing board. So, while some begin to successfully rule relationships over their clients, others continue to be more forcefully ruled.

While early graphic design practitioners like Schleger and Henrion had, by the end of the 1950s, slowly began to gain some independence from the advertising industry, by the 1960s they were competing for jurisdiction with practitioners from beyond traditional design contexts. Take for example the development of Michael Farr's design management business, Michael Farr (Design Integration), MFDI hereafter. The growth of MFDI can be considered indicative of the development of an increasingly contested field, with a broader base of practitioners from varied educational backgrounds now seeking to benefit from the opportunities of design's growing status. In this way Farr is comparable with other entrepreneurial design consultants such as James Pilditch and Wally Olins. Like Farr, Pilditch led his own successful group, Allied International Designers, while Olins led the influential consultancy Wolff Olins with his partner Michael Wolff. While Farr's business only prospered for ten to fifteen years, Pilditch and Olins played major roles in the later proliferation of corporate identity as a central tenet of the marketing mix, with Pilditch's Allied International Designers being the first design consultancy to float on the London Stock Exchange, thus reconceptualizing what it meant to practice as a design consultancy. The examples of Farr, Pilditch and Olins reflect a broadening out in the conception of brand identity design, away from the earlier preoccupations of graphic designers and their concern for the unification of corporate aesthetics, to a more fully rounded strategic conception of the brand as a nexus of different design sensibilities beyond the conventional graphic veneer.

The designer as leader

With greater jurisdiction over their work came greater administrative responsibility for designers, as we have seen in the case of Misha Black who seemed to rue his own transmutation from the role of the designer to that of the design leader. According to Black (1967), the position he described as the 'client/designer' was one wherein the designer distanced themselves from the concerns of the drawing board to direct their energies to the management of their employees. Though Black and his partner Milner Gray came to accept the growing disjunction between the management of design and what could be described as the more conventional production side, many commercial artists of pre-war were not as willing to give over their role in the production process. Thus, we saw Schleger and Henrion reluctant to cede the 'hands-on' craft of their design labour.

In each of the three consultancies the practitioners in question adapted their roles, as well as the skills and routines of their practice, to accommodate the collaborative group work required when handling unwieldy brand identity commissions. This is key, as it shows that the emergence of brand identity design had significant impacts on the patterns of practice for design consultants. So, as I show throughout the book, individuals grouped together to handle ever more complex brand identity programmes. For Schleger, this meant adopting something akin to an atelier, or master and apprentice model, with the craft and artistry of design taking precedence over the formal codification of work life. Henrion, by comparison, emphasized the depth of specialist knowledge spread across his team, frequently referring to the trained mathematicians within his group. Here he directed his energies into the formalization of work processes in a bid to appear more institutionalized to the corporate clients he wished to serve. For Black and Gray, group practice was not unfamiliar, given that they had trialled collaborative working first with Bassett Gray and then later with the Industrial Design Partnership; but whereas their earlier groups had operated as loose collectives of artists and designers, DRU, by comparison, sought to develop a more tightly knit team ethos. Although this was largely successful, by the late 1960s the harmony of the group came under stress as the they took on more institutional tendencies.

Of the three consultancies studied here it is apparent that the central personalities heading each group came to have an important influence over the identities of the collective groups they fronted, acting as the veritable face of their firms – although Black and Gray's names were not in the name of the company their personalities were synonymous with public impressions of the firm. As a result, the businesses in question struggled to sustain themselves once the involvement of the founders became uncertain.

The DRU were the only group of the three to have made significant attempts to impose a more distributed management structure, with the idea being that this would enable leadership to be reattributed and allow a succession to a younger generation. However, these efforts came late in their development as a group, with founder partners so deeply entrenched in their existing roles that they were unwilling, or perhaps unable, to step out of the limelight.

When HDA International became Henrion Ludlow Schmidt, Henrion stepped aside, taking on an advisory role that enabled Chris Ludlow and Klaus Schmidt to take the firm in new directions. There seems to have been little attempt to smooth this transition, with Ludlow and Schmidt moving the operation away from its long-standing base at Henrion's home in Hampstead. It was perhaps the disjunction between the two phases of the group that had allowed its new incarnation to prosper, with the group still active until Schmidt's passing in 2007.

Schleger by comparison appears to have had little desire to sell on his business, rejecting hierarchical systems outright and considering the practice a family to be nurtured, as opposed to a corporate institution to be sold on or sustained.

Models of group practice

In terms of practising in groups, we saw a varied range of models in the consultancies presented, from the informal and organic, to the more mechanical and codified. Thus, we had the case of Schleger, who rejected formal hierarchy, embracing instead the idea of his studio as a family and his employees as his children or *'kinder'*. By comparison, we saw Henrion reporting on the new technocratic methods he had developed to coordinate both his design work and the collection of employees working under his command. Finally, we observed the case of the DRU, as led by Black and Gray, and their attempts to embrace a non-hierarchical and transparent group structure, where the values of all practitioners were considered equal. So, whereas Schleger and Henrion had operated their businesses as one-man teams, placing themselves as the central figureheads, the DRU relied on the diarchy of Black and Gray, with Read and Brumwell acting in support as business partners with a financial interest in the venture.

In their influential text *The Management of Innovation*, Burns and Stalker (1961) explain how technology firms of the 1960s had moved away from conventional mechanistic forms of governance to more flexible and organic structures better equipped to deal with growing instability and more rapid rates of change. Yet, as we saw in the practices presented here, within the domain of design during the same period the inverse trend can be witnessed, with design organizations seeking to present themselves as *more* bureaucratic and rule governed than they had previously been. This is not to suggest that design practitioners moved from one extreme to another, but rather that they adapted gradually to more closely resemble the formalized structures and operations of their corporate clients.

Centralized and formalized organizational structures are said to privilege efficiency gains above all, whereas decentralized, unformalized structures are more well suited to fostering creativity and invention. According to Jerald Hage's (1965) axiomatic theory of organizations, the individualized commercial art practices of pre-war can be understood as high on invention, but low on efficiency. By comparison the technocratic corporate design practices of the post-war era can be understood as an attempt to find a more equitable balance between invention and efficiency, as per Tushman and O'Reilly's (1996) 'organisational ambidexterity', wherein highly flexible and adaptive organizations manage to be simultaneously inventive and efficient.

In all three cases the four key figureheads were of central importance to the public image of their firms. As a result, they have typically been celebrated as individual design heroes, rather than design leaders fostering creative collaboration amongst a wider team. In the case of DRU, Black and Gray spent most of their careers working in tandem, yet the Design Council published individual monographs about their work and the V&A Museum holds separate archives of their working lives. Challenging the dominant design hero narrative is thus problematic in this context and it is necessary to concede that the personas and status of the individuals were actually paramount to the companies' success.

From socio-cultural to economic capital

As design slowly began to gain traction as a recognized professional activity it went through a process of increasing commercialization, from which the highly prized cultural capital of commercial art came to be challenged by more explicit drives towards the imperatives of economic capital. During this period the imperatives of some designers were radically modified, as they sought to rationalize design labour processes and manage the risks inherent in their work. Business values thus began to take precedence over traditional design values and the principles of social betterment that had initially followed in the aftermath of the Second World War.[3] As we saw in Part One of the book, many British design practitioners distrusted the increasingly commercialized nature of design in the 1950s and 1960s, questioning whether the burgeoning corporate opportunities of the design world conflicted with their own sense of ethics and social purpose.

Within the three consultancies presented here we saw how the practitioners involved had engaged with corporate communication design in their own particular ways. So, whereas Schleger's studio was against standardization and the all-powerful corporation, Henrion's studio embraced the opportunities of big business, seeking to model his group on the institutions for whom they wished to work. One factor worth consideration here is their respective ages at the time, with Henrion being sixteen years younger than Schleger and more in the prime of his career at the time. DRU, meanwhile, comprised of Misha Black (b. 1910), who could be considered the same generation as Henrion (b. 1914), and Milner Gray (b. 1899) who was a contemporary of Schleger (b. 1898). Together, their group transitioned towards techno-scientific methods as the business grew in scale and became more established. So, although they had once loathed the 'stereotyped' treatment of chain stores, they gradually came to embrace corporate standardization as a core facet of their approach to brand identity design.

Design practitioners rooted in specialist forms of craftsmanship are known to have struggled to balance commercial imperatives with their puritanical craft ideals, but this was not an issue for the emergent new design entrepreneurs – as characterized by Pilditch and Olins – who appear to have had few qualms about the morality or ethics of design and consumption. The emergence of these increasingly entrepreneurial individuals forced art-school-trained design practitioners to direct their energies towards more strategic, business-minded endeavours in order to remain competitive and continue to have a say over the governance of their work.[4] So, while the emergence of the design entrepreneur was an occurrence of great significance, I have also shown how individual commercial artists and designers transmuted towards new ways of practice that incorporated more entrepreneurial dimensions.

Despite their efforts to be more business-like, many of the burgeoning design groups of the 1950s and 1960s struggled with profitability. DRU, the first group to really get going in Britain after the war, had by 1951 become a firm of supposed worldwide repute. However, the socio-cultural success of their work was not matched in economic terms, with records showing a loss over their first decade of operation. Like many groups of the era, they favoured a certain utopian idealism, being described as, 'less of a business enterprise or a firm than a common way of thinking about design' (Beresford Evans, cited in Brumwell, 2010: 56). Still, they managed to grow their staff base and increase their turnover through the 1960s and 1970s, posting profits between 1957 and 1969.[5] As they developed to become more viable in economic terms, their approach hardened. With more technocratic forms of governance and communication in place, tensions began to emerge that put strain on the non-hierarchical ethos of the group. The social idealism that was evident in their early endeavours and exemplified by the utopian exhibitions of the 1940s and 1950s, slowly gave way to a more institutionalized culture of work. Black soon recognized that the rationale supporting design labour was at least equally significant to clients as the actual work itself, leading some practitioners to exaggerate or even fabricate the reasons for their design decisions – much like we have seen in the case of HDA and their rationalizations of the KLM logotype. As Black (cited in Blake, 1983: 63) explains, 'the acceptance of his [the designer's] work will depend not on rational judgement but on his own powers of persuasion, on his capacity for convincing argument, which often must deliberately falsify the real reason for his decisions'.

Hans Schleger, meanwhile, is noted to have had a certain nonchalance for the economies of design, with employees commenting on his relative disregard for cost efficiency – hence, he worked in the studio at weekends to calculate how many of the hours actually worked could reasonably passed on to their clients. In this sense Schleger accepted that certain costs could not be passed to the client, treating his business as a labour of love rather than a strict profit-making enterprise. As the business operated from his home, junior design staff were known to have acted as babysitters to his children, with family and creative life blurring into one. Though F. H. K. Henrion had begun from a similar base to Schleger as a successful individual commercial artist, he embraced the opportunities of brand identity design more fully, adapting his working practices to reflect and benefit from changes in the industry. Having practised commercial art with a sense of fluidity and individuality earlier in his career, his design methods now became more formalized and systematic. Though he lamented the demise of the poster as a heroic individualistic medium, he had been quick to capitalize on the economic possibilities of programmatic brand identity design. The group he founded in 1951 was slow to develop at first, but by the late 1950s his vision of group practice became more fully realized with a slew of major identity design commissions. As a consequence, HDA prospered well into the 1970s, before Henrion ceded control of the group in 1981.

Although design had become an increasingly viable career path in the postwar era, by the 1970s, many practitioners were becoming less optimistic about the possibility for design to make a meaningful contribution to the world. Looking ahead to the prospects of the coming decade, Misha Black wrote in 1972:

> The period of enthusiasm and self-confidence is ended. Few designers now believe that they can change the world by the excellence of their work. Even if they are comforted by the conviction that their activity influences the environment and is thus an aspect of the external forces which affect social development, they know that they are part of political and economic systems which permit execrable social conditions which are tolerated only because they are a fractional improvement on the past.
>
> (Black, cited in Blake, 1983: 258)

Black's despondent attitude about the prospects of the British design scene compare unfavourably with the optimistic principles that had underscored his earlier work at DRU. When they first formed, DRU promoted themselves as having been established for a higher purpose beyond financial gain, asserting their intent to serve the needs of consumers and society at large; Black's later pessimism indicates how radically some designers' attitudes had changed. Established designers now came to reluctantly accept that they were part of more complex systems beyond their control, with Black rueing the increasingly commercialized nature of the design scene and complaining about how the designer's ideas were hindered by the whims of their uneducated clients.

Writing in the early 1980s, design commentator James Woudhuysen (1981: 17) echoes Black's sentiments about the state of the profession, claiming: 'In industry ruthlessness is the order of the day and in government the "wets" lose every Cabinet debate; in design, by contrast, ideology of any kind has long been dead.' Moreover, contemporary commentators (Blauvelt, 2012; van der Velden, 2012; Shaughnessy, 2014) note how designers' control and authority over the corporate design process began to wane from the mid to late 1970s onwards, with practitioners focused on strategy and design management coming to the fore and taking a commanding role in the management and direction of corporate design programmes. So, while designers of the 1960s had become accustomed to an unprecedented level of influence and control, this state of relations was relatively short lived. Van der Velden argues that designers' diminishing control over corporate design work led many to seek alternate opportunities, ushering in a new era where the notion of the 'designer as author' was particularly celebrated and valorized – he suggests that in current times, so called, 'important design' is typically generated by the designer himself and serves as nothing more than a 'commentary in the margins of visual culture' (van der Velden, 2012: 17).

8
THE LEGACY OF POST-WAR CORPORATE DESIGN METHODS

The emergence of a new approach

In this book I have surveyed how practice routines radically changed for consultant designers in post-war Britain as they embraced a systems approach, shifting their focus from individual design artefacts to comprehensive brand identity programmes. I have shown how British designers were at the forefront of efforts to codify the practice of brand identity design, developing new esoteric knowledge that bestowed professional legitimacy upon the practice. By developing methods centred around the coordination of brand collateral, these designers took a lead in establishing brand identity design as a recognized practice complete with its own unique rhetoric and principles. The adoption of the programmatic approach was aligned with the development of British consultant design groups specialized in graphic design. Whereas in the United States design groups had emerged in the interwar years as a response to investment in industrial design and the streamlining of products, in Britain, by comparison, consultant design groups took root after the Second World War in line with rising investment in corporate communications.

My focus within this book has been the phase of emergence during which the new consultant design groups sought to develop programmatic branding as a tenable labour practice that would provide a stable income stream for their burgeoning businesses. This phase of early development concentrated around the 1950s and 1960s, a period previously neglected by most scholars of branding. To understand how designers' practice routines were transformed during the period I focused on the material apparatus of everyday design work life within three representative design consultancies. While such apparatus may seem inconsequential or unappealing aesthetically, in their ability to script stable and routine labour patterns, such entities can be seen as the bedrock of neoliberal capitalism. Anyone attempting to understand the behaviour of corporate designers would do well to consider the apparatus upon which their cognitive and creative processes are scaffolded.

Through the three representative design consultancies we saw how various technical entities were deployed to exert power within the workplaces of commercial design. Some entities were used to closely control and monitor designers' work, while others were developed and used by designers themselves to seek heightened control within client and collaborative relationships. In these examples there were several instances where the moral and ethical basis of post-war design came under stress from growing commercial imperatives. The idea of a holistic corporate image now took centre stage and with 'the whole' taking precedence over its constituent 'parts', the ad hoc individualism of pre-war came under increasing strain. Much of the early focus lay in consistent application of recurrent design elements that would foster recognition among consumers of the brand. Yet some practitioners understood that design standardization could lead to sterility.

Hans Schleger's group reoriented their practice to work around these pressures, moving focus away from corporate marketing clients and taking on smaller brand design work in the cultural sector, which enabled them to retain a playful spirit of dynamism. By comparison, Henrion's group embraced corporate standardization, adopting techno-scientific methods to manage the design process and mitigate against the increased risks associated with larger projects involving more staff and resources. The individualistic wit of Henrion's early work was dropped in favour of an aesthetic homogeneity founded upon tightly controlled design standards and brand specification manuals. Meanwhile, like Schleger, the Design Research Unit had been opposed to the 'stereotyped' homogeneity of corporate design and their first branding programmes reflected this, adopting a controlled eclecticism that combatted the repetitiveness of formulaic design systems. But over time the polyvocal tone apparent in their early work began to fade from view as they embraced a more controlled and homogenous approach in line with the systematic methods of Henrion's group.

The programmatic approach to brand design prioritized systems of consistency above all else and the corporate identity manual was key to this, acting as an inscription device that controlled and managed all conceivable manifestations of a company's image. So, whereas the pre-war 'commercial artist' had been understood as a virtuoso responsible for heroic individual designs, the post-war 'graphic designer' typically worked collaboratively with brands and was concerned with notions of organization, structure and method. These imperatives aligned well with the needs of their corporate clients, and over time the International Typographic Style gradually became dominant in Britain as well as in the wider Western world. Traditional serif fonts went out of fashion, as the painterly whimsy of commercial art was replaced with modernist sans serifs and bold splashes of colour (Henrion's branding work for KLM exemplifying this transition, or equally Design Research Unit's work for British Railways). The stark modernist simplicity of the International Typographic Style fitted perfectly with the need for brand visuals to be reproduced easily at different scales and across different media. Furthermore, the grid systems upon which the style was based provided a rational framework from which designers could develop their work. The corporate identity manual became a dominant focus for designers working with brands in the late 1960s, through to the 1970s and 1980s. During this period many corporations began to scale operations, transitioning from local to national, or national to international markets. For those graphic designers wanting to practice professionally, programmatic brand identity design was thus a means to capitalize on new investment within corporate communications.

Part of my focus in this book has been directed to an explication of the interrelationship between advertising and graphic design professionals, with the three case studies showing how graphic designers used brand identity design to gain jurisdiction and competitive advantage over the advertising agencies they had previously depended upon. By adopting more rigorous, systematic and technical approaches, many were able to establish their work as distinct from that of interrelated but competing marketing professionals. As a result, corporate design strategy developed as a long-term business endeavour, distinct from the more cyclical nature of the advertising campaign. Graphic designers thus stole a march on advertising practitioners by claiming this endeavour as their own, emphasizing the enhanced recognition and loyalty they could foster for their clients by coordinating their brand identity. During this period graphic designers came to dominate brand identity design practice in Britain, but their monopoly over the domain was short-lived, with the practice soon becoming contested by those from outside the design bubble.

The three case studies

Henrion Design Associates

The evolutionary development of HDA demonstrates the radical shifts that occurred in the ways and means of graphic design consultants practising in the post-war era. We saw F. H. K. Henrion and his colleague Alan Parkin developing a new approach to practice to tackle the scale and complexity of brand identity design programmes. So, while Henrion the pre-war commercial artist used traditional intuitive methods, Henrion the post-war graphic designer embraced the principles of technical rationality, employing mathematically trained rationalizers and seeking to scientize the design process.

I deployed the notion of mapping as a collective enabling enterprise to show how complex information systems had been central to the consultancy's methodology. The mapping systems devised by HDA gave them control over the flow of project data, thus enabling them to direct working relationships with their clients. Examples discussed included indexing systems to catalogue data about their client's operations, as well as diagrams to re-present data back to clients in a more persuasive fashion. HDA's control over the collection and shaping of data gave them agency over their clients, enabling them to act like kingmakers seeking to redistribute power within the organizations for whom they consulted. Yet these initiatives were not without complication, for as we saw in the case of the Post Office, a breakdown in communications led to much of the work being disregarded.

Most of their new apparatus centred around servicing clients, but some were used to aid in the smooth running of internal operations, with network planning tools being adopted to enhance their capacity to manage their own employees, carefully pre-plan project schedules, distribute staff, as well as estimate time and cost to clients. This was a significant shift away from the ad hoc methods of the individual commercial artist of pre-war times. Their next move was to rationalize the act of innovation at the heart of their service. Creative decision making had typically been made on an intuitive basis, but in the KLM example we saw how intuitive design decisions were reframed to be presented as the outcome of codified, technically rational processes, when in actuality they had emerged from tacit, unplanned acts. This attempt to mask the human judgement inherent within design thus reinforced the perceived illegitimacy of intuitive methods, as well as the apparent vulnerability of creative work.

Many of the business practices developed at HDA can be understood as forms of risk management conceived to optimize success with their clientele, reducing unwanted friction and economic uncertainty wherever possible. They published articles about their methods in English and German trade journals, marketing themselves internationally and influencing wider patterns of practice in Britain and beyond. The influence of their methods also spread through those who had worked with them before going on to establish their own consultancies, with Sampson Tyrell being a strong case in point.

Hans Schleger & Associates

HSA embraced brand identity on their own terms, resisting the homogenization of corporate design and the explicit rationalization of design processes. Focusing on a pair of Guard Books I showed how the group were governed closely by the advertising agency Mather and Crowther (Mathers) acting on behalf of their client Mac Fisheries. Mathers set out 'rulings' to forbid certain design permutations, constraining the consultancy's creative work. This resulted in a tussle for power that led to inconsistency and a low level of standardization in terms of the precise implementation of the programme. Despite the hierarchical line of command, Schleger's team continued with their dynamic approach, playfully exploring different renderings of the firm's trademark.

By comparing design artworks with published press advertisements, I identified discrepancies in the implementation of the scheme, with poor standards of typographic reproduction and arrangement leading to imprecise execution. The difficulties involved in implementing large-scale brand identity programmes became apparent here, as well as the ramifications for those designers working with organizations scaling their business operations from a local level to a national or international scale. Various members of the team had been required to illustrate characters for the brand, leading to further inconsistencies in the implementation of the programme. Furthermore, practitioners working outside the Schleger studio had contributed designs for the client too, further diluting the coherence of the brand. Yet despite these discrepancies, the programme was considered a great success, with key figures from the design community commending the significance of the work.[1] It featured extensively in the international design press too, indicating the wider influence of British identity design.

We saw Schleger act as a reflective practitioner who shunned techno-scientific rationality to embrace a heterogeneous form of design coordination distinct from the homogeneity of typical corporate programmes. His ethos was to avoid strict standardization, leading him to adopt handwritten lettering for the Mac Fisheries identity. This was astute for two reasons. Firstly, it stopped the campaign from becoming repetitive, with each instance of lettering created anew. Secondly, the handwritten script referenced the fishmonger's chalk board, thus connecting his designs back to the product and insinuating a certain freshness, which was desirable for the seafood being publicized.

Over many decades HSA worked to create dynamic brand identity programmes that were coordinated, but never standardized. We saw how this approach could be traced back to Schleger's time on Madison Avenue in the 1920s, with the same method persisting well into the 1970s when he died. As the consultancy became more independent from the advertising industry, they sought to redirect their practice away from global corporations and towards organizations and institutions in the public and cultural sectors. In their work for these clients, they embodied a designerly form of practical rationality, not so far removed from the traditional intuitive methods of commercial artists. The identities they produced could be said to have a 'family resemblance' as opposed to a standardized consistency, thus mirroring the current trend for dynamic branding that balances consistent and variable elements to produce an image that is recognizable, but never static.

Design Research Unit

Misha Black and Milner Gray of the Design Research Unit (DRU) were accustomed to collaboration, with Gray having engaged in group practice since the 1920s and Black joining him by the 1930s. Whereas Henrion and Schleger's groups were one-man teams with a known personality at the head, the leadership of the DRU was more distributed, with the diarchy of Black and Gray leading the operation. Through the 1950s commercial artists relied on the advertising industry for employment, yet DRU's dependency on advertising was altogether different, with the financial backing of contacts at the Advertising Service Guild enabling them to set a divergent path. It is ironic that investment from the advertising industry enabled them to be independent of this industry in a way that other design practitioners simply could not.

Given the relatively stable basis of their operation, the DRU were more forceful in setting out their ideals, positioning themselves as a non-hierarchical, transparent and highly principled design consultancy. Much of their initial work centred on cultural and social reconstruction, with commissions for exhibitions like Britain Can Make It and the Festival of Britain. Staff numbers fluctuated at first, but they were the only British design group of significant scale during this time. So whereas Henrion and Schleger led operations from design studios based at their homes (Henrion at Pond Street in Hampstead and Schleger at Sydney Mews in Fulham), DRU moved business premises frequently as they went through phases of growth and contraction in their early years.

The cross-disciplinary expertise within the group allowed them to take on distinctive commissions that brought two- and three-dimensional design together in unison. Their early architectural work on exhibitions set a precedent here, with the commission for The Civic Trust at Magdalen Street, Norwich leading on from this. Later the multidisciplinary nature of the firm led to organizational issues, with a rupture emerging between the architectural and graphic design sections, which were operating largely independent of one another by the mid to late 1960s.

Project reports and manuals prepared for clients showed how DRU transitioned from soft, suggestive forms of governance, to stricter assertive 'rulings' that forbid those implementing their designs from straying from their guidance. Initially they had been opposed to the perils of homogenous design, loathing 'stereotyped' chain stores like Woolworths. But their idealism soon waned as they took on large national projects such as the identity for British Railways. Their position now moved closer to that of Henrion, as they embraced opportunities presented by brand identity programmes and transformed their working methods to capitalize on this.

I analysed several examples of the consultancy's brand reports and manuals, demonstrating how these files had become more carefully and precisely designed over time. The notion of inscription was used here to show how DRU's brand identity manuals can be interpreted as 'immutable mobiles' conceived to assert control over others from a distance.

Here we saw a marked difference by comparison to the case of Schleger who had been ruled by the advertising agent in their capacity as intermediary. By comparison, DRU lay down rules and specifications to control other designers, applied artists and manufacturers.

From emergence to proliferation

While group practice in design became gradually more commonplace in the 1950s and 1960s, the number of consultancies increased rapidly in subsequent decades as opportunities in the corporate design sector grew. As the number of groups increased, so too did the relative scale of these groups, with staff numbers increasing as design offices expanded. The early post-war phase of development covered in this book ultimately set in motion a long-term development path that led to the proliferation and entrenchment of corporate design practice. My book can thus be interpreted as a pre-history of contemporary neoliberal corporate design, with the legacy of these post-war design methods having a lasting impact on patterns of practice up to the present day.

Through the 1970s, 1980s and 1990s the corporate design sector developed, with agencies competing in what had become an important domain for the national economy. Graphic design grew in status too, and as opportunities to study the subject expanded, it slowly became more widely recognized as a form of labour and potential career path for aspiring creatives. The emergence of entrepreneurially minded design practitioners from outside conventional design contexts was highly significant too, and what followed on the whole was a closer imbrication between design and management practices, with James Pilditch's Allied International Designers and Wally Olins's Wolff Olins being front-runners in this regard. The success of entrepreneurs like Pilditch and Olins reflects a broadening out that occurred in the ways that design was now conceptualized. So, while design had originally been understood narrowly as an aesthetic practice dependent on craftsmanship and production, in the latter half of the twentieth century it became increasingly understood in broader terms, reflecting Herbert Simon's (1968) contention that anyone who 'devises courses of action aimed at changing existing situations into preferred ones' is a designer.

The idea that anyone can design continued to develop in the twenty-first century, with 'design thinking' (Brown, 2009) popularized as a way for stakeholders from a range of contexts to partake in the creative process. Adopting collaborative methods, design thinking advocates facilitate workshops that attempt to simulate the cognitive phases of professional designers' work.

THE LEGACY OF POST-WAR CORPORATE DESIGN METHODS

The popularity for design thinking outside the design studio has played a role in the so-called 'dematerialization' of design, with strategy, conceptual thinking and design research often understood as hierarchically dominant over production and implementation. As a consequence, production is commonly perceived by non-designers to be a 'downstream' activity wherein concepts and ideas are realized in isolation from senior stakeholders working 'upstream' who conceive and plan them.[2]

These developments led typographic scholar Catherine Dixon (2017) to argue that strategy alone does not sufficiently capture the gamut of the designerly act. Dixon claims that workmanship and craft are fundamental to design activity, with ideas being transformed through the process of making as designers' fashion the means to carry out a design. Such an approach sees design not only as the implementation of a plan, but rather as an open-ended, inventive and improvizational practice of situated and material doing, where making informs the shape and concept of the outcome.

Within corporate branding circles, entrepreneurs like Olins sought to downplay the visual aspects of brand design, arguing that the corporate identity of the 1970s constituted a more fully rounded behavioural form, as opposed to the shallow aesthetic preoccupations of earlier 'House Style' practitioners. Olins (1979) thus underscored the need for well-rounded strategic practitioners with business skills that transcended a concern for the purely visual. The business success of strategically-minded branding experts coincided with the development of design management from the mid 1960s onwards. British practitioners played an important role in the professionalization of these practices, with Michael Farr's *Design Management* (1966) and *Control Systems for Industrial Design* (1973) being key early texts. The Royal Society of Arts initiated their Presidential Awards for Design Management in 1965 and the Design Management Institute was established a decade later in 1975. Elsewhere Peter Gorb and Naomi Gornick were important, with Gorb having pioneered the teaching of design management at the London Business School from the late 1970s onwards, and Gornick working to similar effect at the Royal College of Art in the late 1980s.

The early development of design management theory and practice is an important subject with untapped potential. Individuals like Farr, Gorb and Gornick provide an entry-point to understanding the historical relationship between the management of design and design management as two interconnected but distinct concerns, one focusing on the value of design to management, and the other on the value of management to design. Although there is an established body of scholarship surrounding the contemporary theorization of design management and the idea of 'managing as designing' (Boland and Collopy, 2004), a more detailed practice theoretical approach to the study of the subject's history would reveal more about how patterns of practice developed in this area.[3]

Anne Marie Dorland's (2009) work on the management of design labour within the contemporary setting provides a strong example of what is possible.

Brand consultants soon adopted design management as a means to bolster their expertise and allow them to stand shoulder-to-shoulder with board room executives. With entrepreneurs like Pilditch and Olins embracing the cut-throat world of business, those wishing to compete had to get onboard or redirect their efforts elsewhere. The new strategic impetus of brand consultancy set in train a trend for the devaluation of the graphic designer within brand practice. Design consultants faced significant challenges, with the recession of the early 1980s leading some to downplay their design expertise and reorient their business offer around the managerial aspects of brand identity. This meant abandoning the graphic design training and ideals that had led them to the field and concentrating on strategic factors instead. This prompted designer John Lloyd (2009) to reflect upon the impact of design's diminishing status within the field:

> The territory, once the preserve of designers, has been colonised by management consultants, accountants, lawyers, business school professors and design managers. Today, you can find books about corporate identity or corporate branding, as it is now more widely known, that cover market research, strategy development, marketing, corporate positioning, brand architecture and brand valuation. These things are necessary in building a compelling identity but in the midst of all this sophisticated theory and analysis there is a danger that the contribution of the graphic designer and the significance of corporate design may be under-valued.

The emergence of the personal computer in the late 1980s was also significant. Designers began to adopt Apple computers and page layout software like QuarkXPress which revolutionized the production of communication design collateral and the workflows associated with it. By the late 1990s brands started to understand the increasing importance of the internet and digital media more broadly. The centrality of print design waned slowly over coming decades, to the point where today we live in a global society where corporate communication is often considered 'digital by default'. These generational changes have ushered in a world of post-print branding, with practitioners increasingly focused on brand experience design for digital products and apps.

During this time the distinction between advertising agencies and corporate design firms has blurred, with businesses from both camps competing for work in a terrain referred to simply as 'branding'. Despite the increased competition, design and advertising agencies continue to exhibit their own distinct occupational formulas and routines, with advertising firms having roles such as the 'planner', 'copywriter' and 'creative' that do not exist in the same way within branding and graphic design agencies.[4] Still, the creative advertising of post-war

Britain has been on the decline for some time, now being the preserve of the few independent agencies operating outside the hegemonic control of multi-national conglomerates. It is interesting that while Britain moved away from the model of the advertising agency as the dominant supplier and conduit for corporate communication, this model is said to have persisted in other countries such as India and Poland.[5]

Within Britain, economic uncertainty linked to Brexit and Covid-19 has led several design consultancies to merge, as was the case in 2018 when the conglomerate WPP, combined five agencies to form Superunion. The businesses at stake – Brand Union, The Partners, Lambie-Nairn, Addison and VBAT – were no industry minnows, but rather long-established, award-winning powerhouses with a significant historical legacy (their lineage can be traced back to Henrion Design Associates, with Terry Tyrrell and Sam Sampson who formed Sampson Tyrrell in 1976, later Brand Union, both cutting their teeth working for Henrion's agency in London). The cycle of mergers continued in 2021, when Landor merged with Fitch to form Landor Fitch (now rebranded as Landor) and Superunion merged again, combining with Design Bridge to form Design Bridge & Partners. Although such practices are implemented under the guise of consolidation and a concentration of expertise tailored to client demands, they can also be read as a sign of a contracting industry wherein corporate design expertise is increasingly homogenized and controlled by a small number of hegemonic conglomerates.

As we come to the mid 2020s a new doctrine is emerging in response to concerns around climate crisis, decolonization and mental health. Strategic brand consultants are coming clean about the destructive social and environmental impacts of corporate branding, offering up a mea culpa and attempting to reframe their expertise around the opportunity to make brands more 'net positive'. The mantra for branding practitioners today increasingly centres around 'people and planet', with 'regenerative practices' being the order of the day. The goal is to help brands 'thrive in balance', sustaining their economic performance, without further damaging our natural environment and human wellbeing. It remains to be seen whether brands and the agencies they commission can move beyond virtue signalling and tactics like greenwashing to play a genuine role in tackling these important societal crises. Those practitioners wishing to envisage another path would do well to revisit the social imperatives at the heart of early post-war brand design programmes. At their very best these projects prioritize a joyful form of design that is driven by social ideals, wit and eclecticism over standardization or corporate homogeneity.

NOTES

Chapter 1

1. Many scholars have focused on the role of brands in society, with attention directed to the impact of consumerism and changing patterns of brand consumption (Lury, 2004; Aronczyk and Powers, 2010), together with the potential of brands to shape personal and collective identities (Lury, 1996). This work has centred on the importance of the 1980s as a time when the concept of brand took on unprecedented levels of significance, with Arvidson (2006) arguing that the brand was first established as a central component of the social fabric during this period; Julier (2000) takes a similar stance. Arvidson posits Bret Easton Ellis's (1991) text *American Psycho* as an example of how brands became aligned to the pursuit of lifestyle and self-realization, and thus, entrenched as a part of global popular culture.
2. In his review of the V&A exhibition brand.new, Stephen Hayward (2001: 147) draws attention to the design firm Fitch's reference to brands as 'the new religion'. The concept of brands as a symbol of worship helps to establish the important position brands would come to occupy in contemporary society.
3. See for instance, US practitioner Saul Bass (1990) and British design commentator Avril Blake (1986: 42).
4. For more on the working routines of pre-war commercial artists, see Preston (2014).
5. DRU were not alone in embarking upon their first brand identity programme at this time; during the same year Hans Schleger & Associates began work on their identity programme for the sock maker W. Raven and Company.
6. Middleton (1967) is the only scholar I have identified to directly link the growth of group practice with the proliferation of brand identity programmes.
7. Describing the conditions of designers in the early half of the twentieth century Milner Gray (1980) recalls that they were typically working in isolation.
8. For an overview of the Design Methods Movement, see Cross (1993). For works by innovators in the movement, see texts by Alexander (1964), Archer (1965) and Jones (1970).
9. Henrion and Parkin (1968) allude to the importance of coordinating the workforce in an article discussed later in this book.
10. In the US the term 'corporate image' was important, but it is difficult to pin down any meaningful relationship between these phrases due to the way that different practitioners in different cultures have defined them.

11 Balmer (2010) suggests that the heightened interest in corporate image at this time was linked to several factors including: the English economist Kenneth Boulding's (1956) book *The Image*; the activities of the Opinion Research Corporation in the US; the work of Burleigh Gardner of Social Research Inc. in the US; and the writing of Pierre Martineau (1958) who undertook corporate image studies for the *Chicago Tribune*.

12 Balmer (1998) writes extensively on different conceptualizations of 'corporate identity', identifying seven different approaches, four of which note the importance of graphic design.

13 Olins (1979: 210) claims the term house style is 'superficial and implies drawing up designs for letterheads'.

14 Although 'branding' and 'brand identity' were not terms used in the post-war period, it was common to refer to 'brand-name' products.

15 See for instance works by Meggs (1983) and Drucker and McVarish (2009).

16 For early reference to the term 'graphic design', see for instance, Dwiggins (1922) and Raffé (1927).

17 For more on graphic design at the Royal College of Art, see Frayling (2007).

18 For Stiff (2009: 9), exhibition design, and especially the exhibition division of the Ministry of Information, had been critical in leading a generation of designers towards the 'small-business model of graphic design practice'.

19 For more on the concept of professional jurisdiction and the system of professions, see Abbott (2010). For a brief overview of the transition towards corporate design, see Preston (2011).

20 One notable example focused on ways of practice in the contemporary studio is Farías and Wilkie's (2015) book, *Studio Studies: Operations, Topologies & Displacements*.

21 One notable exception to this tendency is Paul Stiff's (1996) detailed account of the role of specification as a practice that influenced the development of graphic design.

22 For more on 'practical rationality', see Sandberg and Tsoukas (2011).

Chapter 2

1 See Haskett (1984) for an early example of the logo design textbook.

2 For an early example of the design agency showcase, see Peter Gorb's (1978) book on Pentagram. For an example of the brand showcase, see John Heskett's (1989) book on Philips.

3 This coming together of design and business, both thought broadly, is evidenced in other work around this time, with the UK-based *Cox Review of Creativity in Business* (Cox, 2005) being a crucial example of this, as well works by Martin (2009) and Neumeier (2009).

4 In terms of the role of the grid in the emergence of corporate design, some scholars argue that typographic practitioners Jan Tschichold (Remington, 2014) and Josef Müller-Brockmann (Shaughnessy, 2014) had a crucial role in laying the groundwork

NOTES

for a rational and objective approach to graphic design to emerge, with their interest in norms and standards linked to the rise of Swiss Style, also known as the 'International Typographic Style' or 'die neue Grafik' (Hollis, 2006).

5 An exhibition of the same name was held in London in 1959, organized by Alec Davis for the Design & Industries Association.

Chapter 3

1 In other work, Mills (2012: 9) suggests that whilst Britain experienced 'its fastest-ever economic growth' between 1950 and 1973, 'relative economic decline proceeded at a rapid rate vis-á-vis its European peer group'. This decline, he suggests, continued until the 1970s, when increased competition helped to reverse Britain's relative economic decline.

2 Marwick organized the first three parts of his book as follows: Social Consensus 1945–57; Roads to Freedom 1958–73; The Time of Troubles 1973–82.

3 Although Conekin et al. (1999: 1) agree that Britain was, during the period, divided between the values of the past and the future, they contend that the Coronation alone came to exemplify these two conflicting states.

4 Nixon (2013) underscores the fact that American advertising practices had already been influenced by the ideas of Europe, with émigrés from the continent bringing over new ideas about motivation research, modernism and the functionalism of the Bauhaus.

5 For more on the development of corporate design agencies in early twentieth century North America see Meikle (1979).

6 Bassett Gray transmuted first to become 'Industrial Design Partnership' in 1935, before later regrouping after the war as the Design Research Unit.

7 Other notable US practitioners include Donald Dohner, Lurelle Guild, George Sakier and John Vassos.

8 For more on the SIA, see Armstrong (2014).

9 Though the intention had been to make an example of Conran, the turn of events transpired to bring the legitimacy of the SIA under scrutiny, for Conran showed that it was possible to be more prosperous working as a designer outside the confinement of the SIA and its strict code of conduct (Armstrong, 2014).

10 Born in New York in 1900, Warde was a writer, scholar and champion of typographic printing. Upon graduation from Barnard College, she became head librarian of the American Type Founders Library. After moving to England in 1924 she found work as a writer, resulting in the production of numerous articles. Later she was employed by the Monotype Corporation, firstly as editor of their journal, then as Publicity Manager. Her appointment lasted over three decades from around 1927 to her retirement in 1960 (Gruendler, 2002).

11 This phrase translates loosely into the rhetoric of contemporary branding, where consultancies commonly refer to the 'look and feel' of a brand (Wheeler, 2018).

12 Dutton established his reputation designing packaging for clients during the 1930s and was considered a pioneer in the field. In 1938 he joined a new design

group, The Design Unit Limited. Consisting of engineers, industrial designers and commercial artists, those involved in the group continued with their individual practices, coming together to offer their services in unison as appropriate projects arose. This was an unusual alliance not afforded time to prosper, being dissolved with the onset of war. Dutton joined the Design Research Unit after the war where he worked on packaging as well as industrial design projects. He would later go on to practice independently, working for his clients such as Cadbury's. He was an early member of the Society of Industrial Artists (Newton, 1949).

13 The term 'idiom' was picked up by Christian Barman (1979: 115), who later explained how London Transport's director, Frank Pink, had instructed architect Charles Holden to join him in his search for 'a new architectural idiom' for the organization.

14 See, for instance, works by Barman (1979), Saler (1999) and Ovenden (2013).

15 Dutton's use of the word 'module' could be viewed as significant here in that it predates the concerns of later influencers. Swiss designers Karl Gerstner, Emil Ruder and Josef Müller-Brockmann have been credited with developing the notion of the modular grid (Evans and Sherin, 2008). Gerstner (1963), in particular, explored how modules influenced visual communication in his seminal text, *Programme entwerfen*.

16 Davis's first article was written on the evolution of the light aeroplane and published in *Design for Today* in 1933. In the 1930s he freelanced for publications such as *Shelf Appeal* and *The Architectural Review*. He later took on the role of editor for *The British Printer* and is known to have redesigned the magazine, a significant achievement for one not trained in design. This publication deeply influenced Davis's career trajectory, with his work as a design consultant being founded on a rich knowledge of printing and the mechanics of typography. By the mid-1950s he described himself as a 'writer and typographical adviser' (Davis, 1956: 14).

17 Given that Stuart Rose worked alongside Davis as Art Editor, it appears that Davis's journalistic expertise was more highly prized than his design skills. In June 1952, Davis and Rose were succeeded by Michael Farr and Peter Hatch, as Editor and Art Editor respectively (*Interview with Michael Farr*, 1991).

18 The concept of the print user was a relatively radical idea within the world of print, pre-dating the rise of 'user centred design' ideas that developed after the publication of Henry Dreyfuss's (1955) *Designing for People*.

19 For more on the history of Crawfords, see Schwarzkopf (2008).

20 Pride and Ferrell (2012) claim that there are three levels of brand loyalty: recognition, preference and insistence. They suggest that recognition is the most basic level, where a brand is readily recognized by the consumer, but not necessarily valued. Preference is the median level, where consumers show favourable opinions of the brand. Insistence, meanwhile, suggests that the consumer is unyielding in their loyalty for the brand in question. Roberts (2004: 66) refers to this as 'loyalty beyond reason', implying that the consumer is so unflinching in their allegiance to the brand that their support may become irrational, resulting in an unreasonable level of devotion.

21 Edited by Michael Farr and with a cover designed by F. H. K. Henrion, Davis's (1956) issue of *Design* is a powerful reminder of the closely knit social connections between influential designers within the British scene. Here in this one artefact several key protagonists are entwined.

22 Examples include Anthony Adams's 'An Industry in Print' articles, which analysed the way that firms within certain industries presented themselves; or Christian Barman's article on 'London Transport Publicity', which surprising failed to touch upon the concept of house style at all.

Part Two

1 Both firms have already been subject to oral history research (see, Roberts, 2001 and Sandino, 2005 respectively).

Chapter 4

1 Landor was advised to study with Milner Gray by the advertising creative Ashley Havinden. In 1935 Landor, together with Gray (and others) co-founded the Industrial Design Partnership (Gallagher, 2009). Industrial Design Partnership were an early, industry-leading design group that preceded the Design Research Unit.
2 HDA were established in 1951, replacing an earlier antecedent started in 1948, Studio H (Hope, 1996).
3 Suschitzky was an important documentarian who captured the spirit of British life in the twentieth century. Held in the collection of the National Portrait Gallery, it is not clear why this image was commissioned, or by whom, but it is not known to have been used for promotional purposes by Henrion.
4 In 1957 Erwin Wasey was merged with Ruthrauff & Ryan to form Erwin, Wasey, Ruthrauff & Ryan.
5 Henrion's response alluded to the fact that the Dutch design scene was not as well developed commercially as Britain's, with no design consultancies of the requisite institutional appearance yet established. Ben Bos (2011: 7) notes how Dutch design groups were a novelty in 1963, recalling how KLM's appointment of a British-based design group had led their designers to feel 'short-changed and underappreciated', but that the decision was understandable given that 'visual communication in Britain had entered a new phase as far back as the war years'.
6 The campaign as a serial concept that grows and evolves with repeating motifs, rhetoric and characters, can be traced back to the beginning of the early twentieth century and shares many similarities with the objectives of the brand identity programme. The most significant difference relates to their relative degrees of permanence. For more on the origins of advertising, see Schwarzkopf (2009).
7 Worthy of note here is Olle Eksell's (1967) modest book, *Corporate Design Programs*, which offered a hand-book style approach, taking the reader step-by-step through a hypothetical case study, demonstrating how a corporate design programme could be initiated and implemented.
8 Studio Vista was a relatively small imprint, publishing exclusively on leisure and design topics, while Reinhold published more broadly on non-fiction, with especially strong representation on art and architecture.

9. By comparison, the Society of Industrial Artists, led by designers themselves, was fundamentally about serving designers interests.
10. In correspondence with Parkin (2012), he confirmed to me, 'Yes, I did all the writing for publication or reports, first a draft which Henri would check and quite often change in emphasis or argument. He was very good at speaking but liked someone else to do the writing.'
11. First released as a series of seven separate articles in *Design* magazine between 1963 and 1964, Archer's texts were later published by the Council of Industrial Design in one single volume.
12. For example, in 'Design Consultants: A New Profession', Henrion (1959: 36) outlines how 'a new kind of design practice has developed in Britain', with the holistically minded General Consultant Designer now competing with more conventional Specialist Designers.
13. The parallels with the advertising profession are notable here, where 'planning' is an established disciplinary practice commonly understood as a form of research-driven strategizing that precedes the creative formulation of the advertising campaign.
14. Whereas the design coordination programme seeks to downplay the role of design by introducing the credibility of science, the contemporary design thinking movement can be understood to 'up-sell' design as a way to bring innovation into business contexts. Curiously both initiatives seek to tackle strategic design and business concerns with a combination of rational (explicit knowing) and intuitive thinking (implicit knowing) – it is notable that the HDA model seeks to mask any intuitive thinking, as if it were a sign of weakness.
15. In the case of the Post Office library, the indexing tools developed by HDA would become redundant, due to irreparable conflicts that emerged between different protagonists involved in the project. As Cabianca (2018) explains, Henrion conflicted with Stuart Rose, who acted as a design advisor for the Post Office. In their capacity as advisors to the same organization Rose and Henrion were at odds with one another, with Rose instrumental in blocking Henrion's proposals. Their conflicting interests were untenable, which meant HDA's ambitious design coordination programme made little meaningful impact on the organization. Their indexing system for the Blue Circle group was more successful, given the wide rollout of HDA's design proposals.
16. Graphic designers have typically been unerring in their desire to keep their operational methods concealed, preferring to garner attention through the visual appeal of the design artefacts they produce.
17. Though these latter two examples bear little resemblance to conventional understandings of map-making, they can be understood as products of a mapping process, in as much that they are recordings, or re-presentations, of a spatial happening (Corner, 1999).
18. According to Nicolini et al. (2012) boundary objects are artefacts that support collaboration across diverse specialist groups, serving as a bridge that spans intersecting social and cultural worlds.
19. Sampson Tyrell were acquired by global communications conglomerate WPP in 1986 and have since been through a series of corporate mergers with other design and marketing agencies.

Chapter 5

1. Kauffer was a prominent figure in the British commercial art scene, due largely to his poster designs for London Transport. Schleger later moved into a penthouse apartment in the same block as Kauffer and his partner Marion Dorn, sharing in the same artistic and intellectual social scene. Havinden remained a close professional contact for Schleger too, though surprisingly, Schleger does not appear to have worked with Crawford's in London, perhaps due to retainer contracts he had in place with other agencies.
2. As previously mentioned, the term 'graphic design' was not widely adopted in Britain until the mid to late 1950s, with the introduction of this new term ushering out the era of the 'commercial artist'.
3. Gray's symbol was combined with a common-colour scheme and distinctive lettering applied to shopfronts and vans. The use of these standardized elements created a unity of style uncommon for the time, making this an early example of effective brand identity design in Britain. Such an approach was not unprecedented, with Eric Gill's standardized alphabet for retailer W. H. Smith also being notable. Gill's first commission for Smith's began in 1903 when he created fascia lettering for the Paris store in the Rue de Rivoli. Between 1906 and 1913, Gill set out standard sample brush-drawn alphabets that other lettering artists could follow to standardize the lettering that appeared on shop fronts, kiosks, vehicles and signs.
4. Fred Taylor and Gregory Brown were popular and successful commercial artists, highly regarded for their poster designs for London Transport and the London & North Eastern Railway. Kennedy North, meanwhile, created designs for Shell Oil and the British Empire Exhibition.
5. 'Guard Book' is a term commonly used in advertising to describe a book or folder used to collate information about a particular campaign.
6. Henrion had a similar contract with another American advertising agency in London, Erwin Wasey.
7. When *Commercial Art* ran a feature on the group of commercial artists Bassett Gray they emphasized how each member of the group actively worked to cultivate their own individual style and approach (*The Work of the Bassett Gray Studio*, 1927).
8. It is notable that Schleger is valorized as a heroic individual designer by *Graphik* magazine (Maiwald, 1952), with no credit for the scheme going to his team of colleagues at HSA.
9. This closely mirrors F. H. K. Henrion's career, where he had acted as a consultant to advertising agents Erwin Wasey from 1954 to 1958, before later concentrating on his own studio practice and facing clients directly. In both cases the advertising agent acted as a bridge between studio work as an individual artist and professional group practice.
10. Schön's ideas originate from a tradition commonly associated with the work of John Dewey (1933).

Chapter 6

1. Gray's style was advertised at this time as 'romantic period work', which contrasts dramatically with the highly corporate visual language he would later come to embrace.

2. Blake and Blake (1969) note that the research element of DRU's practice never truly materialized in the manner they had first planned, primarily because they were more adept at other services and unable to extend themselves into so many different fields of work.

3. Negus (1997) notes that Gray served on various SIA committees until 1984, when he was 85 years old.

4. The Tcherny family changed their name to Black (the English translation of Tcherny) by deed poll.

5. The Festival was a formative experience for practitioners of the time, giving them a taste for the type of organizational challenges they would face later in their work lives. As Blake and Blake (1969: 26) explain, 'As co-ordinator of the upstream section, Black was faced with the kind of organisational problem that was to recur increasingly in the years that followed'. Black also had prior experience of collaborating with other designers, having taken on the role of coordinator for the 1938 MARS exhibition.

6. This follows the present day model of the 'T-shaped designer' where the horizontal cross bar of the letter 'T' represents the designer's breadth of knowledge and expertise, while the vertical stroke represents the depth of their technical and creative skills.

7. Gray was known particularly for his work in packaging design, but also had a strong command of typography and graphic design. Black, meanwhile, had made his reputation in exhibition design, and from a position of relatively little training successfully integrated himself into the professional networks of the London architectural scene. By the 1950s Black had a team of newly graduated architects working under his command, with Gray following suit with his own team of graphic designers (Timings, 2012). The backing of Read and Brumwell extended their network of influences and helped them capture a wider range of commercial opportunities.

8. Gaby Schreiber of Gaby Schreiber & Associates is important as a significant competitor to the DRU. She offered a broad range of services founded on her expertise in interiors and industrial design and was notable in her capacity as an independent female design consultant (Schreiber, 1991).

9. Garland's third categorization of practice is the *design consultancy group,* which employs many skilled people and situates itself closer to the advertising agency, in as much that it is seen to deploy pushier, hard-sell tactics and is likely to be floated on the stock exchange. Groups of this ilk began to take form only in the 1970s, and as such, they reside outside the study period of this book. Garland notes that medium sized groups like DRU increasingly had to work for larger sized businesses by the 1980s due to the culture of mergers and takeovers which had led to a diminishing number of the medium sized businesses considered their natural clients.

NOTES

10. The DRU Bulletin supports this notion of departments separated by floors. Reporting on the addition of a new work cafe, the author noted: 'it is hoped everyone will come for their coffee and tea break and to meet people from other floors whom they do not normally come into contact' (Black, 1964–76).

11. Halftone is a reprographic printing technique that simulates continuous tone imagery using dots, varying either in size or in spacing, thus generating a gradient-like effect.

12. Henrion featured in Bendixson's (1963: 34) article for *Design*, with his group structure described as 'a pyramid in love with a rakehead'. Henrion is noted as 'clearly the leader'.

13. Dick Negus and Philip Sharland formed Negus & Sharland in 1951, later becoming Negus & Negus, 1968 (Adams, 2011); Colin Banks and John Miles formed Banks & Miles in 1958 (Myerson, 2002); Derek Birdsall, George Daulby, George Mayhew and Peter Wildbur formed BDMW Associates in 1959 (Wildbur, 2005); Alan Fletcher, Colin Forbes and Bob Gill joined forces to become Fletcher/Forbes/Gill in 1962 (Dempsey, 2017), later to become Crosby Fletcher Forbes, 1968, and then Pentagram, 1972; Jimmy Main and Michael Wolff formed Main Wolff in 1963 (Garland, 1996: 75), later Wolff Olins; and Marcello Minale and Brian Tattersfield formed Minale Tattersfield in 1964 (*Obituaries: Marcello Minale*, 2001).

14. Henrion, for example, is known to have produced posters well into the latter part of his career, continuing to work on design proposals right up to the year of his death in 1990.

15. The October 1964 edition of the DRU Bulletin notes the release of a Japanese translation of the text. This is indicative of the international influence of design ideas emerging from Britain.

16. Schatzki (2002: 193) defends what he calls 'residual humanism' in which human agency is considered central. Postill (2010) meanwhile, claims that the first two waves of practice theorists understood the human body as the nexus of people's practice engagements with the world. By comparison, ANT scholars view the social and natural world as part of a constantly shifting network of relationships, seeing humans and non-humans as equal in agential terms.

17. This was the Civic Trust's first street refurbishing scheme but is said to have influenced over 500 other civic programmes.

18. The treatment of colour appears to have been dealt with more precisely, with each swatch labelled in accordance with the British Standards Institute's range of 101 Colours.

19. Milner Gray acted as chairman of a working party responsible for the development of the design programme.

20. The myriad of interrelated terms deployed within the field is a problem that persists to this day, with Balmer (2001) having drawn attention to the fog of confusion surrounding the discipline and its discourse.

21. Michelle Cotton (2012), for example, concludes her monograph of the group in 1972. With her study beginning in 1942, Cotton's dates closely resemble the focal period of this book (1945–1970).

22. This is a subject business theorist Chris Argyris (1957) covers well in his early work on the conflict between individual human needs and the requirements of organizations as systems.

23 See for instance, March, 1991.
24 Whereas Taylor's (1911) managerialist vision posited the organization as a machine deployed solely to achieve the purposes of the shareholders or owners, Follett (1940) considered the organization as a composite of the individuals of which it comprised.

Chapter 7

1 In 1957 Erwin Wasey merged with Ruthrauff & Ryan to become Erwin, Wasey, Ruthrauff & Ryan.
2 The same could also be said of HDA's corporate design manuals, though they have not been the focus of attention within this book.
3 Others (Shaughnessy, 2014) have also noted how the probity of early post-war designers was slowly eroded as corporate communications came to have an ever greater influence over the design profession.
4 Sparke (1983, 75) reflects on the shifting focus of design consultancy Lloyd Northover – a design group formed in 1975 on a traditional art school basis – and their move away from 'skilled work on the drawing board' towards 'research and analysis' to combat the financial challenges of the recession of the period.
5 For more on the economic development of DRU see Brumwell (2010) and Cotton (2012).

Chapter 8

1 This conflict between the tightly controlled public relations representation of events as opposed to the lived experience of the identity programme remains a discrepancy to this day.
2 The development of generative artificial intelligence threatens to make certain aspects of design production near instantaneous, further exacerbating the idea that production is a low cost, second-order discipline that can be separated from the strategic and conceptual aspects of design.
3 For more on design management theory see, Martin (2009) and Neumeier (2009).
4 Fore more on planning in advertising, see literature on Stanley Pollitt (Feldwick, 2000) and Stephen King (Lannon and Baskin, 2007).
5 For more on this, see Burgoyne (2011), *Who's Winning the Brand Identity Turf War.*

REFERENCES

Abbott, A. (2010), *The System of Professions: An Essay on the Division of Expert Labor*. Chicago: University of Chicago Press.
Adams, G. (2011), 'Obituary: Dick Negus', *The Independent*, 3 July. Available at: http://www.independent.co.uk/news/obituaries/dick-negus-designer-celebrated-for-his-work-with-british-airways-and-other-national-institutions-2306210.html (Accessed: 21 March 2025).
Akrich, M. (1992), 'The De-Scription of Technical Objects', in Bijker, W. E. and Law, J. (eds) *Shaping Technology/Building Society: Studies in Sociotechnical Change*. Cambridge, MA: MIT Press, 205–24.
Akrich, M., Callon, M. and Latour, B. (2002a), 'The Key to Success in Innovation Part I: The Art of Interessement', *The International Journal of Innovation Management*, 6 (2): 187–206.
Akrich, M., Callon, M. and Latour, B. (2002b), 'The Key to Success in Innovation Part II: The Art of Choosing Good Spokespersons', *The International Journal of Innovation Management*, 6 (2): 207–25.
Alexander, C. (1964), *Notes on the Synthesis of Form*. Cambridge, MA: Harvard University Press.
Anderson, S. (2000), *Peter Behrens and a New Architecture for the Twentieth Century*. Cambridge, MA: MIT Press.
Archer, B. (1954), 'Artist Versus Engineer', *Design*, 67: 13–16.
Archer, B. (1960), 'Consultant – but how General?', *Design*, 138: 65.
Archer, B. (1963), 'Systematic Methods for Designers', Part Two: *Design*, 174: 70–4.
Archer, B. (1965), *Systematic Method for Designers*. London: Council of Industrial Design.
Archer, B. (1968), 'The Structure of Design Processes', PhD thesis, Royal College of Art, London. Shelfmark: Document Supply DRT 484530.
Argyris, C. (1957), *Personality and Organization: The Conflict Between System and the Individual*. New York: Harper.
Armstrong, L. (2014), 'Designing a Profession: The Structure, Organisation and Identity of the Design Profession in Britain, 1930–2010', PhD thesis, University of Brighton. Available at: https://research.brighton.ac.uk/en/publications/designing-a-profession-the-structure-organisation-and-identity-of (Accessed: 21 March 2025).
Arnheim, R. (1954), *Art and Visual Perception: A Psychology of the Creative Eye*. Berkeley: University of California Press.
Aronczyk, M. and Powers, D. (2010), *Blowing up the Brand: Critical Perspectives on Promotional Culture*. New York: P. Lang.
'Art designer forms own firm' [press cutting] (1957), *World's Printing News*, 5 April. Hans Schleger Archive, V&A Archive of Art & Design, 2009/11/9.

Artmonsky, R. (2011), *FHK Henrion (Design)*. Woodbridge: Antique Collectors' Club Ltd.

Arvidson, A. (2006), *Brands: Meaning and Value in Media Culture*. Oxford and New York: Routledge.

Baker, S. (1989), 'Re-reading the Corporate Personality', *Journal of Design History*, 2 (4): 275–92.

Bakker, W. (2005), 'Man to manual?: The diverse roots of corporate identity'. Paper read at the *European Business Historians Association Annual Conference*, 1–3 September, Frankfurt.

Bakker, W. (2006), 'The obvious choice: an evolutionary approach towards trademark design', *Design and Evolution: Design History Society Conference*, Delft University of Technology, The Netherlands, 6 September 2006. Available at: https://www.academia.edu/1397545/W._Bakkker_The_obvious_choice_An_evolutionary_approach_towards_trademark_design_paper_DHS_Conference_Delft_2006 (Accessed: 21 March 2025).

Bakker, W. (2011a), *Droom van helderheid: Huisstijlen, ontwerpbureaus en modernisme in Nederland, 1960–1975*. Rotterdam: nai010.

Bakker, W. (2011b), 'Housestyle Imported: The Long Way of KLM', in *Droom van helderheid: huisstijlen, ontwerpbureaus en modernisme in Nederland, 1960–1975* [Bakker's own English translation]. Rotterdam: NAI Uitgevers.

Balmer, J. M. T. (1998), 'Corporate Identity and the Advent of Corporate Marketing', *Journal of Marketing Management*, 14: 963–96.

Balmer, J. M. T. (2001), 'Corporate Identity, Corporate Branding and Corporate Marketing – Seeing Through the Fog', *European Journal of Marketing*, 35 (3–4): 248–91.

Balmer, J. M. T. (2010), 'Weathervanes or Signposts? Constructs or Philosophy? Scrutinizing and Explicating Corporate Image, Corporate Identity, Corporate Communications, Corporate Reputation, Corporate Brands and Corporate Marketing', in Podnar, K. and Balmer, J. M. T. (eds) *Contemplating Corporate Marketing, Identity and Communication*. Oxford and New York: Routledge, 3–35.

Balmer, J. M. T. (2014), 'Corporate Identity, Corporate Identity Scholarship and Wally Olins (1930–2014)', *Corporate Communications: An International Journal*, 20 (1), 4–10.

Balmer, J. M. T. and Greyser, S. (2003), *Revealing the Corporation: Perspectives on Identity, Image, Reputation, Corporate Branding and Corporate Level Marketing*. London: Routledge.

Banks, C. (1994), *London's Handwriting: The Development of Edward Johnston's Underground Railway Block-letter*. London: London Transport Museum.

Barbieri, C., Klevgaard, T., Messell, T. and Preston, D. (2014), 'Designing Identity', in Faust, C. (ed) *Prova 2: Humanities Research Forum Journal 2014*. London: Royal College of Art, 63–7.

Barman, C. (1954), Letter from Christian Barman to Hans Schleger, 21 November. Hans Schleger Archive, V&A Archive of Art & Design, 2009/11/9.

Barman, C. (1979), *The Man Who Built London Transport: A Biography of Frank Pick*. London: David & Charles.

Barmas, J. (1952), 'Men of Vision: Hans Schleger' [press cutting], *Sales Appeal*, November/December. Hans Schleger Archive, V&A Archive of Art & Design, 2009/11/9.

Bendixson, T. (1963), 'Professional Practice: Does the Versatile Designer Make Sense?', *Design*, 177:29–38.

REFERENCES

Bernays, E. (1923), *Crystallizing Public Opinion*. New York: Liveright Publishing.
Best, K. (2015), *Design Management: Managing Design Strategy, Process and Implementation*. London and New York: Fairchild Books.
Black, J. (2012), 'For the People's Good: Hans Schleger (1898–1976), Poster Design and British National Identity, 1935–60', *Visual Culture in Britain*, 13:169–90.
Black, L. and Pemberton, H. (2004), *An Affluent Society?: Britain's Post-war 'Golden Age' Revisited*. Aldershot: Ashgate.
Black, M. (1958), 'Manual for Magdalen Street, Norwich'. Milner Gray Archive, V&A Archive of Art and Design, AAD/1999/103.
Black, M. (1964–76), DRU Bulletin. Misha Black Archive, V&A Archive of Art and Design, AAD/1980/3.
Black, M. (1967), 'Leadership and Rewards', in Middleton, M. (ed) *Group Practice in Design*. London: Architectural Press, 285–93.
Black, M. (1973), Letter from Misha Black to Marcus Brumwell, 8 January. Marcus Brumwell papers, TGA 20046, Tate Archive.
Black, M. (1974), 'The Designer and the Client, Misha Black, 1956', in Banham, R. (ed) *The Aspen Papers: Twenty Years of Design Theory from the International Design Conference in Aspen*. London: Pall Mall Press, 63–71.
Blaikie, N. (2009), *Designing Social Research*, 2nd edn, Cambridge: Polity Press.
Blake, A. (ed) (1983), *The Black Papers on Design: Selected Writings of the Late Sir Misha Black*. Oxford: Pergamon Press.
Blake, A. (1984), *Misha Black*. London, Design Council.
Blake, A. (1986), *Milner Gray*. London, Design Council.
Blake, J. and Blake, A. (1969), *DRU: The Practical Idealists: Twenty Five Years of Designing for Industry*. London: Lund Humphries.
Blauvelt, A. (2012), 'Brand New Worlds', in Blauvelt, A. and Lupton, E. (eds) *Graphic Design: Now in Production*. Minneapolis: Walker Art Center, 190–208.
Boland, R. and Collopy, F. (2004), *Managing as Designing*. California: Stanford Business Books.
Bos, B. (1994), *The Image of a Company: Manual for Corporate Identity*. London: Phaidon Press.
Bos, B. (2011), *TD 63–73: Total Design and its Pioneering Role in Graphic Design: An Insider's View*. London: Unit Editions.
Bos, B. and Bos, E. (eds) (2007), *AGI: Graphic Design Since 1950*. London: Thames & Hudson.
Boulding, K. (1956), *The Image*. Ann Arbor: University of Michigan Press.
Bourdieu, P. (1986), 'The Forms of Capital', in J. Richardson (ed) *Handbook of Theory and Research for the Sociology of Education*. New York: Greenwood, 241–58.
Bourdieu, P. (1990), *The Logic of Practice*. Cambridge: Polity Press.
Brech, E., Thomson, A. and Wilson, J. F. (2010), *Lyndall Urwick, Management Pioneer: A Biography*. Oxford: Oxford University Press.
Breward, C. and Wood, G. (2012), *British Design from 1948: Innovation in the Modern Age*. London: V&A Publishing.
Brown, T. (2009), *Change by Design: How Design Thinking Transforms Organizations and Inspires Innovation*. New York: HarperCollins.
Brumwell, J. (2010), *Bright Ties Bold Ideas: Marcus Brumwell, Pioneer of 20th Century Advertising, Champion of the Artists*. Truro: The Tie Press.
Bueger, C. and Gadinger, F. (2015), 'The Play of International Practice', *International Studies Quarterly*, 59 (3): 449–60.

Burgoyne, P. (ed.) (2011), 'Who's winning the brand identity turf war?', *Creative Review* [blog], 1 December. Available at: https://www.creativereview.co.uk/whos-winning-the-brand-identity-turf-war (Accessed: 21 March 2025).

Burns, T. and Stalker, G. M. (1961), *The Management of Innovation*. London: Tavistock Publications.

Burke, C. (1992), 'Peter Behrens and the German Letter: Type Design and Architectural Lettering', *Journal of Design History*, 5 (1): 19–37.

Cabianca, D. (2018), 'An Examination of the 1960s Attempt at a new Brand Identity for the General Post Office', *Journal of Design History*, 31 (2): 121–37.

Callon, M. (1981), 'Struggles and Negotiations to Define What is Problematic and What is Not: The Socio-Logic of Translation', in Knorr, K. D., Krohn, R. and Whitley, R. (eds) *The Social Process of Scientific Investigation*. Dordrecht: Springer, 197–219.

Callon, M. (1986), 'Some Elements of a Sociology of Translation: Domestication of the Scallops and the Fishermen of Saint Brieuc Bay', in Law, J. (ed) *Power, Action and Belief: A New Sociology of Knowledge?* London, Routledge, 196–233.

Carter, D. E. (1977), *Corporate Identity Manuals*. New York: Art Direction Book Company.

Chia, R. C. H. and Holt, R. (2009), *Strategy Without Design: The Silent Efficacy of Indirect Action*. Cambridge: Cambridge University Press.

Conekin, B., Mort, F. and Waters, C. (1999), *Moments of Modernity: Reconstructing Britain, 1945–1964*. London: Rivers Oram Press.

Corner, J. (1999), 'The Agency of Mapping: Speculation, Critique and Invention', in Cosgrove, D. (ed) *Mappings*. London: Reaktion, 1999, 213–52.

'Corporate Image Issue' (1959), *Print*, XIII (3), May–June.

Cotton, M. (2012), *The Design Research Unit: 1942–72*. London: Koenig Books.

Cox, G. (2005) *Cox Review of Creativity in Business: Building on the UK's Strengths*. London: Design Council.

Crafts, N. and Mills, T. (1996), 'Europe's Golden Age: An Econometric Investigation of Changing Trend Rates of Growth', in Van Ark, B. and Crafts, N. (eds) *Quantitative Aspects of Post-War European Economic Growth*. Cambridge: Cambridge University Press.

Cross, N. (1993), 'A History of Design Methodology', in de Vries M. J., Cross N., Grant D. P. (eds) *Design Methodology and Relationships with Science*. NATO ASI Series (Series D: Behavioural and Social Sciences), 71. Dordrecht: Springer, 15–27.

Cross, N. (2001), 'Designerly Ways of Knowing: Design Discipline Versus Design Science'. *Design Issues*, 17 (3): 49–55.

Davis, A. (1950a), 'Printing Design and the Print User', *Design*, 14: 2–5.

Davis, A. (1950b), 'Van Lettering as Part of a Consistent Design Policy', *Design*, 19: 8–9.

Davis, A. (1952), 'Typography and House Style in Industry', *The Penrose Annual*, 46: 36–8.

Davis, A. (1956), *Design* [House Style special issue], 95.

Davis, A. (1957a), 'House Style for Household Appliances', *Design*, 98: 36.

Davis, A. (1957b), 'House Style for Confectionary', *Design*, 100: 57

Davis, A. (1957c), 'House Styles Evolving', *Design*, 104: 38–40.

Davis, A. (1957d), 'House Style for a Printer', *Design*, 108: 44–6.

Davis, A. (1958a), 'House Style Programmes and Progress', *Design*, 113: 33–6.

Davis, A. (1958b), 'House Style by Remote Control', *Design*, 118: 45–7.

Davis, A. (1959), 'House Style: The Face of the Firm', *Design*, 124: 32–7.

Davis, A. (1960), 'Public House Style', *Design*, 139: 40–1.

REFERENCES

Deleuze, G. and Guattari, F. (2004), *A Thousand Plateaus*. London: Continuum.
De Majo, W. (2009), Willy De Majo Archive, University of Brighton Design Archives, GB 1837 DES/WMD.
Denzin, N. K. (1989), *The Research Act: A Theoretical Introduction to Sociological Methods*. Englewood Cliffs, NJ: Prentice Hall.
Department of Typography & Graphic Communication (n.d.), 'Banks and Miles Graphic Design Archive', Collections and Archives, Department of Typography & Graphic Communication, University of Reading.
Dewey, J. (1933), *How We Think*. Chicago: Henry Regnery.
Dixon, C. (2017), 'Strategy is Never Enough', *Eye*, 94 (24): 22.
Dorland, A. (2009), 'Routinized Labour in the Graphic Design Studio', in Julier, G. and Moor, L. (eds), *Design and Creativity: Policy, Management and Practice*. Oxford: Berg, 105–21.
Dreyfuss, H. (1955), *Designing for People*. New York: Simon and Schuster.
Drucker, J. and McVarish, E. (2009) *Graphic Design History: A Critical Guide*. New York: Pearson Prentice Hall.
Durepos, G. and Mills, A. J. (2012), *ANTi-history: Theorizing the Past, History, and Historiography in Management and Organization Studies*. Charlotte: Information Age Publishing.
Dutton, N. (1946), 'Living Design—London Transport', *Art & Industry*, 41 (244): 98–122.
Dwiggins, W. A. (1922), 'New Kind of Printing Calls for New Design', *Boston Evening Transcript* (29 August).
Easen, P. and Wilcockson, J. (1996), 'Intuition and Rational Decision-making in Professional Thinking: A False Dichotomy?' *Journal of Advanced Nursing*, 24 (4): 667–73.
Easton Ellis, B. (1991), *American Psycho*. New York: Random House.
Eksell, O. (1967), *Corporate Design Programs*. London: Studio Vista.
Escobar, A. (2018), *Designs for the Pluriverse: Radical Interdependence, Autonomy, and the Making of Worlds*. Durham, NC: Duke University Press.
Evamy, M. (2007), *Logo*. London: Laurence King.
Evans, P. and Sherin, A. (2008), *Forms, Folds, Sizes*, 2nd edn, Beverley, MA: Rockport.
Farías, I. and Wilkie, A. (eds) (2015), *Studio Studies: Operations, Topologies & Displacements*. London: Routledge.
Farr, M. (1955), *Design in British Industry: A Mid-Century Survey*. Cambridge: Cambridge University Press.
Farr, M. (1966), *Design Management*. London: Hodder and Stoughton.
Farr, M. (1973), *Control Systems for Industrial Design*. Epping: Gower Technical Press.
'Feature: Erik Spiekermann' (2014), *Creative Review* [blog], 1 November 2014. Available at: https://www.creativereview.co.uk/erik-spiekermann (Accessed: 21 March 2025).
Feldwick, P. (2000), *Pollitt on Planning: Three Papers on Account Planning*. Oxfordshire: Admap.
Felsing, U. (2010), *Dynamic Identities in Cultural and Public Contexts*. Baden: Lars Muller.
Findeli, A. and Bousbaci, R. (2005) 'L'Eclipse de L'Objet dans les Théories du Projet en Design' (The Eclipse of the Object in Design Project Theories), *The Design Journal*, 8 (3): 35–49.
Follett, M. P. (1940), *Dynamic Administration: The Collected Papers of Mary Parker Follett*. New York: Harper.
Franklin, U. M. (1999), *The Real World of Technology*. New York: House of Anansi.

Frayling, C. (2007), 'Richard Guyatt' [obituary], *The Guardian*, 27 October.

Frenzel, H. K. (1931), 'Interview of the month: Hans Schleger' [press cutting], *Gebrauchsgraphik*, December. Hans Schleger Archive, V&A Archive of Art & Design, 2009/11/9.

Gallagher, B. (2009), *Walter Landor: Portrait of a Pioneer* [Landor company documents]. Available at: https://web.archive.org/web/20101230143820/http://www.landor.com/one/?do=aboutus.walterlando (Accessed: 5 February 2025).

Gantz, C. (2014), *Founders of American Industrial Design*. Jefferson, NC: McFarland & Co.

Garland, K. (1964), *First Things First: A Manifesto*. London: Independently published and distributed.

Garland, K. (1996), *A Word in your Eye: Opinions, Observations and Conjectures on Design, from 1960 to the Present*. Reading: University of Reading.

Garland, K. (2012), 'Last Things Last', *Eye*, 83 (21): 78–83.

Garland, K. (2017), 'Michael Farr (Design Integration)' [work profile]. Available at: https://web.archive.org/web/20190909211556/http://www.kengarland.co.uk/KGA-graphic-design/michael-farr (Accessed: 21 March 2025).

Geertz, C. (1973), *The Interpretation of Cultures*. New York: Basic Books.

Gerstner, K. (1963), *Programme entwerfen* [Designing Programmes]. Teufen: A. Niggli.

Gorb, P. (ed) (1978), *Living by Design: The Pentagram Partnership*. London: Lund Humphries.

Goslett, D. (1960), *Professional Practice for the Designer*. London: Batsford.

Gowing, M. (1956), 'The Creative Mind in Advertising: Hans Schleger', *Art & Industry* (December), 204–9.

Grant, J. and Vodeb, O. (2023), *What Is Post-Branding?: How to Counter Fundamentalist Marketplace Semiotics*. Eindhoven: Set Margins' publications.

'Graphic Art Annuals' [press cutting] (1954), *Printing World*, 26 March. Hans Schleger Archive, V&A Archive of Art & Design, 2009/11/9.

Gray, M. (1935), 'Bassett Gray Becomes a Partnership' [unidentified press cutting], 23 May. Milner Gray Archive, V&A Archive of Art and Design, AAD/1999/8.

Gray, M. (1950), 'Report on proposed design policy and estimated expenditure on sales promotion equipment and material for 1950'. Milner Gray Archive, V&A Archive of Art and Design, AAD/1999/81.

Gray, M. (1956), 'A report and recommendations on the establishment of a design policy for Watney, Combe, Reid & Company Limited.' Milner Gray Archive, V&A Archive of Art and Design, AAD/1999/85.

Gray, M. (1964), 'British Railways Board, Corporate Identity Programme, Design Manual'. Milner Gray Archive, V&A Archive of Art and Design, AAD/1999/113.

Gray, M. (1970), 'SIAD: The First Forty Years', *Designer*, October.

Gray, M. (1977), Photocopy of a letter sent from Milner Gray to F. H. K. Henrion, 27 August. Milnhive, V&A Archive of Art and Design, AAD/1999/8.

Gray, M. (1980), 'Preface', in Holland, J. (ed) Minerva at Fifty – The Jubilee History of the Society of Industrial Artists and Designers, 1930 to 1980. Westerham: Hurtwood Publications, viii–ix.

Gray, M. (1999) Milner Gray Archive, V&A Archive of Art and Design, AAD/1999/8.

Gruendler, S. (2002), 'Beatrice Warde', *First Annual Friends of St Bride Conference*, September 24 and 25.

Hage, J. (1965), 'An Axiomatic Theory of Organizations', *Administrative Science Quarterly*, 10: 289–320.

REFERENCES

Harwood, J. (2011), *The Interface: IBM and the Transformation of Corporate Design, 1945–1976*. Minneapolis: University of Minnesota Press.

Hasler, C. (1950), *Specimen of Display Letters Designed for the Festival of Britain*. Taunton: Festival of Britain.

Haskett, M. S. (1984), *Design Your Own Logo: A Step-by-step Guide for Businesses, Organizations and Individuals*. Seattle: International Self-Counsel Press.

Hastings Bristol, L. (ed) (1960), *Developing the Corporate Image: A Management Guide to Public Relations*. New York: Scribner.

Havinden, A. (1952–3), 'The Designer's Part', in Society of Industrial Artists (ed), *Designers in Britain 4*. London: Allan Wingate, pp. iii–vi.

Havinden, A. (1953), Letter from Ashley Havinden to Hans Schleger, 16 December. Hans Schleger Archive, V&A Archive of Art & Design, 2009/11/9.

Havinden, A. (1955), 'The Importance of "Company Handwriting"', *The Penrose Annual*, 49: 58–61.

Hayward, S. (2001), 'The Branding of Modern British Culture: Consumer Citizenship and the Age of Anxiety – A Response to the Exhibition brand.new at the V&A', *Journal of Design History*, 14 (2): 141–9.

Heller, S. (1995a), 'Advertising: Mother of Graphic Design', *Eye*, 17 (5): 26–37.

Heller, S. (1995b), *Paul Rand*. London and New York: Phaidon.

Heller, S. (2011), 'The Master Race's Graphic Masterpiece', *Design Observer* [blog], 7 February. Available at: https://designobserver.com/the-master-races-graphic-masterpiece (Accessed: 21 March 2025).

Henning, W. (ed) (2016), *British Rail Corporate Identity Manual*. London: Henning Limited.

Henrion, F. H. K. (1956), 'Graphic design in England' [conference paper/presentation notes], *6th International Design Conference in Aspen*. F. H. K. Henrion Archive, University of Brighton Design Archives, GB 1837 DES/FHK.

Henrion, F. H. K. (1959), 'Design Consultants: A New Profession', *Impulse*, February, 36–40.

Henrion, F. H. K. (1968), 'Designpolitik – Ziele, Kriterien, Methoden' [photocopy of unattributed journal article]. F. H. K. Henrion Archive, University of Brighton Design Archives, GB 1837 DES/FHK.

Henrion, F. H. K. (1979), 'FHKH Book – 13 September 1979' [unpublished manuscript]. F. H. K. Henrion Archive, University of Brighton Design Archives, GB 1837 DES/FHK.

Henrion, F. H. K. (1990), Interview with Mike Hope, in Hope, M. (ed) *F. H. K. Henrion: Five Decades a Designer* [Video VHS]. Flaxman Productions.

Henrion, F. H. K. and Parkin, A. (1967), *Design Coordination and Corporate Image*. London: Studio Vista.

Henrion, F. H. K. and Parkin, A. (1968), 'Systematic Methods for Design Coordination', *DIA Yearbook 1967/68*. London: Design and Industrial Association, 33–42.

Heskett, J. (1989), *Philips: A Study of the Corporate Management of Design*. London: Trefoil.

Hewison, R. (1977), *Under Siege: Literary Life in London 1939–45*. London: Weidenfeld & Nicolson.

Hewison, R. (1981), *In Anger: Culture in the Cold War, 1945–60*. London: Weidenfeld & Nicolson.

Hewison, R. (1986), *Too Much: Art and Society in the Sixties, 1960–75*. London: Methuen.

Hollis, R. (1994), *Graphic Design: A Concise History*. London: Thames & Hudson.

Hollis, R. (2006), *Swiss Graphic Design: The Origins and Growth of an International Style, 1920–1965*. London: Laurence King.

Hope, M. (ed) (1996), *F. H. K. Henrion International Design Archive* [Compact Disc], ICOGRADA International Design Archive.

'How "Operation Mac Fish" was planned and launched' [press cutting] (1954), *Advertiser's Weekly*, 4 February. Hans Schleger Archive, V&A Archive of Art & Design, 2009/11/9.

Howes, J. (2000), *Johnston's Underground Type*. London: Capital Transport.

Hutheesing, O. K. (1990), *Emerging Sexual Inequality Among the Lisu of Northern Thailand*. Leiden: E. J. Brill.

Hyland, A. and Bateman S. (2011), *Symbol*. London: Laurence King.

'Interview with Michael Farr' [transcript] (1991), 15 August. Michael Farr Archive, V&A Archive of Art & Design, AAD 7-1989.

Jacobsen, E. (ed) (1952), *Seven Designers Look at Trademark Design*. Chicago: P. Theobald.

Janser, A. and Junod, B. (eds) (2009), *Corporate Diversity: Swiss Graphic Dand Advertising by Geigy, 1940–1970*. Baden: Lars Müller.

Jones, J. C. (1970), *Design Methods: Seeds of Human Futures*. New York and Chichester: John Wiley & Sons.

Julier, G. (2000), *The Culture of Design*. London: Sage.

Julier, G. (2007), 'Design Practice Within a Theory of Practice', *Design Principles & Practices: An International Journal*, 1 (2): 43–50.

Julier, G. (2017), *Economies of Design*. London: Sage.

Julier, G. and Narotzky, V. (1998), 'The Redundancy of Design History', *Practically Speaking Conference*, Wolverhampton University, December. Available at: www.designculture.info/reviews/ArticleStash/GJVNRedundancy1996.pdf (Accessed: 21 March 2025).

Kamekura, Y. (1965), *Trademarks and Symbols of the World*. New York: Van Nostrand Reinhold.

Kaplan, A. (1963), The Conduct of Inquiry: Methodology for Behavioral Science. New York: Chandler.

Kaufmann Jr., E. (1948), 'Borax – or the Chromium-Plated Calf', *Architectural Review*, August: 88–93.

Kepes, G. (1944), *The Language of Vision*. Chicago: Paul Theobald and Company.

Khazraee, E. and Gasson, S. (2015), 'Epistemic Objects and Embeddedness: Knowledge Construction and Narratives in Research Networks of Practice', *The Information Society: An International Journal*, 31 (2): 139–59.

Kiechel, W. (2010), *Lords of Strategy: The Secret Intellectual History of the New Corporate World*. Boston, MA: Harvard Business Press.

Kimbell, L. (2009), 'Beyond design thinking: Design-as-practice and designs-in-practice', *CRESC Conference*: *Objects – What Matters? Technology, Value and Social Change*, University of Manchester, 1–4 September. Available at: http://www.lucykimbell.com/stuff/CRESC_Kimbell_v3.pdf (Accessed: 21 March 2025).

Kinross, R. (1988), 'From Commercial Art to Plain Commercial', *Blueprint*, 48: 29–36.

Kinross, R. (1990), 'Emigré Graphic Designers in Britain: Around the Second World War and Afterwards', *Journal of Design History*, 3 (1): 35–57.

Klanten, R. (ed) (2002), *Los Logos*. Berlin: Gestalten Verlag.

Klein, N. (1999), *No Logo*. New York: Picador.

Kussin, W. (1954), 'Das Firmengesicht', *Graphik*, 8: 424–7.

REFERENCES

Kuwayama, Y. (1973), *Trade Marks & Symbols*. New York: Van Nostrand Reinhold.
Kynaston, D. (2007), *Austerity Britain, 1945–1951*. London: Bloomsbury.
Kynaston, D. (2009), *Family Britain, 1951–1957*. London: Bloomsbury.
Kynaston, D. (2013), *Modernity Britain, 1957–1959*. London: Bloomsbury.
Labuz, R. (1993), *The Computer in Graphic Design: From Technology to Style*. New York: Van Nostrand Reinhold.
Laidlaw, J. (2010), 'Agency and Responsibility: Perhaps You Can Have Too Much of a Good Thing', in Lambek, M. (ed) *Ordinary Ethics: Anthropology, Language, and Action*. New York: Fordham University Press, 143–64.
Laing, J. and Saunders-Davies, R. (1986), *Graphic Tools & Techniques*. Poole: Blandford Press.
Lannon, J. and Baskin, M. (eds) (2007), *A Master Class in Brand Planning: The Timeless Works of Stephen King*. Chichester: John Wiley & Sons.
Latour, B. (1983), 'Give Me a Laboratory and I will Raise the World', in Knorr-Cetina, K. D. and Mulkay, M. (eds) *Perspectives on the Social Study of Science*. London: Sage, 141–70.
Latour, B. (1986), 'Visualisation and Cognition: Drawing Things Together', in H. Kuklick (ed) *Knowledge and Society Studies in the Sociology of Culture Past and Present*. Greenwich, CT: Jai Press, 1–40.
Latour, B. (1990), 'Technology is Society Made Durable', *The Sociological Review*, 38 (1): 103–31.
Latour, B. (1992), 'Where are the Missing Masses? The Sociology of a few Mundane Artifacts', in Bijker, W. E. and Law, J. (eds) *Shaping Technology/Building Society: Studies in Sociotechnical Change*. Cambridge, MA: MIT Press, 225–58.
Latour, B. and Woolgar, S. (1986), *Laboratory Life: The Construction of Scientific Facts*. Princeton, NJ: Princeton Architectural Press.
Lave, J. and Wenger, E. (1991), *Situated Learning: Legitimate Peripheral Participation*. Cambridge: Cambridge University Press.
Law, J. (1992), 'Notes on the Theory of the Actor Network: Ordering, Strategy and Heterogeneity', *Syst* 5 (4): 379–93.
Law, J. (2009), 'Actor Network Theory and Material Semiotics', in Turner, B. S. (ed) *The New Blackwell Companion to Social Theory*. Chichester: Wiley-Blackwell.
Lippincott, J. W. and Margulies, W. P. (1958a), *Sense* [Corporate Identity: Part One], 13, New York: L&M.
Lippincott, J. W. and Margulies, W. P. (1958b), *Sense* [Corporate Identity: Part Two], 14, New York: L&M.
Lloyd, J. (2009), *The Art of Corporate Design*. Available at: https://www.johnlloyd.uk.com/reflection/2 (Accessed: 21 March 2025).
Lorenz, M. (2021), *Flexible Visual Systems: The Design Manual for Contemporary Visual Identities*. Karlsruhe: Slanted Publishers UG.
Lott, J. (1982), 'Interview: Drawing People Together', *Design*, 402: 25.
Lubliner, M. J. (1994), *Global Corporate Identity: The Cross-Border Marking Challenge*. Beverly, MA: Rockport Publishers.
Luna, P. (2011), 'Marks, Spaces and Boundaries', *Visible Language*, 45 (1–2): 139–60.
Lury, C. (1996), *Consumer Culture*. Cambridge: Polity.
Lury, C. (2004), *Brands: The Logos of a Global Economy*. Abingdon: Routledge.
Maguire, P. and Woodham, J. (1997), *Design and Cultural Politics in Postwar Britain: The 'Britain Can Make It' Exhibition of 1946*. London: Leicester University Press.
Maiwald, H. (1952), 'Extract of letter from Mr Heinrich Maiwald' [to Hans Schleger], Hans Schleger Archive, V&A Archive of Art & Design, 2009/11/9.

Maiwald, H. (1953a), 'Zero: Wirbt für frische fische: Neuer werbestil für Mac Fisheries', *Graphik*, 1: 16–27. Hans Schleger Archive, V&A Archive of Art & Design, 2009/11/9.

Maiwald, H. (1953b), 'Zero's publicity campaign for Mac Fisheries' [English transcript of article for *Graphik*, 'Zero: Wirbt für frische fische: Neuer werbestil für Mac Fisheries']. Hans Schleger Archive, V&A Archive of Art & Design, 2009/11/9.

MacCarthy, F. (1986), 'Introduction: Pushing the Tank Uphill: The British Tradition in Design', in Royal Society of Arts (ed) *Royal Designers On Design.* London: The Design Council, 1–26.

MacCarthy, F. (2001), 'Hans Schleger – The Art of Desire', in Schleger, P. (ed) *Zero: Hans Schleger, A Life of Design*. Aldershot: Lund Humphries, 11–17.

March, J. G. (1991), 'Exploration and Exploitation in Organizational Learning', *Organization Science*, 2 (1): 71–87.

Margolin, V. (1994), 'Narrative Problems of Graphic Design History', *Visible Language*, 28 (3): 233–43.

Maria Ricci, F. and Ferrari, C. (1973), *Top Symbols & Trademarks of the World*. Milan: Deco Press.

Martin, R. (2009), *The Design of Business: Why Design Thinking Is the Next Competitive Advantage*. Boston, MA: Harvard Business Press.

Martineau, P. (1958), 'The Personality of the Retail Store', *Harvard Business School Press*, January–February, 47–55.

Marwick, A. (1982), *British Society since 1945*. London: Pelican.

Massey, A. (1996), *The Independent Group: Modernism and Mass Culture in Britain, 1945–1959*. Manchester: Manchester University Press.

Mather and Crowther (1951–58), Mac Fisheries Guard Books, History of Advertising Trust, Raveningham, Norfolk.

McLuhan, M. (1951), *The Mechanical Bride: Folklore of Industrial Man*. New York: The Vanguard Press.

Meggs, P. B. (1983), *Meggs' History of Graphic Design*. New York: John Wiley & Sons.

Meggs, P. B. (1990), 'Saul Bass on Corporate Identity', *AIGA Journal of Graphic Design*, 8 (1): 4.

Meikle, J. (1979), *Twentieth Century Limited: Industrial Design in America 1925–1939*. Philadelphia: Temple University Press.

Mercier, A. G. and Nunnally, R. S. (1965), 'The Critical Path Method: Its Fundamentals', Masters thesis, United States Naval Postgraduate School, Monterey. Available at: https://core.ac.uk/download/pdf/36705239.pdf (Accessed: 5 February 2025).

Merholz, P. and Skinner, K. (2016), *Org Design for Design Orgs: Building and Managing In-House Design Teams*. Sebastopol: O'Reilly.

Middleton, M. (1967), *Group Practice in Design*. London: The Architectural Press.

Middleton, M., Lord, P. and Pilditch, J. (1971), *Professionalism and the Designer* [report of a commission by the Society of Industrial Artists and Designers]. London: SIAD.

Mills, T. (2012), 'British Relative Economic Decline Revisited: The Role of Competition', *Explorations in Economic History*, 49 (1): 17–29.

Moor, L. (2007), *The Rise of Brands*. Oxford: Berg.

Moor, L. (2008), 'Brand Consultants as Cultural Intermediaries', *The Sociological Review*, 56 (3): 408–28.

Moving Brands (2009), *Living Identity*. London: Moving Brands.

Moving Brands (2012), 'Mitigating against risk in social media', *Moving Brands* [website]. Available at: https://web.archive.org/web/20140821015537/http://www.movingbrands.com/insights/mb-white-paper-mitigating-against-risk-in-social-media/ (Accessed: 21 March 2025).

REFERENCES

Myerson, J. (2002), 'Obituary: Colin Banks', *The Independent*, 16 March. Available at: https://www.independent.co.uk/news/obituaries/colin-banks-9272633.html (Accessed: 21 March 2025).

Nakanishi, M. (1979), *Corporate Design Systems 1: Case Studies in International Applications*. Tokyo: SANNO Institute of Business Administration.

Nakanishi, M. (1985), *Corporate Design Systems 2: Identity through Graphics*. New York: PBC International.

Naylor, G. (1966), 'The Designer v Jack With the Paint Brush', *Design*, 210: 40–51.

Negus, D. (1997), 'Obituary: Milner Gray', *The Independent*, 7 October. Available at: http://www.independent.co.uk/news/obituaries/obituary-milner-gray-1234647.html (Accessed: 21 March 2025).

Neumeier, M. (2009), *The Designful Company. How to Build a Culture of Nonstop Innovation*. Berkeley, CA: New Riders.

Newton, J. (1949), 'The Intellectual Approach', *Art & Industry*, 47 (282): 230–3.

Nicolini, D. (2009), 'Zooming In and Out: Studying Practices by Switching Theoretical Lenses and Trailing Connections', *Organization Studies*, 30 (12): 1391–418.

Nicolini, D. (2012), *Practice Theory, Work, and Organization: An Introduction*. Oxford: Oxford University Press.

Nicolini, D., Mengis, J. and Swan, J. (2012), 'Understanding the Role of Objects in Cross- Disciplinary Collaboration', *Organization Science*, 23: 612–29.

Nixon, S. (2013), *Hard Sell: Advertising, Affluence and Transatlantic Relations, c. 1951–69*. Manchester: Manchester University Press.

Nonaka, I. (1994), 'A Dynamic Theory of Organizational Knowledge Creation', *Organization Science*, 5 (1): 14–37.

Nonaka, I. and Takeuchi, H. (1995), *The Knowledge-Creating Company: How Japanese Companies Create the Dynamics of Innovation*. New York: Oxford University Press.

Nonaka, I. and von Krogh, G. (2009), 'Perspective—Tacit Knowledge and Knowledge Conversion: Controversy and Advancement in Organizational Knowledge Creation Theory', *Organization Science*, 20 (3): 635–52.

'Obituaries: Marcello Minale' (2001), *The Telegraph* [newspaper], 4 January. Available at: http://www.telegraph.co.uk/news/obituaries/1313052/Marcello-Minale.html (Accessed: 21 March 2025).

Olins, W. (1978), *The Corporate Personality*. London: Design Council.

Olins, W. (1979), 'Corporate Identity: The Myth and the Reality', *Journal of the Royal Society of Arts*, 127 (5272): 208–23.

Ovenden, M. (2013), *London Underground by Design*. London: Penguin Books.

Packard, V. (1957), *The Hidden Persuaders*. New York: David McKay Company.

Parkin, A. (2012), Email to David Preston, 4 May.

Paulus, P. B. and Nijstad, B. A. (2003), *Group Creativity: Innovation Through Collaboration*. Oxford: Oxford University Press.

Perkins, S. (2024), *North: Extracts From Visual Identities*. London: Unit Editions.

Pevsner, N. (1952), 'Lettering and the Festival on the South Bank', *Penrose Annual*, 46: 28–34.

Pilditch, J. (1970), *Communication by Design: A Study in Corporate Identity*. London: McGraw-Hill.

Polanyi, M. (1966), *The Tacit Dimension*. London: Routledge & Kegan Paul.

Portelli, A. (1998), 'What Makes Oral History Different', in Perks, R. and Thomson, A. (eds) *The Oral History Reader*, London: Routledge, 63–74.

Postill, J. (2010), 'Introduction: Theorising Media and Practice', in Bräuchler, B. and Postill, J. (eds) *Theorising Media and Practice*. Oxford and New York: Berghahn, 1–34.

Poynor, R. (2004), *Communicate: British Independent Graphic Design since the Sixties*. London: Laurence King.

Preda, A. (1999), 'The Turn to Things: Arguments for a Sociological Theory of Things', *The Sociological Quarterly*, 40 (2): 347–66.

Preston, D. (2011), 'The Corporate Trailblazers', *Ultrabold*, 10 (Summer): 14–21.

Preston, D. (2014), 'Tom Purvis: At Work', in Artmonsky, R. and Preston, D. (eds) *Tom Purvis: Art for the Sake of Money*. London: Artmonsky Arts, 38–110.

Pride, W. M. and Ferrell, O. C. (2012), *Marketing*, 16th edn, Masori: Cengage Learning.

Rand, P. (1947), 'Too Many Cooks', *Art & Industry*, August: 52–3.

Rand, P. (1952), 'The Trademark as an Illustrative Device', in Jacobson, E. (ed) *Seven Designers Look at Trademark Design*. Chicago: Paul Theobald, 60–76.

Raffé, W. G. (1927), *Graphic Design*. London: Chapman & Hall.

Reckwitz, A. (2002), 'Toward a Theory of Social Practices, a Development in Culturalist Theorizing', *European Journal of Social Theory*, 5 (2): 243–63.

Reichardt, J. (1968), *Cybernetic Serendipity: The Computer and the Arts* [exhibition catalogue]. London: Studio International.

Remington, R. R. (2014), 'On the Laws of Form: A Contextual View of Graphic Standards Manuals', in Shaughnessy, A. (ed) *Manuals 2: Design & Identity Guidelines*. London: Unit Editions, 21–9.

Rennie, P. (2001), 'Fat Faces All Round: Lettering and the Festival Style', *Twentieth Century Architecture: The Journal of the Twentieth Century Society*, 5, 107–16.

Ritzer, G. (1992), *The McDonaldization of Society – An Investigation into the Changing Character of Contemporary Social Life*. Thousand Oaks, CA and London: Pine Forge Press.

Roberts, K. (2004), *Lovemarks: The Future Beyond Brands*. New York: PowerHouse Books.

Roberts, L. (2005), *Drip-dry Shirts: The Evolution of the Graphic Designer*. Lausanne: AVA Publishing.

Roberts, M. (2001), 'The Oral History of Wolff Olins', *Sounds* [website], Available at: http://cadensa.bl.uk/uhtbin/cgisirsi/x/0/0/5?searchdata1=CKEY6153224&library=ALL&_ga=2.5679856.258680879.1530473898-677620898.1525867179 (Accessed: 25 June 2018).

Rubinstein, W. D. (1993), *Culture and Decline in Britain, 1750–1990*. London: Routledge.

Rubinstein, W. D. (2001), 'The British Industrial Decline (Review)', *Victorian Studies*, 43 (2): 348–50.

Rushin, E. (2011), Conversation with David Preston, 15 December.

Saler, M. (1999), *The Avant-Garde in Interwar England: Medieval Modernism and the London Underground*. New York: Oxford University Press.

'Sampson Tyrrell Enterprise' (1998), *Design Week*, 27 March. Available at: https://www.designweek.co.uk/issues/26-march-1998/sampson-tyrrell-enterprise (Accessed: 21 March 2025).

Sandberg, J. and Tsoukas, H. (2011), 'Grasping the Logic of Practice: Theorizing Through Practical Rationality', *Academy of Management Review*, 36 (2): 338–60.

Sandino, L. (2005), 'Alex Maranzano (b. 1943) Designer, Chairman, Minale Tattersfield' [interview], *Viva Voices* [website]. Available at: http://www.vivavoices.org/website.asp?page=Alex%20Maranzano (Accessed: 25 June 2018).

REFERENCES

Schatzki, T. R. (2002), *The Site of the Social: A Philosophical Account of the Constitution of Social*. Pennsylvania: The Pennsylvania State University Press.

Schatzki, T. R., Cetina, K. K. and von Savigny, E. (eds) (2005), *The Practice Turn in Contemporary Theory*. London: Routledge.

Schleger, H. (1959), 'The New Mac Fisheries Packs for Fresh Frozen Foods' [company report]. Hans Schleger Archive, V&A Archive of Art & Design, 2009/11/9.

Schleger, P. (ed) (2001), *Zero: Hans Schleger, A Life of Design*. Aldershot: Lund Humphries.

Schleger, P. (2011), Interview with David Preston, 14 December.

Schön, D. A. (1983), *The Reflective Practitioner: How Professionals Think in Action*. New York: Basic Books.

Schreiber, G. (1991), 'Papers, Diaries and Designs'. Gaby Schreiber Archive, V&A Archive of Art & Design, AAD/1991/11.

Schwarz, F. (1996), 'Commodity Signs: Peter Behrens, the AEG and the Trademark', *Journal of Design History*, 9 (3): 153–84.

Schwarzkopf, S. (2008), 'Creativity, Capital and Tacit Knowledge', *Journal of Cultural Economy*, 1 (2): 181–97.

Schwarzkopf, S. (2009), 'What Was Advertising? The Invention, Rise, Demise, and Disappearance of Advertising Concepts in Nineteenth- and Twentieth-Century Europe and America', *Business and Economic History On-Line*, 7: 1–27.

Schweizer, R. G. (1968), *Design Research Unit Report No. 1 Review of Organisation and Management*, 12 January. Marcus Brumwell papers, TGA 20046, Tate Archive.

Shaughnessy, A. (2012), *Ken Garland: Structure and Substance*. London: Unit Editions.

Shaughnessy, A. (2013), *FHK Henrion: The Complete Designer*. London: Unit Editions.

Shaughnessy, A. (ed.) (2014), *Manuals 1: Design & Identity Guidelines*. London: Unit Editions.

Shaughnessy, A. (ed.) (2023), *Pentagram: Living by Design*. London: Unit Editions.

Shove, E., Watson, M., Hand, M. and Ingram, J. (2007), *The Design of Everyday Life*. Oxford: Berg.

Simon, H. (1981), *The Sciences of the Artificial*. Cambridge, MA: MIT Press.

Sparke, P. (1983), *Consultant Design: The History and Practice of the Designer in Industry*. London: Pembridge Press.

Spinosa, C., Flores, F. and Dreyfus, H. L. (1997), *Disclosing New Worlds: Entrepreneurship, Democratic Action, and the Cultivation of Solidarity*. Cambridge, MA: MIT Press.

Stake, R.E. (2005), 'Qualitative Case Studies', in Denzin, N. K. and Lincoln, Y. S. (eds) *The Sage Handbook of Qualitative Research*. Thousand Oaks: Sage Publications, 119–49.

Steel, M. (2016), 'Why a Coherent Brand Identity is Stronger Than a Consistent Logo', *Parisleaf* [blog], 14 October. Available at: https://parisleaf.com/why-a-coherent-brand-identity-is-stronger-than-a-consistent-logo/#:~:text=If%20we%20treat%20coherence%20as,in%20and%20around%20people's%20lives (Accessed: 5 February 2025).

Stiff, P. (1996), 'Instructing the Printer: What Specification Tells About Typographic Designing', in Stiff, P. (ed) *Typography Papers 1*. London: Hyphen Press, 27–74.

Stiff, P. (2009), 'Austerity, Optimism: Modern Typography in Britain after the War', in Stiff, P. (ed) *Typography Papers 8*. London: Hyphen Press, 5–68.

Stonier, G. W. (1935), 'Style Attracts Us Underground', *Commercial Art & Industry*, May: 186–91.

'Systematic method for designers' [advertisement] (1965), *Design*, 204, December 1965: 73.

Taylor, F. W. (1911), *The Principles of Scientific Management*. New York and London: Harper & Brothers.

'The Work of the Bassett Gray Studio' (1927), *Commercial Art*, 3: 282–5.

Thrift, N. (2005), *Knowing Capitalism*. London: Sage.

Timings, C. (2012), Interview with David Preston, 23 November.

Triggs, T. (2009), 'Designing Graphic Design History', *Journal of Design History*, 22 (4): 325–40.

Tushman, M. L. and O'Reilly, C. A. (1996), 'The Ambidextrous Organization: Managing Evolutionary and Revolutionary Change', *California Management Review*, 38: 1–23.

Twemlow, A. (2013), 'Purposes, Poetics, and Publics: The Shifting Dynamics of Design Criticism in the US and UK, 1955–2007', PhD thesis, Royal College of Art. Available at: https://researchonline.rca.ac.uk/1659/1/TWEMLOW_THESIS_NOV_2013.pdf (Accessed: 21 March 2025).

Twyman, M. (1970), *Printing 1770–1970: An Illustrated History of its Development and Uses in England*. London: Eyre & Spottiswoode.

Twyman, M. (2013), *A History of Chromolithography: Printed Colour for All*. London: British Library.

van der Velden, D. (2012), 'Research and Destroy: Graphic Design as Investigation', in Blauvelt, A. and Lupton, E. (eds) *Graphic Design: Now in Production*. Minneapolis: Walker Art Center, 16–18.

van der Velden, D. and Kruk, V. (2009), *Uncorporate Identity: Metahaven*. Baden: Lars Muller Publishers.

van Nes, I. (2012), *Dynamic Identities: How to Create a Living Brand*. Amsterdam: Bis Publishers.

Venturi, R. (1966), *Complexity and Contradiction in Architecture*. New York: Doubleday.

Verganti, R. (2009), *Design Driven Innovation: Changing the Rules of Competition by Radically Innovating What Things Mean*. Boston, MA: Harvard Business Press.

Vinti, C. (2007), *Gli anni dello stile industriale 1948–1965*. Venice: Marsilio.

Warde, A. (2014), 'After Taste: Culture, Consumption and Theories of Practice', *Journal of Consumer Culture*, 14 (3): 279–303.

Warde, B. (1932), 'An Account of the LNER Type Standardization', *The Monotype Recorder*, 36 (4): 7–11.

Wheeler, A. (2018), *Designing Brand Identity: An Essential Guide for the Whole Branding Team*, 5th edn, Hoboken, NJ: John Wiley & Sons.

Wiener, M. (1981), *English Culture and the Decline of the Industrial Spirit, 1850–1980*. Cambridge: Cambridge University Press.

Wildbur, P. (1979), *International Trademark Design*. London: Barrie and Jenkins.

Wildbur, P. (2005), 'Obituary: George Daulby', *The Guardian*, 17 October. Available at: https://www.theguardian.com/news/2005/oct/17/guardianobituaries.artsobituaries (Accessed: 21 March 2025).

Wills, F. H. (ed.) (1954), *Das Firmengesicht: eine Ausstellung internationaler Werbegraphik* [exhibition catalogue], Georg C. Marshall-Haus, Messe Berlin.

Woodham, J. M. (1997), *Twentieth Century Design*. Oxford: Oxford University Press.

Woudhuysen, J. (1981), 'Perspectives: Golden Age, Mk 2', *Design*, 392: 16–17.

Woudhuysen, J. (1986), 'FHK Henrion: graphics as propaganda in World War II', *Blueprint*, December 1986/January 1987. Available at: https://www.woudhuysen.com/fhk-henrion-graphics-as-propaganda-in-world-war-ii (Accessed: 9 January 2013).

York, P. (1984), *Modern Times: Everybody Wants Everything*. London: Heinemann.

INDEX

activity objects 95–6, 98, 103
actor network theory 103
  translation 103, 132
advertising
  Adbusters 12
  Erwin Wasey 3, 81, 207
  guard book 73, 118, 121–9, 143–4, 147–9, 209, 219
  Mather and Crowther 118–157
Advertising Service Guild 159, 221
Akrich, Madeline 19, 74, 172
Allgemeine Elektricitäts-Gesellschaft (AEG) 29–31, 33, 36, 50
Americanization 41–3
Archer, Bruce 48, 93, 116, 163
architecture 24, 29–30, 89, 92, 161–2, 167, 183–190
Arnheim, Rudolf 107, 116
Azerbaijan 6, 161

Baker, Steve 25
Bakker, Wibo 29–31, 53, 85, 107
Balmer, John M. T. 25–6, 31
Banks & Miles 70, 168
Barman, Christian 53, 131
Bass, Saul 32, 34
Bassett Gray 42, 82, 159–161, 211
BDMW Associates 168
Behrens, Peter 29, 30, 33, 36
Bernays, Edward 42
Blue Circle Cement 84, 89, 92, 96–8, 102, 104–5
Bos, Ben 85
boundary objects 110, 116, 231
Bourdieu, Pierre 154, 172
Brand Union 225
branding
  brand loyalty 61, 176

  contemporary scene 27–28, 222–225
  as corporate communication and marketing 26–28
  dynamic identity 220
  gurus 24–26
  post-branding 28
  programmatic branding 28–36
  stereotyped approach 176, 195, 199, 213, 217, 221
  terminology 11–12
  uncorporate identity 27
  visual unification 4, 23–4, 29, 31, 43, 46–49, 52, 79, 84
Braun 24, 34
British Empire 37
British Overseas Airways Corporation (BOAC) 55–7
British Rail 164, 171, 190–9, 221
Brownjohn, Chermayeff & Geismar 70
Brumwell, Marcus 159, 164, 166–8, 201, 208, 212, 214

Callon, Michel 103, 114, 172
capital 6–7, 21, 45, 114, 152, 203, 212–213
Ciba-Geigy 33
Columbia Broadcasting System 33
commercialism 40, 42–5
conglomerates 164, 225
Conran Associates 202
Conran Design Group 71
Conran, Terrence 44
consultant design group 32, 41–43, 118, 138, 207–9, 216
consumerism 38–9, 154
Container Corporation of America 30, 33, 50
Corner, James 94–95, 100, 108, 116

Courage Brewery 172–9, 181–2, 189–90, 195
Crawfords 58, 71
critical path method 103, 112

Das Firmengesicht 33
Davis, Alec 11, 13, 32, 54–8, 62–6, 85–86, 156, 176
de Majo, Willy 33, 71, 164
Design
    as labour 14–16
    material apparatus of design 16–18
Design Bridge 225
design coordination 10–11, 20, 54, 74, 85–110, 121, 146, 220
Design Council 54, 68, 191, 212
design discourse 6, 8, 17, 20, 22, 27, 33, 45, 76, 85
Design & Industries Association 87
design management 21, 87, 100, 111, 153, 167–9, 202–3, 209, 215, 223–4
    Design Management Institute 223
Design Methods Movement 11, 77, 111–12, 153
Design Research Unit 7, 42, 75, 79, 142, 158–204, 217–18, 221
    Black, Misha 78–9, 87, 158, 160, 162, 164, 168–9, 185–6, 200–1, 201, 213, 215
    Gray, Milner 78–9, 142, 158–60, 164, 169, 174, 177, 185, 191, 200, 202, 210, 213
Dorwin Teague, Walter 30, 43
Dutton, Norbert 45, 50–3, 61, 63–5, 164

Edinburgh International Festival 136–8
education
    Central School of Arts and Crafts 79, 160–1
    London Business School 223
    London College of Printing 79
    Royal College of Art 13, 79, 161–2, 169, 223
    Yale University 13
Eksell, Ole 24, 33, 34
emergent strategy 156
émigré designers 3, 6, 160
epistemic objects 172

Farr, Michael 24, 27, 40, 71, 209–10, 223
Festival of Britain 40, 79, 142, 150, 162, 164, 174, 189, 221
Fitch 202, 225
Fletcher/Forbes/Gill 168
France 33, 77–8

Garland, Ken 40, 44–5, 165
Germany 6, 30, 33–4, 77–8, 87, 112, 118–19, 132, 219
Gerstner, Karl 33
    Gerstner+Kutter 70
gestalt theory 107, 109
Gill, Eric 46, 48
Gorb, Peter 167, 168, 223
Gornick, Naomi 223
Goslett, Dorothy 13, 166, 169–70
Gowing, Mary 132, 151, 154
graphic design
    in relation to brand 25, 52, 217–218, 222–225
    historiography 13, 15, 40
    as labour 14–16
    professionalism 4, 12–14, 31, 43–45, 207–210
greenwashing 225
grid 30, 108, 196, 218, 227, 229
Gropius, Walter 33
group practice 4, 10–11, 18, 41–3, 101–4, 141, 159–60, 164–8, 200–4, 207–12, 214, 221–22
Guyatt, Richard 13

Havinden, Ashley 45, 58–61, 64, 66, 120, 130, 131, 141
Henrion, F. H. K.
    Design Coordination and Corporate Image 3, 24, 33, 85–7, 107, 112–13, 191
    Henrion Design Associates 73, 75, 77–117, 218, 225
    ideas poster 3, 4, 109, 112
Hermann Miller 33

IBM 24, 32, 34
ICA 163
Ilford 7, 57, 164, 172–3
industrial design 13, 32–3, 41–3, 54, 69, 89, 161–2, 216

INDEX

Industrial Design Partnership 79, 82, 159, 162, 164, 211
industrial revolution 29, 37
inscription 17, 19, 64, 74, 103, 109, 154–5, 158, 170–1, 182, 189, 217, 222
    de-scripting 18–20, 74
    immutable mobile 19, 171, 184, 222
    inscription device 19
intermediaries 14, 75, 152, 208
International Typographic Style 196, 217–18
intuitive methods 89, 218–20
Italy 30, 33–4, 50, 92

Julier, Guy 15, 35–6, 41–2, 153

Kepes, György 107, 116
Kinross, Robin 13, 31, 45
Klein, Naomi 12, 22
KLM 3, 59, 81–4, 89, 92, 106–10, 112–16, 207–8, 214, 218–19
Knoll 33

Landor 78, 160
Landor, Walter 70, 78–9, 160
Latour, Bruno 16, 19, 74, 171–2, 184, 197
Lever Brothers 121
Lewitt-Him 33
Lippincott & Margulies 32, 70
Lloyd, John 224
Loewy, Raymond 42–3, 70
logos 23, 29–30, 64, 95, 106–9, 126–7, 133, 142, 171, 192–3
    logo-centric 7, 22–4
London & North Eastern Railway 7, 30, 45–51, 64–5, 142
London Transport 7, 30–1, 45, 50–5, 65, 87, 120
Lonsdale-Hands, Richard 71

Magdalen Street 183–90, 191, 193, 196, 199, 221
Main Wolff & Partners 168
management
    leadership 21, 85, 101–2, 118, 163, 168, 200–4, 210–11, 221

    scientific management 103, 139, 153, 201
    Taylorism 103, 121
Management and Organization Studies (MOS) 17, 74
Margolin, Victor 15
Marketing 8, 12, 24–8, 32–3, 38, 41, 43, 81, 84, 122, 124, 156, 163, 207, 210, 217–19, 224
    corporate communications 4, 22, 25–7, 216, 218
Mass Observation 178
materiality 4, 14, 16, 67, 171, 181
McKnight Kauffer, Edward 120
McLuhan, Marshall 42
Meggs, Philip B. 29, 32
Metahaven 27–8
Middleton, Michael 8, 10, 45, 101, 169, 200–3
Minale Tattersfield 69, 168
modernization 31, 37, 39–40
Moor, Liz 6, 35–6

Nazi party 30, 170
Negus & Negus 101, 168
neoliberalism 6, 28, 35–6, 42, 203, 217, 222
Netherlands 3, 31, 34, 53, 82
Nicolini, Davide 14, 17–18, 67, 74, 95, 98, 110, 116, 172
Notley, Cecil 159
Noyes, Eliot 32–4

Olins, Wally 24–5, 27, 87, 210, 222
Olivetti 24, 30–1, 33–4, 50
Operations Research 77, 103, 112

Packard, Vance 42, 81
Penrose Annual 8, 45, 54–60, 68, 130
Pentagram 24, 69
Pest Control of Cambridge 3, 5
Philips 24
Pick, Frank 30, 53, 87, 120
Pilditch, James 24, 26–7, 34–5, 42, 45, 71, 87, 210, 213, 222, 224
    Allied International Designers 35, 42, 71, 202, 210, 222
Post Office 10–11, 79, 89, 92, 96–100, 120, 208, 219

Poynor, Rick 14, 40
practice theory 14, 17–20, 67, 74, 223
printing 10, 13, 16, 45, 48–9, 54–7, 64, 68, 80, 84, 145, 150–1, 164–5, 181, 224
product design 24, 163, 165
professionalization 12, 223
    jurisdiction 13, 21, 75, 77, 207–210, 218
public relations 33, 42, 132, 207

Rand, Paul 32–4, 135–6, 178, 196
rationality
    practical rationality 7, 118, 154, 220
    techno-scientific rationality 18, 81, 89, 91, 106, 111, 115–16, 155, 157, 218, 220
Read, Herbert 159, 164, 167, 201, 208
regenerative branding 225
Royal Society of Arts 79, 223

Sainsbury's 55, 57
Sampson Tyrell 111, 219
Schleger, Hans
    Hans Schleger & Associates 73, 75, 79, 118–157, 219
    in New York 119
Schön, Donald 154–5
Schreiber, Gaby 71
Schweppes 33
Science and Technology Studies (STS) 17–18, 74
Scott Brownrigg 202
Second World War 7, 31–2, 35–6, 40, 46, 69, 79, 122, 162, 168, 213, 216
Simon, Herbert 222
Simpson of Piccadilly 33
Society of Industrial Artists 43–5, 79, 124, 161–3, 202
Sparke, Penny 41–2, 162

Stiff, Paul 13, 151
streamlining 43
Superunion 225
Switzerland 33–4, 70, 193, 196
systems
    systematic methods 7, 10, 20, 89, 91, 98, 115–16, 217
    systems thinking 89, 118

tacit knowledge 18, 115, 155, 184
technical entities 19, 75, 208, 217
technology 16, 18–19, 38, 49, 74, 181, 201, 212
Texaco 30–1
The Civic Trust 173, 183, 185, 221
The Corporate Personality 24–5
Tootal 30
trade journals
    Art & Industry 9, 32, 45, 50–53, 68, 132, 154
    Design 5, 9, 11, 32, 54, 56, 62, 82–3, 93, 162, 202

van der Velden, Daniel 215
Venturi, Robert 121
Vinti, Carlo 30

W. H. Smith 30
Warde, Beatrice 17, 45–50, 61, 64–5
Watneys Brewery 13, 164, 173, 179–83, 189–90, 193, 199
Weber and Heilbroner 12, 133–6
Wolff, Michael 25, 210
    Main Wolff 168
Wolff Olins 25, 69, 210, 222
Wolsey 33
Woodham, Jonathan 29, 35, 38, 41
Woolworths 196, 221
WPP 225